COURTENAY STUDIES IN
REFORMATION THEOLOGY

1. JOHN CALVIN

JEAN CALVIN (1509-1564)   Attributed to Holbein
Reproduction by courtesy of Baroness von Pölnitz

COURTENAY STUDIES IN
REFORMATION THEOLOGY

1

JOHN CALVIN

F. L. Battles, *Hartford*, U.S.A.
J. D. Benoît, *Strasbourg*
J. Cadier, *Montpellier*
R. N. Caswell, *Belfast*
B. Hall, *Cambridge*
J. I. Packer, *Oxford*
T. H. L. Parker, *Cambridge*
R. Peter, *Strasbourg*
G. S. M. Walker, *Leeds*
G. E. Duffield, *Oxford*, EDITOR

THE SUTTON COURTENAY PRESS
APPLEFORD, ABINGDON, BERKSHIRE

Printed in Great Britain by
Billing and Sons Limited, Guildford and London

CONTRIBUTORS

F. L. Battles
Philip Schaff Professor of Church History, The Hartford Theological Seminary, Hartford, Connecticut, U.S.A.

J–D. Benoît
Professor of Theology, University of Strasbourg, France

J. Cadier
Professor, Faculty of Theology, Montpellier, France

R. N. Caswell
Head of the Religious Education Department, Coleraine Academical Institution, Northern Ireland

B. Hall
Professor of Church History, Westminster College, and University Lecturer in Ecclesiastical History, Cambridge

J. I. Packer
Warden, Latimer House, Oxford

T. H. L. Parker
Vicar of Oakington, Cambridge

R. Peter
Lecturer in Theology, University of Strasbourg, France

G. S. M. Walker
Lecturer in Church history, University of Leeds

TRANSLATORS

G. S. R. Cox
Vicar of Gorsley, Ross-on-Wye, Herefordshire

P. G. Rix
Assistant Chaplain, Wrekin College, Shrewsbury

G. E. Duffield, EDITOR

Contents

Frontispiece

ABBREVIATIONS

CO *J. Calvini Opera quae supersunt omnia* from the *Corpus Reformatorum*

CTS Calvin Translation Society

Doumergue Emile Doumergue: *Jean Calvin, Les hommes et les choses de son temps.* 7 vols., Lausanne 1899-1927.

ET English Translation

Inst. *Institutio Christianae Religionis*

LCC The Library of Christian Classics

OS P. Barth and W. Niesel: *Calvini Opera Selecta*

PL J. P. Migne: *Patrologiae*

Wendel François Wendel: *The Origin and Development of his Religious Thought,* tr. from the French by Philip Mairet, London 1963. All references are to the ET

Introduction

G. E. Duffield

EVER SINCE HIS DEATH in 1564, and indeed even before it,
the name and theology of John Calvin have aroused intense
feelings and vigorous reactions. To some he is the great hero.
To others his very name is anathema. The issue is not the simple
one of Roman Catholics assailing a leading Reformation theologian with Protestants defending him. There have been Romans
who showed considerable sympathy and understanding, just as
there have been Protestants among Calvin's strongest critics,
both in his own day and subsequently. The very fact that
Calvin has been much studied and attracted so much attention
speaks of his significance in theology and Church history. But
his influence has been wider than that, for Calvin's theology
was not restricted to narrowly ecclesiastical horizons, but
rather reached out into the realms of politics, social theory,
economics and culture. That Calvin is one of the key figures in
the history of Christendom, it is impossibe to deny. What
exactly his significance was is not so clear, for there have been,
and still are, schools of Calvin-interpretation. These essays do
not reflect the standpoint of any school. They seek simply to let
the historical Calvin speak for himself. Together they form
volume 1 in the *Courtenay Studies in Reformation Theology*, a
series of contemporary studies of the Reformers and their
teaching. The approach, in this volume as in the whole series, is
sympathetic, yet strictly within the accepted canons of modern
historical scholarship.

It remains for me as editor to record my gratitude to those
who have helped in the production of this book. Some of the

essays were written for the volume, some appear in English for the first time, some are revisions and expansions of articles in learned periodicals now hard to obtain. Thanks are due to the editor of *The Churchman*, in which earlier versions of chapters 1 and 9 appeared, to the *Huguenot Society of London*, in whose journal an earlier draft of chapter 2 was published, to the editor of *La Revue reformée* for permission to translate chapters 5 and 6, the former of which was originally an address delivered in 1959 at the fourth centenary of the founding of Geneva University, and to the proprietors of the *Revue d'Histoire et de Philosophie religieuses* for allowing the translation of chapter 10 and providing the illustration. The frontispiece appears by courtesy of Hedwig Freifrau von Pölnitz. Mr. A. H. Gordon has helped much in the preparation of the book, and my wife has endured the domestic upheavals and piles of paper round the house, the trials of which only an author's wife appreciates.

1 The Calvin Legend

Basil Hall

IN APRIL 1595 William Barret, a fellow of Caius College, Cambridge, 'preached *ad Clerum* for his degree of B.D. in St. Maryes', wherein he attacked Calvin, and was therefore summoned before the 'Consistory of Doctors, and there enjoined a Recantation' in which he said '. . . . I uttered these words rashly against Calvin, a man that hath very well deserved of the Church of God; viz., that he durst presume to lift up himself above the High and Almighty God. By which words I confess that I have done great injury to that most learned and right godly man; and I do most humbly beseech you all to pardon this my rashness.' This passage from Thomas Fuller's *History of the University of Cambridge* is quoted in a collection of 'Opinions and Testimonies' concerning Calvin and his writings which was added to the English version of Calvin's *Commentary on Joshua* in the Calvin Translation Society series over a century ago. There are many other passages also quoted there illustrating the admiration, or at least respect, with which so many distinguished divines, Catholic and Protestant, from the sixteenth to the nineteenth centuries, wrote of Calvin. In view of what follows later below, it may be interesting to note that among these divines were Bishops Bilson and Andrewes, who were opposed to Puritanism in England, yet held Calvin in honour. Bilson is cited as writing: 'Mr. Calvin is so well known to those who are learned and wise, for his great pains and labours in the Church of God, that a few snarling friars cannot impeach his name.' Andrewes is cited as writing: 'Calvin was an illustrious person, and never to be mentioned without a preface

of the highest honour.' Also it is interesting to see seventeenth
century Roman Catholic scholars like Bishop Bossuet and the
Oratorian Richard Simon giving at least qualified praise to Calvin, and to learn that John Donne, writing with approval of
Calvin thus, 'St. Augustine, for sharp insight and conclusive
judgment in exposition of places of scripture, which he always
makes so liquid and pervious,hath scarce been equalled therein
by any of all the writers in the Church of God except Calvin
may have that honour', added, 'for whom (when it concerns
not points in controversy) I see the Jesuits themselves, though
they dare not name him, have a high degree of reverence'.[1]
Nevertheless, in part because of the strength and cohesion of his
life's work, and the integrity, force, and competence of his theological writing, Calvin has never lacked considerable detraction.
One major difference between the older denigration of Calvin
and that of our own time is that once those who sought to
attack him first read widely in his writings. Now it would
seem that the word 'Calvinism' can be used as a self-justifying
pejorative without regard to what, in the context, the word is
supposed to mean.

Misunderstandings

CALVIN and his thought will always be subject to misunderstanding until it becomes sufficiently realised that those things
Calvin said and did are by no means to be regarded as identical
with the work of Protestant successors who either claimed to
follow the aims he proposed, or who were described by their
adversaries, or later writers, as the spiritual heirs of Calvin.
When Calvin died in 1564 the synthesis of biblical studies,
humane learning, and the welfare of the small city state of
Geneva, died with him. A change of emphasis came with Beza,
his successor there, who altered the balance of Calvin's theology,
saw, and in part approved, that successful repristination of
Aristotle among Protestants which led to the Reformed scholasticism that distorted the Calvinist synthesis[2] and used his
contacts with Protestant leaders elsewhere in Europe and in
Britain for ends more politically sophisticated than Calvin
would have conceived or desired. Further, for Englishmen, two
aspects of their own later Protestantism come between them and
2

this original synthesis of Calvin—Puritanism and the Evangelicalism of the eighteenth century. There are elements in common between Calvin's own teaching and that of Puritan and Evangelical writers in the seventeenth and eighteenth centuries both here and in North America: but much in the aims and methods of these writers, together with their self-imposition of certain limitations, separates their work from Calvin's balancing of the proportions in his work. In the reign of Elizabeth, when the Puritan effort failed to modify in a Genevan direction the provisions of the settlement of religion and its interpretation by the bishops, the next generation of Puritans turned to the more intense cultivation of personal piety. It is arguable, for example, that, when the Civil War came, the Puritan fervour—especially in its more sectarian forms—failed to relate adequately their passion for the sanctification of life to the limitations of politics, the nature of the constitution, and the economic and cultural factors in their environment. Here was the failure to do what Calvin had seen was imperative, that is, that one must come to terms with institutions, political and cultural, through a Church established, visible and centralised in authority, and functioning through an effective parochial as well as synodical discipline. (The work of the Westminster Assembly of Divines which owed much to Federal Theology and less to Calvin was, in the circumstances, incapable of fulfilment at the time, and its full programme was soon lost to view in England.) This Puritan failure to face what Anglicanism, for good or for ill, had to face, has left its mark on our subsequent religious history. Evangelicalism was the successor to that intense concern for the sanctification of personal life which was at the heart of Puritanism. European pietism (which owed little to Calvinism) was a spur to, rather than a primary source of, English Evangelicalism. The Evangelicals were the spiritual heirs of those seventeenth century Puritans who, while to some extent admirers of Calvin, had sought, by different emphases, a way of sanctification which Calvin would have approved in principle, but would have criticised for the failure to relate sufficiently this sanctification to the objective existence of the church and sacraments as means of grace, to church order and through these to the political and economic environment.

These assertions of the preceding paragraph would need the

3

support of closer argument and supporting evidence before satisfying conclusively historians of the period. Nevertheless, I make them in order to persuade my readers—if to nothing more—to hesitate before assuming that Calvinism means William Perkins, the Westminster Catechisms, George Whitefield, A. M. Toplady, and Jonathan Edwards. If, however, this seems to some to be an elementary truth, then they should notice how remarkable it is that so few who write and speak of 'Calvinism' are aware of the implications of this truth. Too often we look back to Calvin through the distorting lens of our own Protestant religious history, which, however admirable and original in its aims and achievements, is not Calvin's calvinism 'englished'. To understand Calvin's work we must come forward from the time and place into which he was born—the vigorous energies of change and renewal in the early sixteenth century—towards the completion of his work in Geneva in mid-century. Only by this approach can we learn to appreciate the whole Calvin and avoid imposing on his work a theological pattern from another age, or modifying his thought by making our own selection of what we approve in it outside of the context of the rest of his writing and life history. Too often, today, those who admire Calvin's theology, are guilty of this eclectic approach which may lead to serious misrepresentation of his work. Those who admire—and do well to admire—the massive theological achievement of Karl Barth may do Calvin less service than they wish if they approach him through the method of Barth, and ignore the fact that Calvin was of the sixteenth century and not of the twentieth. For example, the ill-posed question whether there is ground for a natural theology in Calvin has obscured the pattern of Calvin's own emphases and distorted our contemporary understanding of him by overlooking the implications of the fact that he was never entirely free of sixteenth century biblical humanism[3] in his theological method. Further, the theologians of the Reformation did not affirm that the 'theology of the Word' was entirely sufficient in itself. Not even Luther was content to say 'the Word alone', and leave it at that, for his doctrine of the sacraments, for example, moderates what some have sought to regard as the mere biblicalism of Luther. Moreover, his sustained admiration for Melanchthon, the man who sought above all to relate the 'theology of the

4

Word' to his contemporary cultural and political situation, should reject that view of Luther's work which oversimplifies it as mere biblicalism. And it should not be forgotten that Calvin had much in common with Melanchthon besides a cordial and lifelong friendship—for Melanchthon Calvin was quite simply '*the* theologian'.

Calvin like Melanchthon saw that the theology of the Word must be realised in society, it must establish a pattern of cultural and political understanding as well as of churchmanship and sacramental life. It is no use anyone saying 'Nein!' to that—as Barth did however justifiably, to Brunner's attempt, at the time of the Church struggle in Germany, to affirm a measure of natural theology in Calvin. It is well for us to challenge natural theology but one cannot, along with this, shout history out of existence. The Reformers were concerned about institutions, about liturgy and church order, about laws and political relations. It is bad history and inadequate theology to fail to recognise the effort of the Reformers in these matters.

Moreover, this assumption that the Reformers were wrong to be preoccupied with these things is being supported by the renewed and widespread interest in the Anabaptists of the sixteenth century—those men who accused the Reformers of failing to join them in their dissociation of the Word from the ways of contemporary society. Many of the proponents of Anabaptism today directly or indirectly attack the Reformers on the ground that they failed to separate the work of Christians from political and cultural affairs. Several examples might be given of this attempt to undercut the significance of the classical Reformation in favour of this theologically null and ecclesiastically incoherent group of men and women who withdrew from the effort of making the visible church effective in society. Calvin is frequently subjected to attack based on these assumptions. It is distressing that those who claim to be his disciples should also assist unintentionally in this misunderstanding of him, either by ignoring certain elements in his work, or by introducing a defective method in studying him. I have sought to show elsewhere in this book what the term 'Calvinism' should describe.[4]

JOHN CALVIN

LET us turn from the misunderstanding of Calvin by applying to him the aims and teachings of others to look at the variety of misrepresentation of him made by his enemies. It is inevitable that Calvin in his own time and ever since should be attacked by polemical writers of the Church of Rome. It is a measure of Calvin's achievement that Rome should be so consistent and energetic in its attack on Calvin. At the highest theological and historical level there are objective and admirable studies of Calvin by Catholic writers, for example, *Calvin et l'Institution Chrétienne* by Imbart de la Tour. But at the more popular level this objectivity is still far to seek. Daniel-Rops of the Académie Française, author of a widely read history of the Catholic Church, has written an introduction to some extracts from Calvin's writings chosen and translated by another Catholic historian, L. Cristiani.[5] In this introduction Calvin is said to resemble Robespierre in his private character, 'one of the terribly pure men who pitilessly enforce principles': in public life he is described as the theocratic dictator of Geneva, a Geneva where there were 'too many policemen, too many pliable judges, too many prisons, and too many scaffolds'.[6] (Yet how many hundreds fled from Catholic France to Geneva in Calvin's time there to enjoy this nightmare, and sought citizenship in what they believed to be a city of freedom as well as of refuge). This method of attack is neither new nor unusual among Catholic polemical or popular writers, but it lacks the particular instances whereby Calvin was once libelled, since no writer of repute dare use material shown again and again to be mere invention, like the story of Calvin being known to his schoolfellows as the 'Accusative Case'. There are already signs, however, partly in consequence of Vatican Council II, that this kind of attack will decrease.

Since the sixteenth century there has gone alongside Roman Catholic polemic against Calvin an attack from the other extreme, the non-doctrinal and liberal religious viewpoint. It began with Castellio who resigned from his post as schoolmaster at Geneva rather than work with Calvin. More recent examples of this attack can be found in the work of Stefan Zweig and Oscar Pfister. Not long ago at the time of the Nazi

6

domination in Germany, Stefan Zweig in his book *The Right to Heresy*, drew a picture of Calvin's Geneva as a régime of dictatorial cruelty based on religious fanaticism. 'Calvin's secret was not a new one, his art was that which all dictators before and since have used. Terror. Calvin's was a Holy Terror.'[7] Here once again there is a suggestion of Robespierre—now completed by a hint of Hitler. More recently Erich Fromm in *The Fear of Freedom* and Oscar Pfister in *Christianity and Fear*, show their desire to undermine current interest in the theological work of Luther and Calvin by accusing them, in effect, of concealed sadism, and of the cruelty born of fear. Fromm says of Luther and Calvin: 'these two men personally belonged to the ranks of the greatest haters in history, certainly among religious leaders' and relates their doctrinal teaching to a basis of repressed hostility.[8] Pfister says: 'It was the fact that Calvin's own character was compulsion-neurotic which transformed the God of Love as experienced and taught by Jesus into a compulsive character, a fanatic of fearful cruelty, bearing absolutely diabolical traits in his reprobatory practice.'[9] He also speaks of Calvin's 'diabolization of God'.

Pfister, whose theological preoccupations are those of late nineteenth century liberalism, disapproves explicitly of the recent renewal of theological interest in Calvin. He followed up his attack in *Das Christentum und die Angst*, 1944 (ET, *Christianity and Fear*, 1948) with his *Calvins Eingreifen in die Hexer- und Hexenprozesse von Peney 1545* in 1947. Here, to prove his general attack in the former book, he concentrates on Calvin's part in the witch trials of 1545. Pfister wishes to show Calvin as cruel, without regard for human suffering, and without that compassion for human folly and sin which is fundamental to Christian faith and practice. He seeks to demonstrate that where the council of Geneva was reluctant to be too severe, through its officers, in inquiring into the extent of witchcraft (and plague-spreading) during the plague-terror of that year, Calvin directly interfered to increase the pressure of 'inquisition', and thereby emphasised torture to procure evidence. Pfister also affirms that Calvin failed to distinguish between black and white magic, and wished to punish by burning those guilty of either practice. The conclusion would thereafter be irrefutable: Calvin was a sadist. To write a book on what

7

amounts to no more than a few sentences in a speech of Calvin to the Council, in an order of the Council, and in Calvin's commentary on *Deuteronomy* 18, verses 10–15, is an achievement—but of doubtful value when one looks more closely at the correct translation of what Calvin in fact said and puts this into the proper context in the Council minute and in the commentary concerned. First, Calvin, representing the *Venerable Company* of pastors of Geneva, spoke to the Council urging a 'légitime inquisition'[10] (i.e. a legitimate or properly conducted inquiry). Thereafter, the Council recommended 'les procureurs', its officers, to proceed 'without fear'. This Pfister turns into meaning that the 'procureurs' appointed should act without fear of Calvin! Neither the Council nor the 'procureurs' were afraid of Calvin: he had no authority in the matter. The words 'without fear' relate either to the instruction to the 'procureurs' that they should proceed without intimidation of the accused, or without hesitation in face of a mob seeking to lynch the accused. Secondly, regarding Pfister's attempt to show Calvin as desirous of punishing practitioners of both white and black magic with equal cruelty, it appears that this turns upon Calvin's comment on the passage in Deuteronomy mentioned above. Here Calvin, following his ordinary pastoral function of expounding the meaning of Scripture, explains, as the passage plainly states, that hearkening to wizards and witches is disobedience to God: since such practitioners of magic obviously deny God they should be punished, but the goal of Calvin lies in the comment on verse 15. Here he says that ministers should be hearkened to as the servants, the prophets, of God, and one must turn from all dealings with lying spirits which deny God. What Calvin is after is not the sadistic pursuit of witches but the pastoral concern to warn his hearers against lying unbelief.

There have been older attempts than these at discrediting Calvin, by trying to show that he was lacking in warm human lovingkindness; but Pfister's is the most recent, the sharpest, and the most documented. Beside this attack and that of Zweig others seem to be too generalised and imprecise. To dwell on them further would be tiresome. Those who wish to read a patient and carefully documented rebuttal of Pfister's attack should consult the effective short work by Ernst Pfisterer, *Calvins Wirken in Genf*,[11] where, among any other misrepresen-

8

tations of Calvin, the witch trials at Peney are dealt with—in fact, over thirty years ago E. Doumergue, in his large-scale *Vie de Calvin*, criticised this and many other legends about Calvin.

Servetus

THERE is, however, a serious charge against Calvin's humanity which cannot be regarded as distorted by polemical writers: this relates to his part in the trials at Vienne and Geneva of Michael Servetus. We would all agree that it should have been impossible in a Christian state for Servetus to have been burned alive for wrong belief. The Genevan Council should not have enforced the old Imperial and Catholic law, derived from the Code of Justinian, against Servetus which required death by burning for those who denied the Incarnation of the Son of God or who denied infant baptism.[12] That Calvin besought the Council to change the form of execution from burning to beheading may be of more interest than some would allow (had he not known close friends in Paris who had been burned over a slow fire, a fact terrible to Calvin's sensitive memory?), but it does not excuse that death. Joyce's Stephen Daedalus replied to a fellow-student who said that Bruno the Nolan was 'a terrible heretic' that 'he was terribly burned'. The burning of Servetus was also terrible; a fact universally agreed. But may there not be something hypocritical in the denunciation so many of us make on this episode? The Protestant heirs of Calvin have erected an expiatory monument at the place where Servetus was executed, not acknowledging his heresy but acknowledging the wrong in his execution. It would be helpful if expiatory monuments were erected by the spiritual heirs of those who in many places had executed heretics. For example, it would be of interest to see some expiatory recognition, by those Englishmen who cry out against Calvin's cruelty, of the burning of Legate and Wightman as late as 1612 at London and Lichfield respectively when, after condemnation by the bishops of these cities, King and Neile, they were handed over to the secular arm.[13] The stirring up of these bitter memories benefits no one. But it is surely unjust to single out Calvin as standing alone in that age for cruelty and doctrinaire intolerance.

JOHN CALVIN

The burning of Servetus was a terrible fact: but there are those who are not content with this as an example of Calvin's cruelty. Aldous Huxley could endorse an old and groundless legend thus: 'Our fathers took the fifth commandment seriously—how seriously may be judged from the fact that during the great Calvin's theocratic rule of Geneva a child was publicly decapitated for having ventured to strike its parents.'[14] Not only is there no evidence for this imagined incident from the Genevan records; but there was no legal ground for its being possible under the criminal code under which Geneva was governed. A popular poet of our time in a poem entitled *An Incident in the Life of Ebenezer Jones* presents a brutal schoolmaster who hurls down a stairway a mongrel dog before the horrified eyes of a pupil. In his poem, Mr Betjeman claims that this was done by the "minister of Calvin's God", who says "God damns a cur. I am, I am His word".[15] Even if there were any basis for this incredible assertion in the source cited at the head of the poem, to perpetuate the theological absurdity in verse would seem a curious misuse of time and language if one did not recollect that for so many popular writers this kind of inaccuracy in relation to Calvin and Calvinism is common form. It is a curious fact that if one were to collect references to 'Calvin', 'Calvinism', and 'Calvinistic' in non-scholarly writing, the majority of instances would be pejorative in tone and in general bear very little relation to what is known to scholars of Calvin's writing, doctrine, and achievements.

Those who wish to focus denigration of Calvin and what he stood for, on his supposed cruelty and dictatorial powers, fail to come to grips with two major facts. First, if Calvin was a cruel man, how did he attract so many, so varied, and so warmly attached friends and associates who speak of the sensitiveness and the charm beneath his shy and withdrawn manner in public life? The evidence is plain for all to read in the course of his vast correspondence. Secondly, if Calvin had dictatorial control over Geneva affairs, how is it that the records of Geneva show him plainly to have been the servant of its Council which on many occasions rejected out of hand Calvin's wishes for the religious life of Geneva, and was always master in Genevan affairs? A reading of Calvin's farewell speech to the ministers of Geneva made shortly before he died should resolve doubt upon this point.[16] To call Calvin the 'dictator of a theocracy' is, in view of the evidence, mere phrase-making prejudice. Calvin in Geneva had less power either in theory or in practice than had Archbishop Whitgift in England, and less again than had Archbishop Laud, or Cardinal Richelieu in France, for he had neither the authority of their office nor the consistent and powerful political support which they received. Moreover, to take the pattern—a pattern so continually used that it has become a historians' cliché—of the 'Geneva discipline' (as it was exemplified by anti-Calvinist Genevan writers in the nineteenth century) out of the context of the variously repressive ecclesiastical disciplines of the Catholic, Lutheran, Anglican and Presbyterian Churches of the sixteenth century, is to lose proportion and come near to caricature. The growth of the principle of 'toleration' in seventeenth century England lay as much in lay detestation of ecclesiastical courts of discipline as in exhaustion from the strife of Church parties and the consequent acceptance of Hobbes's views of church and state relations.

English writers

THERE is also an English tradition, a tradition of misrepresentation of Calvin which derives from a few English church historians who have a common line of descent reaching back most probably to the wilful rejection of Protestantism, without examining its sources, by R. Hurrell Froude. In the posthumous publication—by former pupils, among whom was Leighton Pullan—of A.L. Moore's *Lectures on the Reformation*, delivered at Oxford, there is a paper entitled 'The influence of Calvinism on modern unbelief'. Here are to be found the strange notions that 'Servetus started from orthodox Calvinism';[17] that Calvinism encourages the transition from Christianity to Arianism and Socinianism or Unitarianism; and the bizarre sentence: 'the most profoundly immoral and revolting tenets of Calvinism are to be found in the *Institutes*.'[18] Leighton Pullan, who had no little of the polemist in his writings, in his Bampton Lectures for 1922 could write: 'The modern capitalist is usually a child of the Ghetto or a grandchild of Geneva.'[19] The illusion that Calvin's theological system and capitalism are comple-

11

mentary has little relation to the facts of economic history and is now much less heard of than it was many years ago.[20] Following Moore, Pullan also argued that 'Calvinism is haunted by the spectre of Socinianism'.[21] Since he makes the very necessary qualification that you cannot accuse Calvin of unorthodoxy on the doctrines of the Trinity and the Incarnation it is difficult, in view of the qualification, to know what Pullan meant.

A recent vigorous attack on Calvin appears in a widely read and moving book by Bishop Trevor Huddleston, *Naught for your Comfort*: '. . . the Calvinistic doctrines upon which the faith of the Afrikaner is nourished, contain within themselves— like all heresies and deviations from Catholic truth—exaggerations so distorting and so powerful that it is very hard indeed to recognise the Christian faith they are supposed to enshrine. Here, in this fantastic notion of the immutability of race, is present in a different form the predestination idea; the concept of an elect people of God, characteristic above all else of John Calvin. . . . Calvinism, with its great insistence on 'election', is the ideally suitable religious doctrine for White South Africa. . . . I believe that Calvinistic theology is largely to blame for the present tragedy in South Africa. . . .'[22] Since it is probable that those who will be reading these *Studies in John Calvin* will have sufficient interest in him either to have read, or to read, what Calvin himself wrote about election and predestination (for example, *Institutio* Book III, xx ff.) there will be no need to outline a reply to the views of Bishop Huddleston on this subject. Bishop Huddleston does not show what connection there can be between the hidden mystery of election (wherein, as Calvin made plain, no man can say what persons are non-elect since the judgment of charity forbids such speculation upon what belongs only to God) and the divisions of men into chosen and rejected, or into superior and inferior races. But Bishop Huddleston's justifiable dislike of *apartheid* is accompanied by so deep an emotional rejection of it that the emotion sweeps him along into denouncing as Calvinism what has no connection with *apartheid* to that degree that the principles of theology, reason and charity are thrust aside in one blind and sweeping condemnation of Calvinism. It is surely plain that he and others of similar opinions condemn here what they have never examined. When he writes of 'Calvinistic doctrines' as

12

being 'like all heresies and deviations from Catholic truth so distorted as to make it hard to recognise the Christian faith they are supposed to enshrine' he apparently did not pause to reflect on the long line of Catholic theology concerning election and predestination which runs from St. Augustine through St. Bernard to St. Thomas and many other scholastic theologians. Further, in view of the Calvinistic theology written into the Confessions of the Reformed Churches it is disturbing as well as uncharitable that Bishop Huddleston's attack assumes that Calvinistic theology, if it does not explicitly support *apartheid*, implicitly does so, and would do so clearly if its principles were consistently carried through. Is it necessary to repeat once again that Calvin's teaching on election explicitly excludes the possibility of *apartheid* being grounded on his theology, and that this is one among other reasons why the Reformed Churches have frequently and openly rejected the concept of *apartheid*?

The Oxford Dictionary of the Christian Church, frequently admirable in patristic and Catholic subjects, is not infrequently less admirable in Reformation subjects: in the article on Calvin it renews the old libels that Calvin was cruel, and an 'unopposed dictator' who prohibited all amusement. Presumably its author had not examined the evidence in the records, or even the secondary sources which have used these records, for no notice is taken of the fact that the Council of Geneva in Calvin's time introduced little in legislation that was new on the suppression of gambling, blasphemy, drunkenness, licentious dancing, luxury in dress, playing of games during the hours of public worship, and so on, for all this had been provided during the episcopal government of Geneva before the Reformation. The Council sought with some additions to make what had been a dead letter a living practice. Again, to assume that Geneva was a city in which 'puritanical' morality became grimly successful is to be more optimistic than either Calvin or the Genevan Council ever were about the success of their aims for the moral life of the city. In view of this attitude it is not surprising that the article on Calvin says nothing of the facts that Calvin was trained as a biblical humanist (the significance of this is in general too little realised), that his doctrinal system (and the word 'system' ought not to be stressed) was essentially Christological, that Calvin was deeply read in patristic and scholastic

13

learning, for example, in the debt of his ecclesiology to the work of St. Cyprian and of St. Augustine, and even to scholastic writers. Calvin's ecclesiology is briefly dismissed with the erroneous statement that he subjected the state to the church. It would be a curious exercise to discover what passages in Calvin's writings could be adduced to validate this assertion, or what reference to the historical evidence concerning the relation of church and state at Geneva could support it.

Conclusion

OF all the leaders of Protestantism Calvin seems to have received a greater weight of denigration and misrepresentation than the rest, for much of the attack on Luther is more abusive than scholarly, and is thereby self-defeating. To go further with the listing and exemplification of misrepresentations of Calvin's life and work would be possible but it would be tedious to continue. What Hooker once wrote amid religious controversy could be written of all those variously motivated writers who mock at or abuse Calvin: 'There will come a time when three words uttered with charity and meekness shall receive a far more blessed reward than three thousand volumes written with disdainful sharpness of wit'—we could add for our purpose 'or disdainful sharpness of denigration'.

Too little space has been given here to the positive contribution of Calvin to the Christian world; this will be made plain elsewhere in this book. Calvin's writings show him to have been no sectary; he sought as did others of his friends and contemporaries no less than the renovation of the Church Catholic and Reformed. Calvin sought passionately, as did his friend Melanchthon, for the restoration of the Catholic Church of the Apostles and the Fathers, and he sought to realise this in the unity of the Churches of Europe, other than that one which held allegiance to Rome. Long ago Hooker in the preface to his *Laws of Ecclesiastical Polity* showed the historical necessity which prevented Calvin from maintaining episcopacy at Geneva, and in our time at least two well-documented monographs have been written abroad to show that Calvin was willing to accept episcopal government of the Church.[23] To ask what side Calvin

14

THE CALVIN LEGEND

would have chosen in the English or Scottish church conflicts of the seventeenth century or in their later developments is to ask the wrong question in the wrong way. Rather it would be more helpful in our contemporary situation to ask what assistance we may gain, from the study of the life and work of Calvin, for the union of the churches on terms which recognise the objective givenness of the Word and of the sacraments, of liturgy and of order, and of the church's duty in the moral well-being of society. There is much that can be learned from Calvin to this end when he is able to stand clear of the weight of misrepresentation and denigration under which so many would wish to obscure him.

A fitting quotation in conclusion can be found in the judicious words of Archdeacon Hakewill who cannot be accused of excess of sympathy for Calvinism in its pejorative, or in its strictly historical, sense: 'I willingly acknowledge him [Calvin] to have been an excellent instrument in the Church of God, and a man of a deepe judgment, specially in the exposition of holy Scriptures (which [i.e. Calvin] I think none condemn more than those who have read him least:) yet withall I freely confesse he had his errors, which being but a man I mervaile not at, but should much rather have mervailed had hee been without them.'[24]

[This chapter has been revised and enlarged from an article under the same title which appeared in *The Churchman*, September, 1959. This in part accounts for the emphasis given to Anglican writers in this chapter. Of course this does not mean that Scottish Presbyterians and English Freechurchmen have failed to present admiration or misrepresentation of Calvin and Calvinism, yet both this admiration (which not infrequently misconceived its object) and this misrepresentation have been more cautiously expressed than the powerful forms of detraction shown in this chapter and for that reason have not called for special comment here.]

1. I cannot trace this quotation in Donne, nor those from Bilson and Andrewes, for the editor of the 'Opinions and Testimonies' very rarely cited a volume or page reference. But on p. 477 of Donne's *LXXX Sermons* (1640) there is a similar statement: '. . . he [Calvin] whom they that even hate his name, (our Adversaries of the Roman persuasion) doe yet so far tacitely reverence, as that, though they will not name him, they will transfer, and insert his expositions of Scriptures, into their works, and passe them as their owne . . . .'

2. This also occurred in Lutheranism when Flacius Illyricus and his aristotelianising successors distorted the original insights and emphases of Luther. The difference of emphasis between Calvin and Beza, generally ignored by more recent writers, did not escape older writers, for example, Peter Heylyn, in no sense sympathetic to 'Calvinism', could distinguish between Calvin and the later Calvinists in his history of the controversy relating to the Five Points of the Synod of Dort: '. . . . only it was permitted unto Beza and his Disciples to be somewhat wilder than the rest, in placing the Decree of Predestination before the Fall, which Calvin himself had more rightly placed in *Massa corrupta* (in the corrupted mass of mankind): and the more moderate Calvinians as rightly presuppose for a matter necessary, before there should be any place for the Election or Reprobation of particular persons.' *Historia Quinquarticularis*, in *The Historical and Miscellaneous Tracts* of Peter Heylyn, 1681, p. 521. See also p. 36 of this book for a similar view of the difference between Calvin and Beza by Bishop Bancroft.

3. As did the other Reformers, Calvin owed a great deal to that renewal of Hebrew, Greek, and Latin studies of the early sixteenth century which made a remarkable contribution to the transformation of biblical learning. Calvin himself studied under the 'Lecteurs Royaux' (later to become known as the *Collège de France*) who represented at Paris the trilingual studies of Christian humanism which so greatly stimulated scriptural learning and assisted in the rejection of the Scholastic methods of, for example, the Sorbonne. See my paper *Calvin and Biblical Humanism* in the *Proceedings of the Huguenot Society of London*, vol. XX. No. 2.

4. See ch. 2, *Calvin against the Calvinists*.

5. *Calvin tel qu'il fût*, 1955, texts selected by L. Cristiani, with an Introduction by Daniel-Rops.

6. *Calvin tel qu'il fût*, Introduction pp. 7–8. Daniel-Rops does not disclose his source for these expressions, but it is most probable that he obtained them, directly or indirectly, from, of all places for a historian, Honoré de Balzac's *Sur Catherine de Médicis*, 1836–41, where more than one resemblance is shown between Robespierre and Calvin. Balzac writes that after Calvin returned to Geneva in 1541: 'Les exécutions commencèrent, et Calvin organisa sa terreur religieuse. . . . L'existence si semblable de Robespierre peut faire seule comprendre aux contemporains celle de

16

Calvin, qui, fondant son pouvoir sur les mêmes bases fût aussi cruel, aussi absolu que l'avocat d'Arras'. Balzac, after providing this setting proceeds to his story by describing Calvin at a later time walking in a Genevan street: 'Gros et gras . . . tout le monde eût tremblé devant cette figure presque aussi large que longue . . . il n'y avait pas plus de bonhomie que dans celle du terrible Henri VIII, à qui Calvin ressemblait beaucoup . . . avec une ample barbe grise'. Those who remember the surviving portraits of Calvin, and his emaciated condition at the time of which Balzac writes, will realise how eccentric this description is. Balzac, *La Comédie Humaine*, tome X (Bibliothèque de la Pléiade), p. 181, and p. 184, 185.

7. Stefan Zweig, *The Right to Heresy*, 1936, p. 80 (translated from the German, *Castellio gegen Calvin*, 1935).

8. E. Fromm, *The Fear of Freedom*, London, 1942, pp. 80 and 81.

9. O. Pfister, *Christianity and Fear*, ET from the German, 1948, p. 401, and p. 399.

10. O. Pfister, *Calvins Eingreifen in die Hexer- und Hexenprozesse von Peney*, 1545, 1947, p. 33 and p. 44.

11. E. Pfisterer, *Calvins Wirken in Genf*, 2nd edition, 1957. (While I have used this work with profit I should state that I have given additional grounds for rejecting Pfister's interpretation.)

12. Servetus had already been condemned by a Catholic tribunal in France to die by fire, but before that sentence was fulfilled he escaped from prison at Vienne.

13. Legate and Wightman held views on the divinity of Christ not far removed from those of Servetus. On the burning of these two men see E. M. Wilbur, *A History of Unitarianism in Transylvania, England, and America*, Cambridge, Massachusetts, 1952, pp. 177–179.

14. A. Huxley, *Proper Studies*, 1949, p. 287.

15. John Betjeman, *Collected Poems*, 1958, p. 55. Another poem entitled 'An Eighteenth Century Calvinistic Hymn' (p. 8) ends:
> 'Oh! I bless the good Lord for my boils
> For my mental and bodily pains,
> For without them my Faith all congeals
> And I'm doomed to HELL'S NE'ER ENDING FLAMES.'

To object to Betjeman's irony here is to lay oneself open to the charge of lacking a sense of humour; nevertheless, risking this, I must observe that the better the poet the more precise the statement and therefore to label the distasteful religious sentiment Betjeman pillories as Calvinistic seems odd when that sentiment is at least as strongly expressed by Catholic as well as by Protestant pietists. It is in that strange poem 'N.W.5 and N.6', (p. 275), where Betjeman loses the usual tone of his sentimental but attractive topography that he shows the probable origin of his fear and hatred of what he conceives to be 'Calvinism'.

16. *Lettres de Jean Calvin*, ed. Jules Bonnet, tome 2, p. 561. ['I have lived amidst extraordinary struggles here; I have been saluted in mockery at night, before my door, by fifty or sixty shots from arquebuses. Think how that would terrify a poor timid scholar such as I am, and, I confess, always have been. Then, later, I was hunted out of this town and went to

17

Strasbourg, whence, having remained some time, I was recalled, but I had no less trouble than before in trying to do my official duty. People, shouting "Blackguard", set their dogs at me which snatched hold of me. When there was a public tumult I went to the Council of Two Hundred and when they said to me in entering, "Monsieur, withdraw, we do not want you here," I replied, "I will not, go on, you scoundrels, and kill me, and my blood will cry against you, even these benches will require it of you." . . . You will experience the same . . . for you are amidst a perverse and ill-natured people . . . whilst I am nothing, yet I know that I have prevented many disturbances that would otherwise have occurred in Geneva . . . God has given me the power to write. . . . I have written nothing in hatred . . . but always I have faithfully attempted what I believed to be for the glory of God.' Cited from *John Calvin* by Basil Hall, Historical Association Pamphlet G.33, 1956, p. 5.]

17. A. L. Moore, *Lectures on the Reformation*, 1890, p. 502.

18. Moore, *op. cit.* p. 506.

19. L. Pullan, *Religion since the Reformation*, 1923, p. 83.

20. See the most recent full discussion of this subject in A. Biéler, *La Pensée économique et sociale de Calvin*, Geneva, 1959.

21. Pullan, *op. cit.*, p. 80.

22. Trevor Huddleston, *Naught for your Comfort*, London, 1956, pp. 63–64, p. 233.

23. Richard Hooker, *The Works of Mr. Richard Hooker*, 2 vols., 1865, Oxford at the Clarendon Press. The earlier quotation is from the Preface, vol. I, p. 100, the later reference on episcopacy is in the same Preface, p. 94. Two monographs on Calvin and Episcopacy are: Jacques Pannier, *Calvin et l'épiscopat*, Strasbourg 1927, and also Jacques Pannier, *Calvinisme et l'épiscopat*, in the *Révue hist. et phil. relig.*, 1926.

24. George Hakewill, *An Apologie or Declaration of the Power and Providence of God in the Government of the World*, 3rd edition, 1635, Book V, p. 110.

2 Calvin Against the Calvinists

Basil Hall

A CATHOLIC OPPONENT wrote of Calvin that God had condemned him since he had no children, to this Calvin replied that there were hosts of his children throughout the Christian world.[1] When Calvin made this bold claim in 1562, two years before his death, he was not boasting—to do so was foreign to his nature—he was stating a fact. Among Italians, Dutchmen, Poles, Swiss, Spaniards, Germans, Englishmen, Scots, and, of course, his fellow Frenchmen, he counted numerous sons and daughters, a great company ever enlarging. There is a sense in which the French Reformed Church would not have come into being if Calvin had never lived, for he was perhaps the greatest of the Huguenots. It was Calvin who gave to French Protestantism a body of writings, an organisation, a flavour and an attitude to life, which have endured through many changes to our own day. Moreover, the word Calvinism has come to be a keyword in the discussion of the history of ideas concerning not only Calvin's theological views and biblical studies, but also the effect of his work on the limitation of monarchical absolutism, the development of democracy, and the rise of the capitalist spirit. And yet the use of the word 'Calvinism' is so wide and varied, and comprehends such contradictory opinions that the question arises, How should Calvinism be defined?, and leads to the further question, To what extent was Calvin himself a Calvinist?

Before his death in 1564 Calvin had prepared the careful balance of his theological doctrines and his organisation of the Genevan Church in relation to the civil power, which constitutes what properly should be called 'Calvinism'. Unfortunately, after his death forces were already at work, not only in the small city-republic of Geneva but also in those parts of Europe where Calvin's disciples were established, which altered Calvin's carefully prepared balance of complementary doctrines. Those who followed him and had some effective claim to be his successors, men like Théodore de Bèze, altered that careful balance in order to meet new needs or because they had never fully accepted or appreciated the whole range of Calvin's thought. Again, there were those who are called Calvinists, but who did not so describe themselves, for example, John Knox, or the English Puritans of the seventeenth century, who omitted or ignored some of Calvin's essential emphases to a degree which would have made Calvin deny that they were satisfactory expounders of his teaching. Calvin himself of course, did not use the word 'Calvinist' and did not think of himself as the founder of something called Calvinism. Besides, it is a sad rule of history that it is the disciples and not the master who make doctrinaire what was intended to be sound doctrine. Calvin did not intend to produce a new church and a new organisation; he claimed to be doing no more than restoring the face of the early church as one cleanses an old painting of disfiguring varnish. He did not wish to deny continuity with the Christian past; he did not wish to leap back to a narrowly conceived apostolic age only as did the Anabaptist sectaries whose principles he abhorred, he wished rather to accept what was useful in the church life into which he had been born in so far as it could be justified by the teaching of Scripture, and subordinately by sound tradition, seen through the works of theologians of earlier times, and from evident and good reason. Calvin had no intention of founding a new church to be called Calvinist or Reformed, nor did he intend to establish a system of ideas to be called 'Calvinism'. Calvin is unjustly treated if he is thought of as a dominating personality wilfully imposing his arbitrarily defined views on those who were compelled to listen to them. His works show a remarkably self-effacing quality (although he can occasionally argue with an opponent like a prosecuting counsel), which is especially shown in the rarity of his references to himself and his own experiences: always he points away from himself to Scripture, to Christ, to the church. It would be unjust

20

to understand his theology as a system in the old scholastic sense, for Calvin would have regarded system-making as an all too human intellectual arrogance. Yet so fresh and profound were his theological insights, given with the lucid precision evident in all his writings, that the major themes of his thought, and the way in which they were articulated, must for want of a descriptive term be called 'Calvinism'. Nevertheless, it should be understood that 'Calvinism' means the careful balance of complementary doctrines which can be seen in his *Institutio*, especially in the final Latin edition of 1559, and it must not be used to mean the choosing of one or more of these doctrines, without reference to the whole, as sufficient in itself to justify, or indeed as the key to understanding, the term 'Calvinism'.

What is Calvinism?

FOR the past century and more there has been argument about the way in which 'Calvinism' should be interpreted. One approach has been to emphasise a particular doctrine as the basis of Calvin's theology, usually the doctrine of predestination, either in its own right or seen as a corollary of a particular emphasis on the sovereignty of God. Alongside of this have gone supporting studies of Calvin's early life showing that he was influenced by nominalist philosophy concerning God's providence; or the Scotist doctrine of God's *potentia absoluta;* or by his relation to a dominating father (this use of psychological analysis of Calvin's motives for insisting on God's absolute power rests upon an assumption, as do the other two supposed influences, since there is no useful evidence). From monographs to large volumes, from encyclopaedia articles to the *Dogmengeschichte* of last century writers have circled round this theme of Calvin's emphasis on God's sovereignty seen in His decrees of predestination. Again, Calvin's work at Geneva has been seen as the focus of his pragmatic theological aims through the discipline of men in obedience to God's laws, thereby forming another variant on the theme of God's sovereign will expressed in laws that must be obeyed. This discipline has been described as a continuation of the medieval ascetic principle in terms of 'open monasticism', or, more intelligibly, as a discipline leading

B

JOHN CALVIN

to bourgeois political self-consciousness in the period 1560–1660. Frequently Calvin is described as being excessively logical, but occasionally it is said that Calvin's views are contradictory; and one scholar in an illuminating study described Calvin's theology as a *complexio oppositorum*.[2] Various grounds might be suggested for these diverse opinions, for example, Lutheran theologians, aware that Luther has the doctrine of justification and forgiveness of sins at the heart of his theological discussion, assume that there must be a centre for Calvin's theology and find it in Calvin's doctrine of God's sovereignty and the consequent decrees of predestination—not without a hint of confessional rivalry in their depreciatory analysis. Again, Calvinism is seen by social historians like Troeltsch as the relationship of Calvin's churchmanship to the social and economic history of the sixteenth and seventeenth centuries, and by economic historians like Weber and Tawney as an important influence, though diversely interpreted, upon capitalist enterprise. Denominational rivalries have led to differing views of Calvinism whereby we are shown Congregationalists and some Anglicans ignoring Calvin's churchmanship while adopting for their own ends other aspects of his teaching, especially his doctrine of grace: but for Presbyterians Calvinism includes the explicit claim that Calvin was the founder and upholder of the Presbyterian system of church government and doctrine—a claim which is not quite justifiable.

Alongside of these conflicting interpretations have developed opposing methods of describing Calvin's thought. Some begin with the older Evangelical scheme of salvation, from the fall of man through substitutionary atonement in Christ's blood, justification, sanctification, to the judgment to come. Here selected passages of the *Institutio* are used to mark the Evangelical pattern. More recently those influenced by the Barthian theology of our time wish to show Calvin as drawing forth from the Scriptures alone not a schematised pattern of thought but a living theology having the immediacy of the Word of God and an emphasis on the Christocentric interpretation of the chief doctrines of the faith. Much new and fruitful work has been done on Calvin because of the seminal power of Barth's thought not least in his own discussion of Calvin's work. However, much of the interpretation of Calvin, based on Barthian

22

theology, shows the putting together of a mosaic of quotations selected mainly from the commentaries and sermons of Calvin. By selected quotations Calvin can be made almost as good a Barthian as Barth: the defect of this method is that it tends to ignore Calvin's advice that the pattern of his theology is his *Institutio*, and thereby a distinct arbitrariness, without a proper standard of reference for the quotations, is introduced. This method has the apparatus of careful scholarship, but often it achieves its results by ignoring what does not fit what the author has in mind to emphasise. In an important, and too frequently overlooked study by Louis Goumaz, *La Doctrine du Salut d'après les commentaires de Jean Calvin sur le Nouveau Testament*,[3] where a group of commentaries is taken together as a whole, there are passages quoted which stand out like rocks in a calm lake showing that in fact Calvin was not a Barth before his time, a fact which the *Institutio* itself would be sufficient to show when taken as a whole and not selectively. This criticism is not to be understood as an attempt to underrate the magisterial achievement of Karl Barth as a theologian of the Reformed Church; it is aimed rather at showing that it is historically unsatisfactory to apply Barthian theological method too narrowly to Calvin's work. Those writers who do so tend either to ignore Calvin's writing on, for example, the church, the state, and the sacraments, or else they tend to allow our contemporary theological needs to dominate their interpretation of Calvin.

The 1559 Institutio

WITH the *Institutio* of 1559 Calvin had arranged his work according to the pattern of the Apostles' Creed: the first book describes the knowledge of God the creator and of ourselves, the second describes the knowledge of God the Redeemer in Christ, the third describes the work of the Holy Spirit making salvation in Christ effective, the fourth describes the church and the means of grace and has a final chapter on civil government. In Book I Calvin discusses the means whereby we can learn to know God and ourselves. He shows that the natural world in its order, and man's conscience, render inexcusable our attempt to ignore God and His laws, but in itself natural theo-

23

JOHN CALVIN

logy becomes merely an idol, for nothing can reveal to us
the truth about God and ourselves save the Word of God made
known through the Scriptures by the Holy Spirit. Thereafter,
he expounds the doctrines of God, the Trinity, man's original
state in innocence, and God's providence which rules all things
and men. This first book, which shows God's sovereign power
in creation and providence is not to be regarded as the chief
to which the other three books are merely subordinate, for
Calvin intended the other three to have equal weight with the
first, and to be held in balance with it. In the second book he
begins with the fall of man which involved the whole race in that
original sin, and led to so great a corruption that the free choice
of obedience to God is lost. He shows that only in God's initiative in grace through Christ can there be renewal for man. The
law of Israel is shown as foreshadowing Christ who is fully
known through the gospel. This close relation of the Old and
New Testaments, of promise and fulfilment, is characteristic of
Calvin's theology. Thereafter follows the discussion of the
Person of Christ. His threefold office as prophet, priest and king,
and His work as Redeemer. In the third book Calvin describes
the work of the Holy Spirit in bringing to us the grace of Christ.
Here are discussed faith, the Christian life with its self-denial,
Justification by faith (and the rejection of Roman Catholic
teaching on the merit of works), prayer, eternal election: it is
important to note that in this final edition Calvin places the
doctrine of predestination at this stage, and not under the
doctrine of God's sovereignty and providence where it had been
for twenty years in the previous editions of the *Institutio*.
In the fourth book Calvin describes how all that he has previously discussed is brought into visible form and obedience
in the church, for outside of the visible church there is no salvation. Here in the longest book of the work he describes the
church's ministry, government, and discipline, gives his full
account of the sacraments, and concludes with a lengthy chapter
on civil government which he regards as associated with the
church in a Christian state, and as an expression of the public
life of the Christian citizen.

Calvin does not show that he wishes one book to be more
important than another, nor is each book to be considered as
self-contained and self-sufficient, all four are closely linked

24

together. One cannot abstract his doctrine of Scripture and ignore the fact that it is only effectively known and understood in the society of the visible church. One cannot talk of God's glory and majesty alone without talking of His revelation in Christ. One cannot talk of predestination without showing that it is related by Calvin to life in Christ through the Holy Spirit, and seeing that the best assurance of one's election lies in the visible life of the Christian within the Church and nourished by Christ through prayer and the sacraments. One may use his sermons, commentaries, treatises, and letters to expound his discussion of the various themes of theology, but this should not be done in such a way that his *Institutio* is ignored, or replaced, or its balance and its emphases are altered. For example, one cannot use an earlier treatise *De Aeterna Dei Praedestinatione* (1552) and say that here is Calvin's essential thought on the subject, and ignore Calvin's last edition of the *Institutio* (1559) in its discussion of the purposes and consequences of that doctrine.

Balance distorted: Beza

CALVIN'S successors nevertheless distorted the balance of doctrines which he had tried to maintain. His successor at Geneva, Beza, together with the Heidelberg theologian Zanchius, the English Puritan Perkins, and their associates and followers, bear much of the blame for this, even if we allow that theological change had to come in order to meet changing situations, yet it is not necessary to assume that only those changes that these men made were necessarily the right ones. When Calvin died in 1564 the close relationship which he had established between biblical exegesis, sound learning, and the well-being of the *Civitas Dei* (which was demonstrated in, though not in Calvin's view coterminous with, the small city-state of Geneva) suffered a loss of balance. The biblical exegesis became subordinated to a restored Aristotelianism, for Protestantism was now recoiling before the victories of the Counter Reformation, and it was beginning to use the weapons of its adversary. Sound learning, *bonae litterae*, could no longer enjoy the freedom and enthusiasm of the thirties of the sixteenth century: the polemic period of Protestant scholasticism now appearing showed less interest in both the classical humanism and the biblical humanism of the earlier period. Geneva became more and more the centre of an international movement combining doctrinaire views of church polity (it was under Beza that disciplined Presbyterianism was urged upon other churches as a polity claiming *de jure divino*) and a political ideology tending to republicanism, or to a limited monarchy, urged with greater sophistication than Calvin had conceived or desired.

The way in which the balance of Calvin's work was altered can be seen in the writings of Beza, and in those of the English Puritan William Perkins. Théodore de Bèze (Beza), ten years younger than Calvin, was born into a French noble family at Vézélay, and after combining the careers of a successful priest and a humanist man of letters, he turned to Protestantism and came to Lausanne to teach Greek in the Academy there. He differed from the Bernese magistrates, to whose rule Lausanne was subject, on church discipline, and left for Geneva where he found the discipline he wanted made effective through the work of his compatriot Calvin. Beza taught in the Academy of Geneva and established an international reputation with his edition of the text of the Greek New Testament accompanied by his own Latin version and annotations. Also he undertook diplomatic work on behalf of the French crown, and other governments, concerning church relations. On Calvin's death he succeeded to the leadership of the Genevan Church with an authority more readily accepted than that of Calvin, who had taken years in that turbulent city to obtain a comparable position, the fruits of whose struggle Beza now enjoyed. Without intending it Beza shifted the balance in Calvin's work. Calvin was not a doctrinaire Presbyterian, and he did not disapprove of episcopacy as long as prelacy, or the secularising of the episcopal office, was avoided: but Beza rejected episcopacy in favour of Presbyterianism with polemic vigour in his treatise *De Triplici Episcopatu* and elsewhere. He hardened the earlier method of scriptural exegesis, and made scripture itself into a corpus of revelation in almost propositional form with every part equal to the other parts in inspiration, thereby developing or encouraging a literalism, in the doctrine of the inspiration of Scripture, which encouraged Reformed theologians to go beyond the more guarded statements of Calvin. Something of scholastic formalism can be seen in Beza's work when it is compared with the more dynamic method and vivid style of Calvin. It was Beza who reverted to the medieval scholastic device of placing predestination under the doctrines of God and providence[4]—the position in which St. Thomas Aquinas discussed it—whereas Calvin had placed it eventually and deliberately under the doctrine of salvation. By doing so, although he was not alone in this, Beza re-opened the road to speculative determinism which Calvin had attempted to close. Beza's writings were largely polemic in origin and contained much less creative theology than Calvin's: it may have been the continuous polemic effort against Catholics and Lutherans that led Beza into exaggeration and distortion in doctrine. Beza taught Supralapsarianism (that is, the view that God decreed from before creation everything relating to man's future, including his fall and total depravity, which comes near to being thoroughgoing determinism)[5] whereas Calvin is not explicit on this point—he would have regarded discussion of it as being impertinently precise in setting out God's purposes. Again, Beza taught the imputation of Adam's sin to all mankind with precision, whereas Calvin, not finding this to be clear in Scripture, had avoided the point: and Beza taught explicitly that Christ did not die for all mankind but only for the elect (that is, the doctrine of limited atonement), whereas Calvin was not so explicit on this, rather he held that the Gospel is offered by God for all mankind, and that we should preach it to all men.[6] In his refutation of the Decrees of the Council of Trent, his *Acta Synodi Tridentinae: Cum Antidoto*, 1547, Calvin wrote that he had no comment to make on that decree which said that Christ died for all men.[7] It is possible to find some evidence in Calvin's writings which might lead to an opposite view (for example, his proposal that 'all men shall be saved' means members of every race and community of men), but taking his discussions of the Atonement and its relation to the elect where these are fully rounded he does not emphasise that well-worn theme of later Calvinism that Christ died only for the elect. He may have been illogical in avoiding this point, but this is typical of his refusal to be too systematic, too logical and too precise about God's purposes—Beza and his successors were not so inhibited. Much of the dislike of the Calvinist view of a limited Atonement stems

27

not from what Calvin said so much as from what upholders of the 'Five Points of Dort' emphasised: this can be seen clearly in the controversial writings of A. M. Toplady, or in Jonathan Edwards's work on *The Freedom of the Will*, where Calvin's name is hardly ever mentioned and his theological aims are ignored. Lastly, Beza not only taught that justification means pardon of sins but also the acceptance of men as righteous,[8] whereas Calvin did not clearly say this. All these points on the Bezan doctrine of grace arose in the discussion on grace in the seventeenth century with men who were unhappy about the decisions made at the Synod of Dort in 1619 where the extreme form of scholastic 'Calvinism' was achieved in the Five Articles which broke the unity of Calvin's theology and replaced his biblical dynamism by formulae. (These Articles were: predestination not dependent on faith, limited atonement, total depravity of man, irresistible grace, the impossibility of falling from grace.) In fairness to Beza it should be added that his treatment of these matters, while it does not show Calvin's careful avoiding of extreme statements, is not so pronounced as that of those seventeenth century writers who supported wholeheartedly the decrees of the Synod of Dort, for example, the Dutchman Bogerman or the Englishman William Twisse. Lastly, it is to Beza, and not to Calvin (who insisted on obedience, martyrdom, or flight) that the principle of resistance to tyrannous princes is due: the Genevan Reformation became suspect because of the incitement to rebellion in his *De Jure Magistratuum in subditos, et officio subditorum ergaMagistratus.*[9]

Balance distorted: Perkins

ANOTHER aspect of the transformation of Calvin's calvinism can be seen in the writings of the Englishman William Perkins whose work profoundly influenced Puritan theology, brought Arminius's refutation of Perkins's doctrine of predestination, and led ultimately, therefore, to the Decrees of the Synod of Dort condemning Arminius. Perkins, a fellow of Christ's College Cambridge, wrote voluminously before his early death at forty-four in 1602. He showed the characteristic English pragmatism which desired to feel the work of grace, and introduced casuistry to Protestant theology in his book *The Whole Treatise of the Cases of Conscience*, thereby opening the way for a number of Puritan works on moral theology of which the most signicant were those of his pupil William Ames, and, later in the century, *The Christian Directory* of Richard Baxter — all this displays an emphasis and a method quite different from Calvin's. With Perkins we can see, as with Beza, a more severe, more speculative and less biblical version of the doctrine of grace lacking Calvin's attempt to give it Christocentric emphasis. Also the element of Puritan pragmatism, the desire for personal feeling in the work of grace (which was to have an influence on the development of Pietism on the continent), the warm assurance of election known within and demonstrated outwardly in one's works of piety, reversed Calvin's purpose for he pointed away from the feelings of the individual to Scripture, Christ, the church and the sacraments for the assurance of salvation. This represents the essential factor in the division between Calvin's own thought and the development of English Protestantism which is miscalled calvinism.

In *A Golden Chaine concerning the Order of the Causes of Salvation and Damnation, according to God's Word*, Perkins, after five articles on Scripture and God, wrote in article 6 of God's decree: 'Therefore the Lord according to His good pleasure hath more certainly decreed every thing and action, whether past present or to come, together with the circumstances of place, time, means, and end. Yea, He hath most justly decreed the wicked works of the wicked. The same decree of God is the first and principal working cause of all things.' Then in article 7: 'God's decree in as much as it concerneth man is called predestination by the which He hath ordained all men either to salvation or condemnation for His own glory.' In article 15: 'Election is seen as the working out of His decree wherein Christ is seen as the mediator of the elect.' In these quotations we see that a determinist viewpoint has taken control: the qualifications and balance of doctrines which Calvin maintained are laid aside, and it is further significant that under article 31, the Covenant of Grace is developed as the prelude to the discussion of the sacraments thereby making the force of the sacraments dependent upon the administration of the Covenant in a way foreign to Calvin's method.[10] This is made even

29

plainer in his turning again to the discussion of how the decrees are efficacious in the individual, thereby undercutting the sacraments and the life of the church: moreover, the doctrine of the church is not given a separate article. The relation between the later modifications of Calvin's doctrine and Perkins himself can be seen in a translation by Perkins of a work of Beza's under the title *A Treatise for comforting such as are troubled about their Predestination* which he appended to a work of his own on predestination.[11] It is significant that he does not go to Calvin for this but to Beza, for here Calvin's concern to give an objective basis to the doctrine of election is overthrown by Beza's statement that Baptism and the Lord's Supper are insufficient help in assuring afflicted consciences, for while he does not deny the value of the sacraments yet he suggests other helps, for example, that 'you should pray so that you feel inwardly'. In his treatise *On the Creed* Perkins can write that to know our election we should look for signs and testimonies in ourselves, and one of these testimonies is 'to pray with groans and sighs' and he uses phrases like 'needing to feel Christ's promises' and 'the affection of Christ'.[12] This is the highroad to that Puritan emphasis on 'groaning in prayer' which will dominate their piety in the seventeenth century, and spread with less beneficial results among the sectaries of the Commonwealth. Again, Perkins appended to his own *A Case of Conscience, the greatest that ever was; how a man may know whether he be the child of God or no*—and the title shows not only the new emphasis on casuistry but also the pietist emphasis on feeling—the little discourse by Zanchius, of the Calvinist university of Heidelberg, which discusses the same problem in a similar way. Lastly, under the title *The Christian Warfare* Perkins shows the personal struggle for the assurance of grace characteristic of Puritan individualism, and concludes with a long discussion on the divine decrees and the state of the elect and the reprobate. What Calvin had described as a profound mystery, a labyrinth, to be avoided in ordinary pastoral oversight, Perkins has made into a commonplace of the religious life.

Changes after Calvin's death

AS has been said above, it is arguable that with the political and theological changes, which came after Calvin's death, within the framework of the national churches of the Reformation and the bitter struggle between Catholic and Protestant in Europe, Calvinism was bound to change. This is true but it is not the same thing as to say that the changes were inevitable and right in the directions which they took. There is not space here to develop this argument, but some suggestions may be made. For example, when Calvin's theological principles crossed the English Channel, like other continental ideas they suffered modification. First, Calvin himself was not always correctly informed about the English religious situation by English correspondents and visitors to Geneva who wished to use the authority of his name to win support for their more radical views. The description of the second Book of Common Prayer of Edward VI, sent by Knox and Whittingham and their friends from Frankfurt to Calvin to seek his aid against Dr. Cox and the Anglican party who wished to maintain the book in its entirety at Frankfurt, is prejudiced and attempts to persuade Calvin by the distortion of certain things in the book: even on this biassed evidence Calvin could find nothing worse to say than that the book—*qualem describitis*—contained *multas tolerabiles ineptias*.[13] In this situation what Calvin wrote about English affairs though shrewd did not seem strictly relevant to the religious problems of England in a clear and precise way. Secondly, there were Englishmen who because of the native tradition of Protestantism, partly based on the old Lollard negations, and to a much greater degree based on devotion to the Reformation principles of Zürich —men who admired Bishop Hooper, that stubborn proponent of a theology which was to be a breeding ground of the more negative aspects of Puritanism—selected certain elements in Calvin's writings and adapted them to English religious needs while claiming that Calvin supported them in their views. Brief evidence for this will be shown later. Thirdly, it was unfortunate that English refugees wrote and printed at Geneva pamphlets attacking government by queens, and implying the need for armed rebellion: Calvin did not understand English and did not know of these proceedings. These publications meant that Queen Elizabeth disliked Geneva and anything or anyone connected with it. As we have seen, Calvin had held that the subject may not rebel against his prince, he must suffer or seek exile: it was a bitter irony that his theological work was distrusted by the English Crown after 1560 by whom he was regarded as a republican and instigator of rebellion, a view that was felt to be justified when Beza began his political activity later. Many who have written on Calvin in the last hundred years appear to accept Elizabeth's view of him, in spite of Calvin's own writings, largely because they wish to make of Calvin a founder of modern democracy, one who recognised the dangers of royal absolutism and explicitly sought and found means for limiting it. If this could be proved then it would be in spite of Calvin. Professor McNeill, whose recent book *Calvin and Calvinism* is a record of the growth and achievement of the Reformed Churches, sees Calvin in their reflected light. In a lengthy note to the cryptic sentence of Calvin in the last chapter of the *Institutio* on the right of the Magistrates to restrain the tyranny of kings, he seeks to establish Calvin's association with the views of Knox, Philippe du Plessis-Mornay, Hotman, and Jurieu, but neither in the sentence to which the note refers nor in the note itself is it clearly established that Calvin agreed with the views of these men.[14] When commanded to blaspheme against God by false worship, Calvin would agree that one could resist to the extent of martyrdom but not to rebellion in arms: his correspondence does not show Calvin supporting the proponents of armed resistance in the Protestant cause. Calvin's legal training in the Roman Civil Law, with its authoritarian attitude to positive law, if nothing else, would have led him to doubt the rights of democracy; in fact, he thought democracy would be as potentially tyrannous as other forms of government save possibly an aristocratic oligarchy. His attitude to François Hotman, who was to write the *Franco-Gallia* after Calvin's death expressing views similar to those of Knox, was guarded; whereas Beza gave Hotman his clear approval, for as has been show above, Beza supported those political writers who urged that monarchy should be limited by a magistracy, a principle that was to be helpful later to the advocates of bourgeois parliamentarianism.

Calvin and England

THE evidence which can be used to discover the nature and extent of Calvin's influence on English religious life is scattered and varied: it can be found in correspondence of the period 1545–1640, and in references to him and his work in books printed in the period. But to glean material from this wide field would require much greater scope than is possible here. Calvin's own letters to Englishmen; the publication of his writings in English with prefatory addresses; and references to Calvin in the controversial literature of Elizabeth's reign will be briefly referred to here. Calvin's letters to England were addressed to Archbishop Cranmer, the Duke of Somerset, Edward VI, Sir John Cheke the king's tutor, William Cecil, and Queen Elizabeth—these letters were, of course, in French or Latin. We can see from them that Calvin did not press the Genevan type of reform, rather he urged the principles of reformation in general terms, proposing the drawing up of a confession of faith, the practice of catechising, more frequent and abler preaching, and the discipline of morals. This is the sort of exhortation one would expect to hear from any Reformer. In one of his letters to Cranmer Calvin's abruptness about Cranmer's delay in advancing Protestant truth was probably the consequence of some harsh judgment of Cranmer sent to Calvin by a zealot who was in the English manner more Protestant than Calvin himself.[15] But on another occasion he cordially agreed with Cranmer's desire for a Council of representatives of the Protestant Churches to find a common agreement, and regretted that he could not leave Geneva.[16] Calvin does not seem to have been well informed about the partisan groups of the Edwardine Church and, as indeed any observer might well have been, he was puzzled by the situation under Elizabeth. It is certainly arguable that Calvin had less real influence on English religion than Bucer of Strasbourg and Cambridge and Bullinger of Zürich. In the more settled conditions of Elizabeth's reign in the Universities and the dioceses Bullinger's *Decades* are referred to as required reading in the training of the clergy, whereas in Kennedy's account of Elizabethan episcopal administration[17] Calvin's *Institutio* is referred to only once under this head. Moreover, Bullinger had been known to many of the English refugees from the Marian persecution, among whom were men of prominence in the Elizabethan Church, Bishops Jewel, Parkhurst, Grindal, and Sandys. John Knox himself, contrary to the received opinion about him, leaned more to Zurich than to Geneva in his theology and something of his practice and he had been the disciple of George Wishart whose theological interests were entirely German Swiss. Sampson, one of the refugees in the English congregation at Geneva, wrote that Grindal, Parker, and Sandys were in Edward's reign, friends of Bucer 'and much approved of Bucer's *De Regno Christi* in private talk.'[18] And it is significant that Bishop Hooper writing from Zürich to Bucer in 1548 could go so far as to say of Calvin's doctrine of the Lord's Supper: 'I had never any intention of using my pen either against Calvin or Farel, although Calvin's commentaries on the first epistle to the Corinthians displeased me exceedingly'—for Hooper was much nearer to Zwingli than to Calvin on the doctrine of the eucharistic presence.[19]

Many of Calvin's works were translated into English, including all of his New Testament and most of his Old Testament commentaries; many of his collections of sermons among them the massive volumes on Job and on Deuteronomy; and some of his treatises, for example, *An Admonicion against astrology judiciall*, in 1561, *A faythful and moste godly treatyse concernying the Sacrament*, in 1549, *A short instruction agaynst the pestiferous errours of the Anabaptists*, in 1549, and his *Treatise on Relics*, in 1561, and perhaps the best translation in English for rendering the flavour of Calvin's style, *The Institution of the Christian Religion*. Some of these works, especially the last, had several editions. Many of the translators were known in the literary and social as well as the religious life of their time. Among them were Thomas Norton, translator of *The Institutio* and author of the tragedy *Gorboduc*; Laurence Tomson, who in 1576 revised the translation of the New Testament in the Genevan English version of the Bible using Beza's notes and text, was secretary to Sir Francis Walsingham, English ambassador in Paris; and the greatest translator of them all, Arthur Golding who produced an excellent version of Ovid's *Metamorphoses* in English verse. That men of this ability translated Calvin shows that he was not merely the favourite of English social and religious radicals. Interesting results can be gained from a study of these translators and their patrons seen as part of the provenance of English protestantism, but this work must be undertaken elsewhere. One of these translators, Clement Cotton, who came latest in date, shows in his prefatory matter the change of tone from Calvin's Calvinism to English Puritanism. He translated some lectures of Calvin on the first five chapters of Jeremiah, and this small work was published in 1620. He addressed the book to Lucy, Countess of Bedford, and the Lady Anne Harrington, and used phrases like these: 'the saving promises of the gospel', 'sweetly preacheth Christ', 'any . . . pricked in conscience and humbled' which have that pietist flavour more reminiscent of English Puritanism than of Calvin himself. Cotton also translated Calvin's commentary on Isaiah and published it in 1609 with a prefatory poem by Francis Hering in praise of the Reformers among whom, after Latimer and others, are 'Diering, Greenham, Perkins, and foreign lights, Beza, Ursinus, Martyr, Musculus in English dress' and then 'great Calvin'. It is significant to look again at some of the names chosen here: Ursinus was of Heidelberg like Zanchius whom Perkins had used in his own work, and his discourse on keeping the Sabbath had been translated into English; Greenham and Perkins were the great lights of that early Puritanism which modified original Calvinism. Before turning to the next point it should be remembered, of course, that Calvin's works were widely used in their Latin, as well, as to a lesser extent in their French, editions by English scholars, so that his influence was far from being confined to the English translations of his writings.

In the controversy between Anglicans and Puritans Calvin's name was more frequently used by the Anglicans in order to show that Calvin would not have agreed with the Puritans in their judgments on the practice and government of the Church of England. The first important stage of this controversy came in the seventies between John Whitgift, the Master of Trinity College, Cambridge, and later Archbishop of Canterbury, and Thomas Cartwright, who was expelled from the Lady Margaret's Professorship of Divinity at Cambridge for teaching Bezan churchmanship or Presbyterianism. In the course of the Admonition Controversy as it has come to be called, Cartwright, when pressed by Whitgift with quotations from Calvin which were against Cartwright's views, replied: '. . . we receive M. Calvin, and weigh of him, as of the notoblest instrument that the Lord hath stirred up for the purging of His Churches, and of the restoring of the plain and sincere interpretation of the Scriptures, which hath been since the Apostles' time. And yet we

35

do not so read his works, that we believe any thing to be true because he saith it, but so far as we can esteem that that which he saith doth agree with the canonical scriptures.'[20] Both Whitgift and Cartwright used the argument that if Calvin had been alive in their time he would have supported them, and in the questions they debated about ceremonies and the contents of the Prayer Book it is probable that Whitgift's claim was justified: 'If M. Calvin were alive and understood the state of our church and controversy truly, I verily believe that he would utterly condemn your doings; . . . your passing over so lightly of quotations from Calvin doth argue your lack of ability to answer them. Indeed they flatly determine this controversy, and in effect overthrow your whole book.'[21] All this shows that they were arguing about an English matter to which Calvin's work did not directly apply, and both men were using him for their own ends, but it is significant that Whitgift can adduce Calvin in support of a churchmanship with which Calvin is not usually associated. Again, Richard Field, Dean of Gloucester, in his book *Of the Church*, published in 1606–1610, written in defence of Protestant churchmanship against Roman Catholic criticism, and regarded as a work claiming the catholicity of the Church of England, frequently quotes Calvin and supports his work against Romanist attack. Whereas Perkins and other Puritans, as has been suggested already, hardly refer to Calvin at all. Richard Bancroft, then Bishop of London and later Archbishop of Canterbury, published in 1599 *Of the Pretended Holy Discipline* in which he combined Whitgift's position with greater polemic truculence, also used Calvin's works to show that Calvin was not a protagonist of the Puritan positions: 'And that you may perceive, what great difference there is betwixt our men's spirits and Maister Calvins; their outrage, and his modestie: their pride and his humilitie: their rashness, ignorance, and giddiness, and his sobrietie, learning, and judgment . . . But it may peradventure be sayd: that, howsoever Calvin did carrie himselfe in this cause, yet Beza is of another opinion. Indeed he is so: but it turneth more and more dayly to his own discredit. He succeeded Maister Calvin in place; but neither in his learning nor in all his vertues.'[22] This shows that at least one contemporary of the so-called calvinists of Elizabethan England did not regard them as being legitimately Calvinists at all.

36

CALVIN AGAINST THE CALVINISTS

NOTES

1. *Responsio ad Balduini Convicia.* CO IX. 576. Dederat mihi Deus filiolum: abstulit. Hoc quoque recenset inter probra liberis me carere. Atque mihi filiorum sunt myriades in toto orbe Christiano.

2. Hermann Bauke, *Die Probleme der Theologie Calvins*, 1922.

3. Nyon, 1917. Goumaz shows the distinctive emphasis of Calvin on 'la notion de causalité dans les commentaires' which has a philosophical root rather than a biblical one: Barth also has pointed to this element in Calvin's thought.

4. Beza, *Tractationes Theologiae*, vol. I, pp. 170 ff. *Summa sive descriptio et distributio causarum salutis electorum, et exitu reproborum.*

5. Beza, *Tractationes Theologiae*, vol. I, pp. 344, 362, 418; vol. III, p. 404.

6. *op. cit.*, vol. I, p. 171 and p. 183.

7. CO VII. 371 ff.

8. Beza, *op. cit.*, vol. III, p. 248, and p. 256.

9. The original edition was in French, 1574, with the title *Du droit des Magistrats sur les subjets: Traité très necessaire en ce temps pour advertir de leur devoir, tant les Magistrats que les subjets.* Printed at Lyons where the Latin edition was printed 1576. See the translation edited by A. H. Murray, with a preface by the late Professor A. A. van Schelven. Cape Town, Pretoria. n.d.

10. *The Works of William Perkins.* 1612. vol. I, pp. 16, 24, 70.

11. *op. cit.*, p. 114.

12. *op. cit.*, p. 284.

13. Calvin, *Epistolae et Responsae*, Geneva, 1576, p. 158. CO. No. 2091.

14. J. T. McNeill, editor, John Calvin: *The Institutes of the Christian Religion*, 1961, vol. II, pp. 1518–9.

15. Calvin, *Epistolae et Responsae*, p. 101. CO. No. 1426.

16. *op. cit.*, p. 100. CO. No. 1619,

17. W. P. M. Kennedy. *Elizabethan Episcopal Administration* (Alcuin Club Tracts), 1924, vol. II. pp. 45, 46, 150, 249, 250.

18. Strype, *Annals of the Reformation in England*, 1709, vol. II, Pt. I, pp. 393–395.

19. *Original Letters* (Parker Society), vol. I, p. 48.

20. *Whitgift's Works* (Parker Society), vol. I, pp. 243–247.

21. *op. cit.*, p. 250.

22. R. Bancroft, *A survay of the Pretended Holy Discipline*, 1593, p. 127

3 The Sources of Calvin's Seneca Commentary

Ford Lewis Battles

THERE ARE in the *Institutio Christianae Religionis* many clear echoes of Calvin's earlier concentration upon classical antiquity. The heavy dependence on Cicero's philosophical treatises in *Inst*. I. i–v is well known; scattered throughout Calvin's master work are quotations from the chief Latin and Greek writers. Furthermore, his very vocabulary and style are steeped in ancient culture. Yet there are two passages which more than any others seem to sum up his verdict, after conversion, upon classical culture and upon his own humanist studies.

The first of these, at *Inst*. II. ii. 15, eloquently asserts the Spirit of God to be the sole fountain of truth and calls upon men not to despise the truth wherever it shall be found; he then turns to the sciences and the arts themselves:

> What then? Shall we deny that the truth shone upon the ancient jurists who established civic order and discipline with such great equity? Shall we say that the philosophers were blind in their fine observation and artful description of nature? Shall we say that those men were devoid of understanding who conceived the art of disputation and taught us to speak reasonably? Shall we say that they are insane who developed medicine, devoting their labour to our benefit? What shall we say of all the mathematical sciences? Shall we consider them the ravings of madmen? No, we cannot read the writings of the ancients on these subjects without great admiration. We marvel at them because we are compelled to recognise how pre-eminent they are. But shall we count anything praiseworthy or noble without recognising at the same time that it comes from God? Let us be ashamed of such ingratitude, into which not even the pagan poets fell, for they confessed that the

38

gods had invented philosophy, laws, and all useful arts. Those men whom Scripture calls 'natural men' were, indeed, sharp and penetrating in their investigation of things below. Let us, accordingly, learn by their example how many gifts the Lord left to human nature even after it was despoiled of its true good.

In this simple catalogue is the sum of Calvin's preparatory studies, and of the content of the Commentary on Seneca's *De Clementia*, his first published treatise. Law, Philosophy, Rhetoric, Medicine, Mathematics and Poetry are mentioned by name. He could well have added History.

He had studied the Pandects and its chief commentators, traditional and contemporary, including what Budaeus called 'the triumvirate'—Alciatus, Zasius, and Budaeus.[1] He had become reasonably well versed in ancient philosophy through Cicero and Seneca, Plutarch, and other writers. Yet at this time —in the midst of his humanist studies at Paris[2]—he had not read Plato[3] and Aristotle[4] in Greek. He had laid a foundation in rhetoric and dialectic as evidenced not only by his use of technical terms, but also by his perceptive criticisms of Seneca's style and thought, and by his own excellent Latin style as well. His interest in and sympathy for medicine are reflected in the pages of the commentary,[5] and he has had occasion to compare various ancient views of the nature of the human body and soul.[6] Even mathematics is represented by a reference to Euclid,[7] and other useful arts, such as agriculture[8] and warfare[9] are not unmentioned. The poets are copiously quoted,[10] but always to make some lexical, philosophical, moral or historical point. The preponderance of Latin over Greek poets gives evidence of his essentially second-hand knowledge of Greek literature.[11] While his use of Latin literature shows some independence, even here he used, as we shall see, contemporary compilations and commentaries for much of his material. The historians are richly represented: not only had he read with some care the chief Latin writers (notably Suetonius, Tacitus, and Livy) but also the lesser Scriptores Rei Augustae, and was to some extent familiar with the main Greek historians of Rome— Plutarch, Arrian, Herodian, Dio Cassius, and Dio Halicarnassus. However, these last were consulted almost entirely in Latin translations, when references to them were not of secondary derivation.

39

These writers do not exhaust Calvin's sources, but they suggest the chief authors he had in mind when he penned his tribute to ancient men of learning. But to stop with this one quotation would give a false impression of Calvin's mature judgment of classical antiquity. The second quotation, from *Inst.* I. viii. 1, traces in a phrase or two Calvin's pilgrimage:

> Read Demosthenes or Cicero, read Plato, Aristotle, and others of that tribe. They will, I admit, allure you, delight you, move you, enrapture you in wonderful measure. But betake yourself from them to this sacred reading. Then, in spite of yourself, so deeply will it affect you, so penetrate your heart, so fix itself in your very marrow, that, compared with its deep impressions, such vigour as the orators and philosophers have will nearly vanish. Consequently it is easy to see that the Sacred Scriptures, which so far surpass all gifts and graces of human endeavour, breathe something divine.[12]

It is with this divided judgment of the Graeco-Roman world, penned by Calvin for the second Latin edition of the *Institutio*, lecarly before us, that we turn to a more detailed examination of his Commentary on Seneca's *De Clementia*.

The two modern pillars: Erasmus and Budaeus

ONCE I penetrated the façade of '74 Latin and 22 Greek Authors', long uncritically attributed to the classical competence of the young Calvin, I realised that the question to answer was not 'what Greek or Latin writers did Calvin cite?' but rather 'how did he come by these citations? Just as important as finding out *what* Calvin read was to learn *where* he read it.

Calvin actually suggests, or at least hints, *where* he read. Twice he uses the figure of 'pillar' to pay tribute to the chief contemporary and ancient authorities for his commentary. Gulielmus Budaeus (1467–1540) is called 'the first ornament and pillar of literature',[13] while Desiderius Erasmus is named 'the second ornament of literature'.[14] In another place, Calvin speaks of Seneca as 'second only to Cicero a veritable pillar of Roman philosophy and literature (eloquence)'.[15] Calvin's preference for Budaeus over Erasmus was not only a reflection of his own national pride, for Budaeus had indeed brought the palm of learning to France.[16]

SOURCES OF CALVIN'S SENECA COMMENTARY

Erasmus

THAT he was indebted to Erasmus, nevertheless, Calvin was quick to acknowledge. Erasmus, in Calvin's phrase had 'twice sweated in the arena',[17] in preparing editions of Seneca in 1515 / and 1529. The need to correct and supplement Erasmus' work was one reason for choosing to comment on the *De Clementia*. 'There are certain things which have escaped the notice of even Erasmus himself . . . and which I say without any ill-will.'[18] Although in the body of the Commentary Calvin refers to Erasmus by name only five times on textual matters, Dr. A. M. Hugo, with whom I am working on a new edition of the Seneca Commentary, has listed some 68 points where Calvin discusses Erasmus' reading in arriving at his own. A reference to Erasmus' use of Virgil is praised as 'learned'.[19] But at other points Calvin joins issue with Erasmus. For example, against Erasmus' assertion that the word *licentia* has only a bad meaning in classic Latinity, Calvin cites instances where it has a good meaning.[20] Even Erasmus' edition of Suetonius draws a small criticism.[21]

Of actual Erasmian sources Calvin mentions the *Adagia* three times,[22] even though there may be as many as 26 uses of it. The *Apophthegmata* may have been quoted 6 times, but not by name. Erasmus' *Panegyric of Philip* is referred to once,[23] but was certainly used at several other points. His *Education of a Christian Prince* (1515–1516), drawn from the standard Greek and Roman writers on the princely office (including Seneca's *De Clementia*) doubtless challenged Calvin to comment independently on the Seneca text.[24] No effort has been made to determine what Erasmian editions of classical and patristic writers Calvin used; but, in addition to the Suetonius he doubtless knew Augustine and other Fathers in Erasmian editions.[25] / No scholar of the time could avoid becoming indebted to Erasmus.

There is on the other hand some evidence that Calvin, at certain points, studiously avoided using Erasmus. Though the Commentary is crammed with proverbial wisdom, it is surprising that so little of it has been drawn from the *Adagia*. It would have been easy for Calvin to turn to this enormous compend for material, but he seldom used it. Of more than passing interest is the fact that, while Calvin's Seneca Commentary went virtually unnoticed, it was extensively plagiarised by Gilbertus Cognatus (Gilbert Cousin), who had been Erasmus' secretary from 1530–35, in preparing a supplement to the *Adagia* which was printed much later. That Cognatus could so use it was a tribute to the relatively independent character of Calvin's work as much as to the aphoristic character of Seneca.

Budaeus

WHEN one turns to Budaeus, however, Calvin's dependence gradually emerges. Budaeus is cited by name 7 times in the text of the Commentary, although only the *Annotationes in Pandectas* and its sequel or continuation are identified. Bohatec's study, *Bude und Calvin*,[26] concentrates mainly on parallels between Budaeus and Calvin's later writings; he refers only a few times to the *De Clementia* Commentary. By contrast, in the course of the present investigation some 90 quotations or clear parallels have been identified. This number far from exhausts Calvin's dependence upon Budaeus.

For many of the problems in annotation, Budaeus is Calvin's starting point. To explain the text of Seneca and to provide in a concise manner the necessary background material, some degree of versatility was demanded of the commentator. It is no wonder that the rich learning of Budaeus was unashamedly used by the young Calvin.

The material suggested by Budaeus[27] comes chiefly from two works: first, the *Annotationes in Pandectas*, and its continuation, *Annotationes Reliquae in Pandectas* (called by Calvin, *Annotationes Posteriores*) and, secondly, the interesting if somewhat miscellaneous treatise on ancient coinage, *De Asse et Partibus eius*. This material may be divided into five main classes: legal terms, Roman institutions and history, political philosophy, philosophy in general, literature.

(1) *Legal terms*. Budaeus' *Annotationes in Pandectas* is an effort to explain a limited number of technical terms and concepts of Justinian's *Corpus Juris Civilis*, within the broadest sort of humanist framework. In fact, the select passages of the Pandects discussed in the *Annotationes* often served as an excuse for extended notes not only on legal terms and institutions, but

42

also on political, theological, philosophical, moral, historical, and other questions. Budaeus' *Annotationes* differed markedly from traditional commentaries on Roman Law, although imitated by jurisconsulti like Alciatus. To understand Roman Law, Budaeus felt, one must immerse oneself in Graeco-Roman history, and it is no wonder that Calvin found this work attractive. Hence, as Calvin came upon legal usages in his text, he turned to Budaeus for assistance.

Such technical terms as *manum iniicere*,[28] *index (indicium)*,[29] *fidem praestare*,[30] *hereditatem adire/cernere*,[31] *aestimare litem*,[32] and the like had been copiously discussed by Budaeus, with historical, oratorical, and even poetic parallels from Roman literature. Procedural terms like *deprecatio*[33] and *cognitio*[34] had been similarly treated. Many of Calvin's numerous Ciceronian and other citations actually stem from Budaeus' juridical exegesis.[35] More important, however, than these isolated terms, is Calvin's grasp of the contrast between *aequum et bonum* and *summum ius*,[36] as expounded by Budaeus,[37] for this concept tempered his critique of Seneca's definition of *clementia*.

(2) *Roman Institutions*. Closely related to legal terminology is the copious material on Roman institutions and society, found in the *Annotationes in Pandectas* and in the *De Asse*. These two treatises overlap at many points, and Calvin drew from both, often for the same context. To sketch the background of Seneca's essay on the political instruction of the young Nero, Calvin needed a clear conception not only of the early empire, but of the whole course of Roman history. Technical questions on the size of Roman legions,[38] the population of imperial Rome,[39] the political offices of Republic and Empire,[40] and the social classes,[41] had to be answered. Fleeting allusions to Actium Sulla,[42] etc., called for brief notes.

Calvin found statistical material on Roman population and wealth already assembled by Budaeus in the *De Asse*.[43] Budaeus had, in his exposition of select passages in the Pandects, dealt at length with the office of dictator,[44] quaestor,[45] centurion,[46] tribune,[47] and the like. But more important Budaeus demonstrated to Calvin a sound method of historical criticism. Budaeus had painstakingly compared Latin and Greek writers on Roman history and suggested canons of evidence.[48] Calvin, apt pupil that he was, treated critically, with use of Latin and Greek

43

sources, many events of the second triumvirate and of Augustus' reign. However, unlike Budaeus (who was a consummate Hellenist), Calvin depended largely on recent Latin translations of Greek writers, yet not without at least one attempt to check translation.[49]

(3) *Political Philosophy*. It was fashionable during the Renaissance for the humanists to write instructive essays for young princes, and moving panegyrics for rulers. To prepare these, the ancients were plundered. Besides Erasmus' *Education of a Christian Prince* there is to be noted the political teaching of Budaeus in the *Annotationes* and the *De Asse*, even if his posthumously-published *L'Institution du Prince* (1547)[50] may not have been known to Calvin in 1532.

Since Calvin had access to a variety of political wisdom in preparing his Commentary, one cannot at a particular point always state his source with certainty. But there is good evidence that the Christianised Plutarch of Budaeus, with Platonic, Aristotelian and Stoic elements (as well as material from Cicero) was determinative in forming Calvin's political philosophy. The Seneca Commentary is an important link between Budaeus' ideas in the *Annotationes in Pandectas* and Calvin's fully formed views at the beginning and end of the *Institutio*. Among the themes common to all three works are the following: rulers as ministers of God or as images of God;[51] Budaeus' understanding of the relation of the ruler to the law is carried over, by way of the Seneca Commentary, to the *Institutio*.

(4) *Philosophy*. Budaeus was probably Calvin's starting point for certain lines of philosophical inquiry. The nature of the soul and its relationship to the body had engaged Budaeus' attention in both treatises and he made a particularly detailed study of this subject in the *De Asse*.[52] Calvin quoted at length from Budaeus' own translation of Plutarch's *De Placitis Philosophorum*.[53] For the Stoic concept of *euthymia*, drawn from Democritus, Calvin first turned to Budaeus.[54] While Calvin used Cicero more than any other ancient writer for philosophical material, the Seneca Commentary suggests that he was largely dependent upon Budaeus for his initial contact with Greek philosophy. In fact, Budaeus' use of Cicero himself was doubtless instructive for the young scholar.

(5) *Literature*. Budaeus taught Calvin the relevance not only

44

of the historians, jurists, and philosophers, to the understanding of life, but also the relevance of the poets and rhetoricians. Budaeus had mined the ancient commentators before him. Thus Calvin came to the Latin poets not less as a literary critic than as a moralist and philosopher; not blind to their beauty of language, but bent on gaining insight into meaning through a comparative study of their vocabulary, with the assistance of their ancient and latter-day commentators. What seems at first a rather strange and utilitarian application of poetry to exegesis when one reads it in Calvin's Seneca Commentary, becomes clear after reading Budaeus' legal commentaries or those of his imitator, Andreas Alciatus. The practice of careful word study learned early by Calvin, served him well in his later career as theologian and Scriptural exegete.

Two other works of Budaeus should be mentioned. While not referred to in the Commentary, Budaeus' vast *Commentarii Linguae Graecae* (Paris, 1530) has presumably been used in at least five places for Greek parallels. Notable among these is Calvin's discussion of *bona fides*,[55] which undoubtedly reflects Budaeus' extended note on *fides*;[56] Budaeus deals in detail with *pistis/fides* in classical antiquity. Budaeus' *Forensia* (posthumously published) may have been available to Calvin in manuscript form. It is a glossary of Roman legal terms with their Latinised French equivalents. In several places in the Seneca Commentary, Calvin has recourse to the same mode of defining meaning.[57] In the absence of definitive modern editions of Budaeus' treatises and of his classical texts, we can only suggest the nature of Calvin's borrowings; we cannot set the extent. In view of the frequent repetition in Budaeus (a quality shared with the other humanists), one cannot always be sure of precise literary relationships between Budaeus and Calvin. The picture of Calvin's use of Budaeus can for the most part be traced in terms of Budaean works published before the year of Calvin's treatise (1532); whether Calvin, as has been suggested, had access also to then unpublished ones cannot be answered.

That Calvin was deeply indebted to Budaeus is beyond question. That he did not, even as a young man, follow him slavishly must also be asserted. Seldom does Calvin quote Budaeus verbatim, unless it be a quotation from another author; not only does he often rephrase—he selects from widely scattered

45

contexts, and often puts his borrowed treasure to new and quite different uses. Even when Calvin praises Budaeus as the *decus et columen*,[58] he is preparing on the evidence of Horace and Curtius, to take issue with Budaeus' flat assertion that *iniicere manus* is never used in the sense of *offerre* or *inferre manus*.[59]

\ Most important of all Calvin never succumbs to the easy allegorical appropriation of things pagan to Christian truth which Budaeus already betrays in the *Annotationes* and *De Asse*, and was later much more explicitly to express in the *De Transitu*. Calvin remained true to the exacting philological discipline of the humanists without practising their excesses. (This is perhaps because he first held his classicism free of Christian piety and made no hasty amalgam before his conversion.) He could not say with Erasmus, *O sancte Socrates, ora pro nobis*;[60] he could not with Budaeus see Christ in the ancient god Hermes:[61] he could not with Zwingli find a place in the Christian afterlife for ancient pagan worthies.[62] As our two initial quotations from the *Institutio* show, he respected, as divinely given, the great achievements of the ancient philosophers and poets, but he had, by 1539, come to take with uncompromising seriousness the superiority of the Bible over all mere human learning—a note frequently struck, one must admit, by Erasmus as well. Yet despite Calvin's profound change of life, his deep study of classical antiquity left an indelible mark upon all that he later wrote.

Philippus Beroaldus the Elder (1453–1505)

\ WHILE Calvin never graced Philippus Beroaldus the Elder with the title 'third modern pillar', use of the noted Bolognese humanist is sufficiently extensive to warrant treating him beside Erasmus and Budaeus. Among the references to various humanist writers scattered through the Seneca Commentary is the following note on the active sense of the adjectival suffix *-bilis* as used in the word *favorabilis*: 'Yet the active sense is found, \ against the observation of Valla and Beroaldus, in Livy' (AUC 22.26.4) etc.[63] In examining this and other allusions I decided to look beyond the works obviously alluded to in Calvin's text. Apart from Erasmus and Budaeus, Beroaldus proved to be the most fruitful indicator of probable literary dependence. His short treatise on the princely office, *De Optimo Statu Libellus* (Basle, 1509) yielded 45 close parallels, many of them proverbs not found in Erasmus' *Adagia* or *Apophthegmata*. Next I turned to Beroaldus' commentaries on classical writers, concentrating on three: the Suetonius, Apuleius, and Cicero (*Tusculan Disputations*) Commentaries.

The combined Beroaldus-Sabellicus Commentaries on Suetonius' *Lives of the Caesars* (Paris, 1512) afforded 33 parallels from Beroaldus and one from Sabellicus. Beyond this, clusters of other references at these points suggested that Calvin closely studied this Commentary in developing his documentation for the historical passages in the *De Clementia*. The Commentary on Apuleius' *Golden Ass (Metamorphoses)*, in its 20 parallels, demonstrated that every acknowledged and unacknowledged reference of Calvin to Apuleius had in fact been copied from Beroaldus. The Commentary on Cicero's *Tusculan Disputations*, studied in the Bologna edition of 1496, provided 19 parallels that 'rounded out' the philosophical sources of Calvin: the materials not traceable (and some that were traceable) to Cicero, Seneca, Plutarch, Erasmus, or Budaeus, could largely be found in this learned work. And the duplicate parallels suggested alternate tracks for Calvin's source materials.

A learned quibble of Calvin's on a point of translation in Angelus Politianus' Latin version of Herodian[64] gave a hint that all Calvin's Latin quotations of the Greek historians of Rome should be checked. Here I discovered that Calvin had used Beroaldus' translation of Appian, *De Civilibus Romanorum Bellis* (15 references).

How may we sum up the place of Beroaldus in the making of Calvin's Commentary? First, Beroaldus provided a store of references which Calvin not only used directly but through which he was led to still others; second, the Suetonius Commentary was the backbone of Calvin's comparative study of the historians of the early Empire; third, the form and method of Beroaldus' commentaries taught Calvin a great deal. He did not fall into the vices of Beroaldus' excessively archaising style or penchant for long digressions,[65] but the types of notes—historical, rhetorical, philosophical, lexical—of Beroaldus were taken into account by Calvin in developing his own format.

JOHN CALVIN

The two ancient pillars: 1. Seneca

'OUR Seneca was second only to Cicero, a veritable pillar of Roman philosophy and literature (eloquence).' With these words Calvin in his preface sums up his defence of Seneca against the ancient critics, Quintilian and Aulus Gellius, and against the low opinion in which the philosopher was held by some contemporaries. Calvin gives Seneca high praise, calling him 'a man of vast erudition and signal eloquence'. In his 'Short life of Seneca, Drawn from the Best Authors', which he sets at the head of the Commentary, Calvin leans almost entirely on Tacitus for biographical details, while ignoring Dio Cassius' less flattering picture.

Competent as Seneca was in 'physics' (doubtless a reference to the *Quaestiones Naturales*), Calvin recognised Seneca's supreme gift to be in ethics, and this judgment is certainly borne out in the course of the Commentary. Of history, Seneca (in Calvin's view) had wide knowledge, but he was guilty of occasional slips, as Calvin points out in the Commentary.[66] His style Calvin finds elegant but perhaps a trifle too luxuriant, and this judgment too, is borne out in the Commentary. In his prooemium to the second book of the *De Clementia*, Calvin notes the contrast between the two books. In the first Seneca accommodated himself to popular understanding; the second he sprinkled with Stoic paradoxes and scholastic subtleties.[67] A real hint of what sort of writer Calvin himself was to become is in these words: 'I also miss the orderly arrangement of matter, which is certainly not the least quality of a good style.'[68]

Here we shall confine our attention to Calvin's use in his Commentary of Seneca's other writings. Dr. Hugo has shown that he consulted all the then extant editions, in establishing his text. That he read the rest of Seneca with some care is evident from his annotations. The tragedies are quoted 23 times by name; the philosophical writings some 74 times. By far the most common citations are of close verbal parallels between the *De Clementia* and Seneca's other works. The *De Clementia* is almost obsessed with the contrast between the tyrant and the clement ruler;[69] nearly every quotation Calvin gives from the tragedies has this theme as well. The parallels are especially

48

close between the *Octavia* and the *De Clementia*, as both writings deal with Nero.

The citations of Seneca's remaining works fall into several well-defined categories. There are the usual philological notes on Latin idioms, chosen not because they express the same thought but rather because they adumbrate some point of syntax or word usage: *ex facili*,[70] *sub manu*,[71] *verba dare*,[72] *ex destinato*[73] are examples. These are part of the general reservoir of Latinity upon which Calvin draws for clarification of doubtful points.

A second class of Senecan citations, already mentioned in connection with the tragedies, is that of close parallels of word or thought. Not only general references to tyrants, but actual historical allusions to Dionysius of Syracuse,[74] Alexander Phalerus,[75] etc., show us the reduplication of subject matter in Seneca as he used his stock of materials again and again. The *De Clementia* suggested a number of themes which Calvin enlarged upon from other Senecan contexts (and from other writers too). Among these are the following: man as a social and political animal,[76] the relation of vices and virtues,[77] the sinfulness of all men (*peccavimus omnes*),[78] and the wise man's serenity of mind in adversity and prosperity alike. The favourite motto of Caligula, twice repeated in the *De Clementia*,[79] *oderint dum metuant*, calls forth a number of analogues from Seneca, Cicero, and others. Cruelty of rulers is abhorred; gentle-dealing enjoined.

The content of the *De Clementia* determines, to a large extent, Calvin's choice of material. The additional references to Seneca amplify and at points sharpen the reader's understanding of the text. On the whole, they underline Calvin's favourable verdict of Seneca, and express admiration for Seneca's psychological insight.

2. Cicero

IF Seneca is the 'second pillar', Cicero is for Calvin the 'first pillar of Roman philosophy and literature'.[80] This is not surprising in an age of Ciceronians. He is cited far more than any other author. Not counting unmarked quotations, one finds about 60 references to the Letters, 95 to the Speeches and to their Com-

JOHN CALVIN

mentator, Asconius Pedianus; 15 to the rhetorical writings; and some 80 to his philosophical treatises. Unquestionably, by sheer bulk, this total is impressive. Even where he is unmentioned, Cicero speaks through Calvin both in direct quotation and in paraphrase.

Calvin's rhetorical and logical terminology is a skilful blend of Cicero and Quintilian with some additions from other rhetoricians such as Rutilius Lupus, Julius Rufianus, and Romanus Aquila. Cicero is also, at this stage in Calvin's career, his main direct source for ancient philosophy.

When we come, however, to examine where Calvin amassed this Ciceronian material, we must single out a fair-sized group of citations which were either part of the traditional 'grist' of the jurisconsults or of the rhetoricians. When, for example, one discusses the terrible Roman punishment for parricide, the sack, one always quotes a certain passage from Cicero's *Pro Roscio*.[81] Every commentary on Roman Law repeats these famous lines. When one wishes to give an instance of *deprecatio*, one turns to the *Pro Ligario*, following Quintilian himself.[82] If one adds to these references a group of philological notes amassed by the earlier humanists from the ancients, the number of Calvin's 'original' citations of Cicero is further reduced. While this may temper our estimate of his knowledge of Cicero, it enhances our respect for his knowledge of contemporary humanist writing and his discrimination in using it.

As intimated above, many of the same references made by Calvin to Cicero, can be found in the *Annotationes* or the *De Asse*.[83] Legal expressions, as one would expect, were tested by Ciceronian usage;[84] numerous quotations from Cicero are used similarly by both writers.

We can now categorise Calvin's use of Cicero, whether direct or through some intermediate source. There is, first of all, the usual substantial number of purely philological notes, at those points where Calvin seeks unimpeachable authority for some of Seneca's turns of phrase.[85] A number of these, together with several grammatical and syntactic annotations, reflect contemporary learned controversies among the humanists.[86] Such notes frankly do not add much to the understanding of Seneca's text, but were obviously included in the Commentary to establish Calvin's reputation as a humanist. All of this, while

50

dealing with minutiae of grammar and rhetoric, does give us a glimpse of the young scholar, painstakingly forming his consummate Latinity.

Secondly, the system of argument set forth in the *Topica* of Cicero is utilised by Calvin in his analysis of Seneca's logic.[87] We have already noted that Calvin drew his extensive rhetorical terminology from a comparative study of Cicero, Quintilian, and lesser writers.

A third group of Ciceronian materials comes mainly from the philosophical treatises; these serve to supplement and temper the Stoic teachings of Seneca. Political philosophy, psychology, and ethics are represented. Calvin's discussion of ultimate blessedness at the beginning of the Commentary[88] stems mostly from Books II–III of the *De Finibus*; when he speculates upon the seat of the soul, Calvin turns to Cicero and to Plutarch for useful compends of ancient philosophy.[89] Epicurus' analysis of *cupiditas* is borrowed from the *De Finibus*.[90] The *Tusculan Disputations* provide Plato's analysis of the mind. The concepts of love as the binding force of human society and of mutual interdependence come from the *De Officiis*.[91]

Far more important, though, than the comparatively small stock of philosophical borrowings, is the evidence of Calvin's intellectual formation. Calvin was later to make a far fuller use of Cicero's philosophical treatises: notably, in *Inst. I. i–v*, where, having asserted the innate awareness of deity in all men, he yet finds them inexcusable in their unregenerate state. Also, when one compares the rather sketchy statement of psychology in the Commentary with the fuller account in *Inst.* I. xv. 2–8; II. ii. 10–27, one sees not only the source of the latter passages, but the further intellectual and spiritual development our author underwent between the two writings.

Three layers of tradition

THE two ancient and three humanist writers just discussed do not exhaust the sources of Calvin's Seneca Commentary. The cumulative tradition of the ancient world, mediated through late classical and recent humanist compilers (whose interests were predominantly philological and moral) coloured for our

51

author and for other authors of his time the understanding of the past.

Three levels of contact with the classics may be discerned in the Seneca Commentary: Classical Authors, Classical Intermediaries, Humanist Compilers. These categories are not completely exclusive: Cicero, as already indicated, was both an author in his own right and a prime channel, for the Latin world, of the Greek philosophical and rhetorical tradition. The same may be said even more strongly of Seneca. Furthermore, one cannot always say with confidence that Calvin has read a particular classical author directly even though he may quote extensively from him. The philological or lexical use to which he puts his classical allusions and the particular combinations of references are often a clue to the derivative character of these citations. More often than not Calvin is tapping the common reservoir of Latinity, used by all his classicising contemporaries.

Classical authors directly used by Calvin

WE cannot say with assurance that certain references to the classics were of Calvin's own original selection; on the contrary, evidence abounds that most were obtained through intermediate authors. A few general principles can, however, be stated concerning his knowledge of the original writers.

(1) At this time Calvin was much less versed in Greek than in Latin literature[92] (by contrast Erasmus, Budaeus, and Beroaldus move freely from one language to the other). All or nearly all of Calvin's Greek references have been garnered from secondary authors. And where he cites some Greek author more fully— e.g. Plutarch, or one of the Greek historians of Rome—he is using a known Latin translation. We can therefore rule out Calvin's Greek references and concentrate on his Latin in considering direct use of classical authors.

(2) The following Latin poets, infrequently quoted, may be eliminated from the category of directly used classical writers: Catullus (2 references), Claudian (4 plus 1 Pseudo-Claudian), Lucretius (1), Martial (3), Persius (3), Propertius (6), Statius (7). Among the Latin poets to whom Calvin may be referring directly out of his own reading of them, are probably to be

included: Horace (37), Juvenal (34), Lucan (14), Ovid (59 plus 3 Pseudo-Ovid), Plautus (8), Terence (31), Virgil (76). The character of his references and the known use of intermediaries may eliminate further all or many of the following: Juvenal, Lucan, Plautus, Terence. There remain Horace, Ovid and Virgil.

(3) Among the historians, Calvin knew especially well Suetonius first and Tacitus second, for they cover the period of Roman history encompassed by the *De Clementia*. Yet Calvin's extensive use of Suetonius was in part mediated by Beroaldus' Commentary. Plutarch's *Lives* and Appian's *History* (in Latin translation) are also used. Of Latin historians employed mainly for non-historical (i.e. lexical) annotations one must mention Curtius, Livy/Florus, Sallust, Ammonianus Marcellinus and the Scriptores Historiae Augustae; Herodian (in Latin translation) is similarly utilised. A third group of historians includes those referred to by name only in strings of citations: Arrian, Dionysius Halicarnassus, Xenophon, Justinus/Trogus, Dio Cassius.

(4) The Rhetoricians, in their analysis of orators and other writers, seem in a sense to be intermediaries, although in our summary they will be included as primary authors. Next to Cicero, Quintilian stands pre-eminent; Calvin's use of him evidences thorough familiarity, even though some references can be attributed to the humanist intermediaries. The 'rhetorici minores'—Romanus Aquila, Julius Rufianus, Rutilius Lupus —were also directly used by Calvin. Together these writers provided a major critical tool for the young commentator in his analysis of meaning and style. Varro's *On the Latin Language* may be included in this class; the references to it seem derivative, although probably Varro's treatise was used as bound in Perottus' *Cornucopia*.

(5) Among the various prose writers who do not fall into the above classes, are Apuleius (see under Beroaldus, above), the Auctores Rei Rusticae—obviously consulted in the study of the 'King' bee,[93] the Panegyrists, and the two Plinies. These last were studied closely, I believe, by Calvin, although some references are second-hand. The Younger Pliny's *Panegyric* (30) was liberally excerpted by Calvin for political maxims and an occasional historical judgment. The *Natural History* of the Elder Pliny (33) was, with the Auctores Rei Rusticae, a chief

C

53

source for animal and plant lore, and (more important) for history, but many of the references were commonplaces. The scattering of other Latin prose writers does not suggest direct use of them by Calvin.

In sum, then, the number of authors used in their original published form by Calvin is far smaller than the impressive list of 74 Latin and 22 Greek alluded to in the Commentary. The basic catalogue of these prime authors is further reduced by the large proportion of derived citations.

Classical intermediaries

BEFORE offering any general comments on 'classical intermediaries', we must speak once again of Plutarch, who, with Cicero and Seneca, serves as an important channel of Greek philosophy, proverbial wisdom, political theory, and ancient biography. Calvin knew Plutarch's *Lives* (41) in the Florentine Latin translation; the *Moralia* (15) he used in the various Latin translations or excerpts of Budaeus, Pirckheimer, Erasmus, etc. Since Plutarch was himself a compiler and widely plundered by the humanists, it is often difficult to determine by what route a Plutarch reference finds its way into the *Commentary*.[94] The longer quotations from the *Moralia* were probably directly obtained, e.g. the extended passage on the seat of the soul; also, the evidence is clearly in favour of Calvin's having collated historical matter directly from Plutarch's *Lives* with that of other historians. A number of the shorter proverbs on the other hand were drawn from the common store of the humanists.

The two chief sorts of classical intermediaries are: (a) the commentators and grammarians, (b) the compilers or excerptors. Three of the commentators are of especial importance. Calvin read Terence through the eyes of his commentator, Donatus; Virgil through Servius' eyes; some of Cicero's speeches through Ascanius Pedianus'. Well-printed and copiously-indexed editions were available to him, containing the text of the poet framed by ancient and modern commentaries. Thus these commentators served a double purpose: they suggested to Calvin a preponderantly philological approach to the poets; they also, in the additional material adduced, greatly

54

expanded Calvin's documentation. Of the 76 references to Virgil, more than 29 contain twin citations of Virgil and Servius. Eighteen of the 31 references to Terence also explicitly mention Donatus. The use of Acron and Porphyrion, Horace's commentators, is minimal and clearly derivative, although similar combined editions of Horace and his commentators were available. Calvin's references to Priscian's *Grammar* give us no hint of the way by which he knew this standard work. Writers like Servius and Priscian treated Greek and Latin as virtually one body of language and literature—a practice later revived by the humanists.

Five Latin writers may be classed as compilers or excerptors: Aulus Gellius (35), Macrobius (10), Pompeius Festus (7), Nonius Marcellus (12),[95] and Valerius Maximus (21). All these authors were well thumbed by the humanists, and may be considered, with the humanist compilers themselves, to constitute a common pool of lexical matter as well as a guide to the determination of word meanings. It is said that Zwingli memorised Valerius Maximus to provide illustrations for his sermons;[96] Calvin uses this writer mainly for historical anecdotes. The others are employed as lexical authorities in defining terms. They are also the source of some quotations of Sallust, Cicero, Servius/Virgil, and others.

Humanist compilers

THE invention of printing in Western Europe called into being a flood of classical materials: texts, translations, commentaries, anthologies, glossaries, specialised treatises, and miscellanies. Calvin enjoyed the fruits of two generations of this intense literary effort. We have already seen how he employed Erasmus, Budaeus, and Beroaldus, his chief humanist mentors, and the shape of his literary dependence is clear. It remains for us to summarise his use of the humanist writers as a group.

Calvin's explicit references to the humanists are meagre and somewhat misleading. Andreas Alciatus is castigated five times in a single context, and refuted in another place.[97] Baptista Egnatius, while styled *vir de studiis humanioribus bene meritus*, is corrected on a point of Roman history.[98] Angelus Politianus' translation of Herodian is, as mentioned above, unjustly criticised.[99] Nicolas Perottus (the excerptor of Phaedrus' *Fables* and a humanist highly respected by Erasmus) is caught in an *insignus error*,[100] in his definition of *muraena* (lamprey). Even the great Laurentius Valla is taken to task four times.[101] Caelius Ludovicus Rhodiginus is pitted against Erasmus on the spelling of 'Vedius'.[102] 'Gabbling' Porcius Latro Vincentinus is bested by Budaeus on Roman coinage.[103] Zasius is praised for an emendation of Justinian's *Digest*.[104] It is quibbles of this sort that delighted the humanists as they waged their pen-and-paper war amongst themselves. One sees here, for example, Frenchmen standing against Italians when the fair name of Marseilles is at stake.[105]

Beneath these explicit points of difference lies a solid, if largely unacknowledged, dependence on the part of Calvin upon at least some of these writers. Undoubtedly, most of the references to military, agricultural, and medical subjects came through humanist compilations. Laurentius Valla seems to have been used at least ten times on questions of syntax and meaning.[106] Rhodiginus, mentioned but once, is probably employed in three additional places on lexical matters.[107] Alciatus and Zasius, beyond Budaeus' *Annotationes*, offer interpretations of the Roman Law.[108] These few references provide only a taste of Calvin's reading in his contemporaries.

We have not in our examination of these traditions mentioned the comparatively few patristic references used in the Commentary. But the same generalisations can be made of them: most have come by way of the Decretals of Gratian, and repeat the same errors of attribution; a few can be noted in the humanist writings used by Calvin.

A key to Calvin's later work

EXCEPT for the extensive plagiarism by Gilbertus Cognatus in his supplement to Erasmus' *Adagia*, the Commentary went unnoticed among his contemporaries. Yet its effect on Calvin's own formation was considerable. In the Commentary can be seen the beginnings of Calvin the exegete. The same attention to the close study of the text will later mark Calvin's Christian writings. The tools of exegesis: grammatical and rhetorical analysis, a wide background in history, philosophy, literature, science, and other studies—these characterise the young Calvin as they will more fully the later Calvin. The 'creative assimilation' of his sources is even at this early stage a trait of our author, for he seldom merely parrots his authorities despite a demonstrable dependence upon them. The same 'free literal' handling of sources will later be observed in his extensive use of such writers as Augustine.

As one reflects upon Calvin's 'pagan apprenticeship' to the Christian life evidenced in the Commentary on Seneca's *De Clementia*, one is reminded of the ambitious classical curriculum which Calvin prescribed for the youth of Geneva in the *Leges academicae Genevensis*, 1559.[109] The same writers which he had read are here, perhaps presented in a more systematic and carefully graded manner. Making due allowance for the widely held humanist educational views of the time, one may yet ask: was not Calvin, perhaps unconsciously, commending his own path to Christian belief to the children of his followers? The only difference, and it is a very significant one, is that these youths were to be effectively catechised in the evangelical doctrine from the start; yet the serious study of the Scriptures was to come only after almost the whole of Greek and Latin literature had been mastered.

In conclusion, one must say that the Commentary—slight though it is when measured by the standard of Calvin's later work—illuminates the latter. Here is a well-formed, disciplined, but not yet full-matured mind at work. Conversion was to bring not an utter repudiation of Calvin's classical learning, but a transformation of it, tested by God's Word. The result was no loose allegorical binding together of classical and Christian; Calvin could not repeat Budaeus' confident assertion that Alexander worshipped Jesus Christ. Rather, the message of Seneca's *De Clementia*—that the mighty should rule with mercy, accountable to God—was recast in the passionate essays in Christian political teaching that introduce and conclude the *Institutio Christianae Religionis*.[110] And something of the high seriousness of the Stoic ethic, also transformed by Christian faith, prevailed at least for a time in Geneva and in her spiritual daughters.[111]

JOHN CALVIN

NOTES

[There have been two recent studies of Calvin's background of classical humanism. J. Bohatec in *Budé und Calvin* (1950) showed Calvin's debt to the French humanist, but did not deal in detail with the impact of Budaeus on the Seneca Commentary. A. M. Hugo in *Cavijn en Seneca* (1957) surveyed the extent of Calvin's classical learning, his work on the text of Seneca and the achievement of the Commentary itself, but did not examine fully Calvin's sources. My own studies began independently but I am now working with Dr. Hugo on a new edition of Calvin's Seneca Commentary.]

1. Budaeus, Epist. to Claudius Contiuncula ICtus, 16 Aug. 1518 (*Opera*, pp. 261–262).

2. Calvin's studies before conversion fall into four periods: (1) University of Paris (1523–28)—Arts; (2) University of Orleans (1528–29)—Law; (3) University of Bourges (1529–31)—Law; (4) under the Royal Readers at Paris (1531–33)—Literature.

3. Plato is mentioned approximately 20 times in the Commentary; of these references at least 4 come through Cicero, and 2 through Aulus Gellius. Where Plato is directly quoted (3 times) Calvin uses the translation of Marsilius Ficinus. 4 references are incorrect. A number of others have been derived from humanistic intermediate sources.

4. Some 20 contexts where Aristotle is mentioned suggest about 32 references, many of which are commonplaces frequently mentioned by the humanists to which Calvin had recourse. There is some evidence that Calvin knew and used Theodore of Gaza's translation of the *Problemata*, but the translation of his one direct Latin quotation of *Politics* (3.5.2) has not been identified.

5. *Comm.* p. 21 n. 2.

6. *ibid.*, p. 32 n. 3.

7. *ibid.*, p. 15 n. 7.

8. There is also the category of natural science and technology, which must include such miscellaneous matter as notes on Seneca's references to lampreys, to pruning fruit-trees, and to bees as well as to allusions to the habits of animals and such natural phenomena as lightning. The Auctores Rei Rusticae, Varro, Columella, Virgil, Pliny the Elder, Aristotle, Alexander Aphrodiseus, are cited on such points. These references are those of an educated person, familiar with the ancient writers and with contemporary humanist use of them.

9. See n. 38.

10. The chief Latin poets used, in descending order of frequency, are: Virgil, Ovid, Horace and Juvenal, Terence. Virgil and Terence are used mainly through the Commentaries of Servius and Donatus, respectively.

11. Epist. 2 (1530, Calvin to Franciscus Daniel, CO. Xa. 3–6) refers to his copy of Homer's Odyssey, lent to Charles Sucquet, a Flemish jurisconsult. In the Seneca Commentary, Calvin alludes three times to the *Iliad*, quotes it twice in Greek (once with Latin translation): at least two of these references are from Erasmus. The *Odyssey* is quoted in Greek twice, both

58

times from Erasmus' *Adagia*; a third quotation is paralleled from other contemporary proverbial literature. How well did Calvin know Homer at this time? The scattered references to other Greek poets tell the same story.

12. The same idea of the innate superiority of the Scriptures to the writings of pagan philosophers is expressed when Calvin introduces (1539) his short treatise on the Christian Life (*Inst.* III.vi–x):

'As philosophers have fixed limits of the right and honorable, whence they derive individual duties and the whole company of virtues, so Scripture is not without its own order in this matter, but holds to a most beautiful dispensation, and one much more certain than all the philosophical ones. The only difference is that they, as they were ambitious men, diligently strove to attain an exquisite clarity of order to show the nimbleness of their wit. But the Spirit of God, because he taught without affectation, did not adhere so exactly or continuously to a methodical plan; yet when he lays one down anywhere he hints enough that it is not to be neglected by us.'

13. *Comm.* p. 42 n. 9.
14. *ibid.*, Pref. p. ii n. 1.
15. *ibid.*, Pref. iii n. 5.
16. *ibid.*, p. 42 n. 9.
17. *ibid.*, Pref. ii. 2–3.
18. *ibid.*, Pref. p. ii lines 4–5.
19. *ibid.*, Pref. p. 132 n. 1.
20. *ibid.*, p. 19.
21. *ibid.*, p. 154.
22. *ibid.*, p. 13, 121, 144.
23. *ibid.*, p. 36.
24. See L. K. Born, ed. tr. *The Education of a Christian Prince by Desiderius Erasmus* (1936), and Ch. 6 of the Introduction in our forthcoming edition of the Commentary.
25. Luchesius Smits, *Saint Augustin dans l'Oeuvre de Jean Calvin*, 1. 201 f.
26. Bohatec, *Budé und Calvin*, p. 406 n. 2, lists Calvin's citations of the *De Asse* in the Commentaries.
27. While the editions of Budaeus' works published prior to 1532 were used initially in preparing the present study, references are given to the Paris edition of 1557, since this is fairly complete and more widely available in libraries. References to single works not included therein (e.g. *Commentarii Linguae Graecae*) are to pre-1532 editions.
28. AP 81B–82C; cf. *Comm.* p. 42.
29. ARP 309B–310C; cf. *Comm.* p. 62.
30. AP 40C; cf. *Comm.* p. 67.
31. AP 52C; cf. *Comm.* p. 103.
32. ARP 326; cf. *Comm.* p. 157.
33. AP 87B, 95B; cf. *Comm.* p. 157.
34. ARP 337B; 338B–339A; cf. *Comm.* p. 102.
35. E.g. *Comm.* pp. 157, 102.
36. *Comm.* pp. 22–23, 111.

37. AP 1 A–B.
38. DA 124; AP 56C; cf. *Comm.* p. 35.
39. DA 124; cf. *Comm.* pp. 46–47.
40. See notes 45–48, below.
41. On social classes, see *Comm.*, pp. 128. 3–12; 88. 8–37; 46.31–47./128. 19–129.8.
42. On Actium, see *Comm.*, p. 78. 23–26. On Sulla, see *Comm.* pp. 83–86, 99.
43. *Comm.* 1.6.1. (46.31 ff.), using Jerome's tr. of Eusebius, *Chron.*, through Budaeus, *De Asse*, p. 124.
44. AP 103B, 111B; cf. *Comm.*, p. 84.
45. AP 111–116; cf. *Comm.* p. 47.
46. AP 54D; cf. *Comm.*, p. 107.
47. *ibid.*
48. DA 120, 124–125.
49. E. g. Politianus on Herodian, pp. 140–141.
50. Chs. 9–16, dealing with the place of history in the education of the prince, afford some parallels.
51. See also Erasmus, *Education of a Christian Prince*, pp. 157 ff., 171, 191.
52. DA 1 (Opera, p. 15); cf. Beroaldus, *Comm. Cic. T.D.*; 7[a–b] [*Comm.* p. 36 n. 13].
53. *Comm.* p. 32 n. 3.
54. DA 284, 294; AP 281D–282C; cf. *Comm.* p. 10 n. 8.
55. *Comm.* p. 70.
56. CLG 145 ff.
57. E.g. tollere filios=elevare filios (élèver les fils); nuncupare vota= facere vota (faire des voeux).
58. See n. 13.
59. See Comm. pp. 42.28–43.5.
60. Erasmus, *Colloquia*, 683DE.
61. Budaeus, DA 5 (*Opera*, pp. 294 ff.). See *Comm.*, p. 10 n. 8.
62. Zwingli, *Fidei Christianae Expositio*, XII, 'Vita Aeterna', SS Opera IV.65, lines 29–37.
63. *Comm.*, p. 74.34–36.
64. See n. 49.
65. For life of Beroaldus see Nicéron, *Memoires pour Servir à L'Histoire des Hommes illustrés*, Tome XXV, pp. 374 ff.
66. Calvin recognises different uses of history (138.6–9): 'Yet to the philosophers and orators, whose job is not to weave lasting history, it is permitted to put to their own use matters of doubtful authenticity, as this passage demonstrates.'
67. *De Clem.*, 2.1.1, *Comm.*, p. 139.5 f.
68. See Preface, p. iii.
69. See *Comm.* pp. 81 ff.
70. See *Comm.* p. 53.5–14.
71. *ibid.*, p. 7. 3–22.
72. *ibid.*, p. 132.32–40.

SOURCES OF CALVIN'S SENECA COMMENTARY

73. *ibid.*, 49.19–33.
74. *ibid.*, pp. 82 ff.
75. *ibid.*, p. 148 n. 4.
76. *Comm.* pp. 28 f.
77. *ibid*, p. 41.
78. *ibid.*, p. 49.
79. *De Clem.*, 1.12.4; 2.2.2.
80. See n. 15.
81. *Pro Roscio*, 25.70 at *Comm.* 1.23.1.
82. *Pro Ligario*, 10.30 at *Comm.* 1.2.1 (p. 22 n. 1).
83. E.g. the classic definitions of *religio* and *superstitio* by Cicero, Lactantius, Augustine, later used by Calvin, *Inst.* I. xii.1, foreshadowed in the Seneca Commentary pp. 150.21–151.5, are conveniently presented in Budaeus, AP 252D–254C.
84. Both Budaeus and Calvin cite the same Ciceronian references for the following terms: aestimare litem (ARP 326C–D; *Comm.*, p. 157); cognitor, cognitio (ARP 337B ff.; *Comm.*, p. 103); cernere hereditatem (AP 52C; *Comm.* p. 103); iudex quaestionis (ARP 317; *Comm.*, p. 48); ius imaginis (AP 53B; *Comm.*, pp. 69, 85):
85. Examples are 'id aetatis' (71.9–15), 'animum abicere demittere' (71.14; 124.4; 159.42); 'animum contrahere' or 'animi contractio' (157.44), 'bene male/audire' (156.36), 'auribus dare' (145.42). 'gratium referre/ deferre' (25.52–54; 63.34–36); 'manus retinere/abstinere' (41.14–15); 'nemo homo' (26.6), 'se dare/applicare' (28.39–52).
86. Laurentius Valla, whose knowledge of Latin, Budaeus had found far superior to that of Greek, is several times 'twitted' by Calvin for his pedantic assertions and hair-splitting distinctions, usually with Ciceronian evidence. Examples are Calvin's assertion that 'licentia' has both good and bad meanings, and is not used exclusively in the bad sense, in the best classical authors (32.9), and that the use of 'quam' as 'how much' is legitimate (66.51 ff.). A study of the *Elegantiae* of Valla suggests the background for some of Calvin's philological notes.
87. Of the thirteen classes of *argumenta extrinsecus*, the first (*coniugata*), fourth (*ex comparatione maiorum aut parium aut minorum*) are employed, together with three others, *a circumstantiis* and *ab utile* (from Quintilian), and *ex remotione* (from Sextus Victor or Quintilian).
88. See *Comm.*, pp. 3–4.
89. *ibid.*, p. 32 n. 3.
90. *ibid.*, p. 17 n. 6, using Cic. *Fin.*, 1.13.45 ff. and *T.D.*, 5.33.93 ff.
91. On peace of mind, see *Comm.* p. 152 n. 8, 9, using Cic. *T.D.* 3.6.12 and 4.23.51. On love as binding force of society, see p. 28. 34, using Cic. *Off.*, 2.3.12–2.4.15; *Fin.* 2.14.45 ff.
92. On Calvin's knowledge of Plato, Aristotle, and others, see notes 3, 4, 6, above.
93. The analogy of the 'King Bee' is developed by Seneca in *De Clem.*, 1.19.
94. This fact is often emphasised by variant Latin renderings of Plutarch's Greek.

95. Pompeius Festus, Nonius Marcellus, and Varro's *De Lingua Latina* were sometimes printed together, twice with Nicolas Perottus' elaborately indexed *Cornucopia* (Venice, 1513; Paris 1529).

96. Oswald Myconius, *Life of Zwingli*, IV: 'He became a priest [at Glarus], devoted himself to studies, especially theological studies, for henceforward he made little account of the heathen classics, unless they assisted him in the sacred things, and in preaching. With this end in view, it should be said in passing, that for the sake of the illustrations he committed Valerius Maximus to memory, and did not forget him.' [Tr. from Jackson, *Works of Zwingli*, I. 5.] After coming to Zürich in 1519 Zwingli continued his studies: 'In the midst of these anxious labors he never omitted his reading of the Greek authors, and went through Homer, Aristotle, Plato, Demosthenes, Thucydides, and in lighter vein Lucian, Theocritus, Hesiod, Aristophanes, and others.' [*ibid.*, VIII.10.]

97. See n. 106.

98. *Comm.*, p. 75.34–37.

99. *ibid.*, p. 140.29.

100. *ibid.*, p. 112. 38–39.

101. On Laurentius Valla, see pp. 19.26; 56.23; 74.34–36; 83.33.

102. On Rhodiginus, see p. 112.20–22.

103. On Vincentinus, see p. 103.24.

104. On Zasius, see p. 104.28.

105. See *Comm.*, p. 102. 7–17.

106. Reference to Valla's *Elegantiae* which have been traced include 1.13, 17; 3.83; 4.17, 101; 5.34; 6.26, 33, 58. See also *In Pogium Antidoti*, 3.

107. Caelius Ludovicus Rhodiginus, *Lectionum Antiquarum Libi* XVI (Basel, 1517), 8.7; 12.52; 14.5.

108. Andreas Alciatus, *De Verborum Significantiae*, ed. Opera, Basel (1558), cols. 143 f.; 161, 203, 257; *Comm. in ff. tit. de liberis et posthum* (ed. Frankfort) (1617) 1.624; *De Praefectio Praetorio*; in *ibid.* 3.508; *Dispunctionum Libri*, 3.7 (in *ibid.*, 2.53 f.).

109. OS II. 366–370.

110. In the Dedicatory Letter to Francis I and *Inst. IV.* 20.

111. See *Consilium De Luxu*, [CO Xa. 203–206] and my article and translation of this interesting document, 'Against Luxury and License in Geneva: A Forgotten Fragment of Calvin', *Interpretation*, April, 1965, pp. 182–202.

The Sources of Calvin's Commentary on Seneca's De Clementia

Use. H—historical or institutional allusions. L—lexical use or literary parallel. P—proverbial saying or political maxim. Ph—philosophy. J—juridical (legal). M—miscellaneous.

Source. A—direct use of classical authors (Latin) by Calvin. B—direct use of ancient compilers by Calvin. C—Humanist compilers used by Calvin. D—Humanist Translations of Classical Writers used by Calvin.

		References	*Use*	*Source*
Aeschines		1	P	C
Aesop		1	P	C
Alciatus		7	J	C
Alexander Aphrodisaeus		2	Ph	C/D
Ambrose		1	P	C
Ammianus Marcellinus		7	PHL	B/C
Appianus Alexandrinus		15	H	D
Apuleius		20	L	B/C
Aristophanes		2	L	C?
Aristotle		35	PhLRM	C/D
Arrian		1	H	C
Augustine		23	PhHLJ	A/C
Ausonius		1	L	C
Beroaldus	Comm. Suet.	34	HL	C
	Comm. Cic. T D	19	PhL	C
	De Opt. St Lib.	45	P	C
Bible		7	PM	
Budaeus		91	JHLPh	C/D
Julius Capitolinus		7	H	A/C
Cato		10	HPL	B/C

63

JOHN CALVIN

	References	Use	Source
Catullus	2	P	C
Celsus	2	M	C
Cicero		LPRPhJHM	A/C
Letters	60		
Speeches	95		
Rhet.	15		
Philos.	80		
Claudian	5	P	C
Columella	5	M	A or C
Corpus Juris Canonici	4	P	A or C
Curtius	45	LHP	A/C
Cyprian	2	P	C?
Demosthenes	1	P	C?
Dio Cassius	8	H	C/D?
Diogenes Laertius	5	Ph	C?
Dionysius Halicarnassus	1	H	C?
Erasmus	44	PPh	C
Euclid	1	L	C
Euripides	3	P	B/C
Eusebius	11	H	C?
Gaius	3	J	B/C
Aulus Gellius	35	LHPM	B/C
Gregorius Magnus	2	P	B/C
Herodian	23	PHL	C/D
Hesiod	1	P	C
Homer	10	P	C
Horace	37	LP	A/C
Isidore of Seville	1	P	B/C?
Isocrates	1	L	C
Jerome	8	PL	A(B)/C
Justinian Corpus Juris Civilis	57	J	C
not found	6	J	B/C
Justinus	4	H	C
Juvenal	34	PL	A/C
Lactantius	3	ML	C
Aelius Lampridius	2	H	A/C
Livy	61	LH	A/B/C
Lucan	14	LHP	A/C
Lucretius	1	L	C
Macrobius	10	LPR	B/C
Martial	3	PH	C?
Nonius Marcellus	12	L	B/C?

64

SOURCES OF CALVIN'S SENECA COMMENTARY

	References	Use	Source
Ovid	59	LHPR	A/B/C
Panegyrici	12	LP	A/C
Asconius Pedianus (Cic)	10	L	B/C
Nicolas Perottus	6	L	C
Persius	3	P	C
Phalerus	1	P	C
Phocylides	1	P	C
Plato	19	PhPL	B/C/D
Plautus	8	PL	A?/B/C
Pliny the Elder	33	HML	A/B/C
Pliny the Younger	30	PhL	A/B/C
Plutarch Lives	41	HPL	C/D
Moralia	15	PPh	C/D
Pompeius Festus	7	LP	B/C
Pomponius Mela	1	H	C
Priscian	3	L	C?
Propertius	6	PLH	C?
Publilius Syrus	11	P	A
Quintilian	93	RLP	A/B/C
Caelius Rhodiginus	4	LP	C
Romanus Aquila	9	R	A
Rutilius Lupus	9	R	A
Sallust	19	LPPh	B/C?
Seneca the Elder	6	LHP	A or C?
Seneca the Younger		PhPLMH	A/C
Tragedies	23		
Philosophical Works	74		
Solon	3	P	C
Sophocles	1	L(P)	C
Aelius Spartianus	1	HL	A?
Statius	7	PL	C
Strabo	2	M	C
Suetonius	120	H	A/B/C
Suidas	1	L	C
Sulpicius Victor	1	R	C?
Synesius	1	L	C?
Tacitus	69	HL	A/B/C
Terence/Donatus	31	LP	A/B/C
Ulpian	1	J	B/C
Valerius Maximus	21	HLM	B/C
Laurentius Valla	10	L	C
Varro	9	LM	A/B/C

JOHN CALVIN

	References	Use	Source
Vegetius	3	M	C
Porcius Latro Vincentinus	1	M (H)	C
Virgil/Servius	76(V)	LPM	A/C (V)
	29(S)		B/C (S)
Vitruvius	1	M	C
Flavius Vopiscus	1	H	A/C?
Xenophon	1	L	C
Zasius	2	J	C

4 Calvin the Letter-Writer

Jean-Daniel Benoît

THERE IS NO better way of getting to know a person than by reading his letters, especially those private ones which he has not the slightest intention of publishing. Here the man himself is revealed without pose or artificiality; here he stands in his weakness as well as his greatness. This is what makes Calvin's letters such an incomparable documentary treasury for those who want to know him as a man.

These letters are a world in themselves, filling no less than eleven large volumes of the *Corpus Reformatorum*.[1] While it is true that a number of these are addressed to Calvin, the majority are his own; they form in themselves an output large enough to assure their author an undeniable literary reputation.

Calvin's correspondents

TO call this chapter 'Calvin and his Correspondents' would have been to change the emphasis, for we must consider for a moment those to whom he wrote. They were the powerful men of the world, the King and Queen of Navarre, the Kings of England, Denmark and Poland, the Prince of Condé, the Duchess of Ferrara, Renée of France, daughter of Louis XII and Anne of Brittany, Admiral Coligny and his wife, the Countess of Roye, sister of the Admiral and step-mother of Condé, the Marchioness of Rothelin, *née* Jacqueline de Rohan, widow of Francis of Orleans, and her son the Duke of Longueville, M. de Falais, descendant of St. Louis and great-grandson of Philip of Bourgogne. It is to such noble representatives of the great families that Calvin writes; he always does so with great respect and with the customary courtesy. But quickly his tone changes to that of the prophet, and he speaks with the boldness, power and force of the spokesman of God, for he is bringing to bear on the duties even of kings and princes the light of the Gospel itself. 'It is a great matter to be a king,' he writes to the young King of England, Edward VI, 'but I am sure that you count it a far greater privilege to be a Christian.' This is not in any way to underrate kingship, but being a Christian is an even greater honour than being a king. Once he has reminded the young prince of the greatness and dignity of the name Christian, he exhorts him to serve the One who is the King of kings. 'God has indeed given you an inestimable privilege, Sire, in making you a Christian king, so that you can be His agent in setting up and maintaining Christ's kingdom in England.'[2] Again Calvin writes to Sigismund Augustus II, King of Poland: 'Remember that in your person God has lit a candle for the whole of Poland, and that you cannot conceal it for long without the most serious consequences.' As always the dynamic of Calvin's faith forces him to emphasise the need for witness. Thus a king's first care must be to bring the lands under his control 'out of that shameful subordination to the Papacy into the obedience of Christ'.[3] But that King, whose hesitation earned him the nickname 'King of Tomorrow' never managed to come to a decision. Calvin writes a second time: 'Shake off your lethargy! You will need every ounce of strength to bring this great task to completion. Now is clearly the right time for action (*agendi maturitas*). Remember that if this God-given opportunity is let slip, nothing may be left but a closed door.'[4] These were prophetic words. The opportunity *was* lost. Protestantism in Poland is no more than a memory, and even now the door is still closed.

Then there were another group of Calvin's correspondents the Reformers, in France, Switzerland, the Netherlands and England. There was no religious leader of any importance at that time in the whole of Europe with whom Calvin did not correspond; Strasbourg, Basle, Berne, Zürich, Lausanne, Neuchâtel, Wittenberg, Wesel, Frankfurt, London, etc. His correspondence with Farel and Viret, in particular, is considerable. This ceaseless round of letters both carried, and commented on, the latest news. The whole history of these troubled times was mirrored here day by day. Indeed nothing of importance occurred without leaving some echo in this correspondence, which on Calvin's side lasted some thirty years. In France there was the death of Henry II, the Protestant Synod of 1559, Colloquy of Poissy, the beginning of the Wars of Religion. The persecution of the Waldensians in Provence deeply moved the Reformer. He wrote everywhere, and set out to stir up the City Councils of Basle, Zürich and Strasbourg to protest. He wrote to Bullinger, 'More than four hundred are in chains, and the galleys are full'. He pleads: 'Can we look on with our arms folded while innocent blood is shed, while wicked men slaughter our brethren with impunity, while Christ is derided?'[5] In England there was the untimely death of Edward VI, and the reaction under Mary Tudor, the 'Bloody Mary' of history. From Scotland John Knox wrote continually to the master he had left in Geneva, whom he called his father, and without whose advice he did nothing. In Germany Calvin corresponded with the Elector Palatine, the Landgrave of Hesse, the Duke of Wurtemburg. Here were all the problems of Imperial politics, the Council of Trent, the Diet of Augsburg, the Interim, and so on. It would not be untrue to say that Calvin's house in the rue des Chanoines was like the Genevan Foreign Office. His position was unique. He had made Geneva 'The Church on the hill', and its light shone over the whole world. From all parts men looked to Geneva. They consulted Geneva. They listened to Geneva, and Geneva meant Calvin. (All this correspondence is even more valuable as a means of knowing the history of those times since there were no newspapers, and even the most important news was transmitted by letter.)

A third group of Calvin's correspondents, and certainly not the least, was made up of prisoners and martyrs. With them we enter deep dungeons or follow the slow procession which leads to the stake. Calvin wrote to these people; his letters were read by the uncertain light from a slit in the wall, or by the flicker of a candle, read by men and women who were going, perhaps the very next day, to seal their faith with their blood. His letters encouraged them, strengthened them, furnished them with answers to the captious questions of their adversaries, opened vistas of the heavenly kingdom, and assured them that no drop of blood would be shed in vain. These letters are sacred, indeed holy, and they deserve much fuller consideration.[6]

But the voice of the Reformer sounds out to a wider audience. This time he does not speak to the mighty of this world, recalling them to their duty. He does not discuss with the leaders of the Reformation the major political and ecclesiastical events, and their repercussions on the life of the church. He does not encourage the imprisoned martyrs where they rot in a living death. This time he reaches out to *all* the faithful, the 'ordinary people', merchants, shop-keepers, businessmen, workers, peasants, the real 'living stones' of the Reformation. Calvin writes truly pastoral letters to Poitiers, Angers, Loudun, Meaux, Dieppe, Montelimar, Valence, Aix and even to Paris. He encourages those near despair, he checks the impatient and calms the hot-headed. He urges faithfulness and perseverance, always pointing to the way of the Gospel. At a time when these churches were scattered throughout the kingdom of France without any real bond to hold them together, Calvin took upon himself the role of bishop, he shepherded the flock, writing like Paul to the churches of Asia or Macedonia.

And so we see Calvin's correspondents surrounding him in a series of greater or smaller circles: kings, princes and potentates of the world; then the Reformers throughout Europe; then the prisoners and martyrs; and finally the entire population of the persecuted churches.

Of course if we were going to treat this subject in such a manner, we would need first to sketch the story of Calvin's life step by step from the start, and then do the same for his times. But that would be tedious and, for the details, would require several volumes. And so in place of such a method, which we may call 'centrifugal', since it would require us to follow wherever Calvin's letters are sent, we have preferred another, which continually leads us back to the centre. Thus instead of the history, even the history of the Reformer, we look for the writer, the man whose mind and heart show themselves in every letter regardless of the addressee, namely John Calvin.

Calvin in his letters

SOME may think it rather ambitious to attempt to fix the reflection of a man in his letters. Who could claim to capture the many facets of such a rich personality? Indeed it is not our intention to paint a full-length portrait from head to foot, missing nothing out, complete in every detail. Rather we intend to focus on a few of those images of the Reformer which seem reflected in this mirror, certain silhouettes of the Reformer. After all, a lightning sketch can be as evocative as a full-scale oil painting. We shall look not at the whole Calvin but only at some facets, each genuine, some perhaps contradictory, but then which of us does not have to say with the demoniac Jesus healed 'I am legion', or at least 'I am many'?

There is at least one aspect of Calvin which we shall try to avoid, namely the theologian, and that for two reasons. First because it is covered elsewhere in this book (see Ch. 8), and second because Calvin's theology can best be studied in his large works on doctrine. That being so, we shall not mention it here. But the question arises, Is this possible? Can we forget theology when we talk of the pastor? Can we leave out theology when we look at the whole man? With Calvin, the theologian cannot be separated from the rest of the man, for the theologian is the man. With him theology permeates everything, inspires everything, and is intermingled with everything—present even in the lowliest thoughts, directing the humblest tasks. You might as well detach life from thought as the Christian life from the doctrine that underlies it. For Calvin theology is the beginning and the end of every journey even when it is not also the intervening way as well. No, it is impossible to leave Calvin's theology out, but we shall not make detailed analyses from the letters of his doctrinal developments on such subjects as the Trinity, Predestination, Baptism or the Lord's Supper. However it should be noted in passing that passages on the Lord's Supper, in particular, which go a long way to defining the Reformer's thought over against Lutheranism would seem essential for any clear exposition of his doctrine.

The man

FIRST we must look at the physical man. 'I prefer not to talk about myself,' said Calvin, and so he rarely enlarged on his ill health. However enough is said to tell us that he was in poor

71

health from a very early age. While still young he had weakened his health with hard work and exaggerated vigils, not to mention the starvation régime of the Collège Montaigu. In 1536 he mentions to his friend Daniel his 'broken health' (*fracta valetudine*).[7] In 1540 at the age of thirty-four he writes to Farel from Strasbourg, 'When I think of my physical weakness and incapacity I am as concerned for those who must come after me as if I were already old, although I am still quite young'.[8] He felt aged prematurely. In fact all his life he was the victim of stomach troubles, of colds and catarrh, while headaches never left him long. Then there were the bouts of malaria, the so-called tertian and quartan agues. He was bothered by haemorrhoids which ulcerated. The gout tormented him cruelly, especially in his right foot. He suffered from gallstones, and towards the end of his life from a crippling nephralgia. Finally in 1559 came tuberculosis; short of breath, coughing blood, almost continually feverish, he suffered another five years, and in all this, when he did complain, it was less of his suffering than of the time which he was wasting.[9]

We must not concentrate on the negative aspect however. In his illnesses Calvin saw the chastisement of God (*castigatio*) and at the same time His call. 'Since the outcome of my illness is uncertain,' he writes to Melanchthon, 'I want you to know that in everything I am ready to answer God's call whenever it comes.'[10] And so he prepared himself for eternity. 'Illness presses me from this world as much as old age does you',[11] he writes to Blaurer, but while he was sometimes heard to say that his life was nothing but a living death,[12] he knew that in the midst of all his illness he was upheld by the power of God. To another sufferer, the Countess of Seninghem, he writes, 'Whatever happens, we may comfort ourselves in suffering with the knowledge that we are upheld by the power of God's Spirit, and that if this earthly dwelling-place should crumble, we shall be refashioned in an instant and for ever.'[13] Calvin was an invalid, but a Christian invalid! The Christian can scarcely be separated from the man, for the Christian *is* the man.

But however much one may be a Christian one cannot escape being the child of one's age, a prisoner of the ignorance and prejudice of one's environment. Thus Calvin was in certain respects still medieval in outlook. In support of this assertion we cite two

72

instances culled from his letters. The plague was ravaging Geneva and as so often in history the terror gave rise to cases of collective hysteria. Groups of men and women, calling themselves 'Plague-spreaders' prepared a sort of paste from infected ingredients and anointed door-latches during the night. They were arrested, interrogated and they confessed. Calvin recalls that twenty-five women have already been burnt alive, and twenty men are in prison. Others have committed suicide, but still in the night latches are being mysteriously infected. 'What dangers we face!' he writes. 'Nevertheless up to now the Lord has preserved our house.'[14] Of course today we would not burn these 'Plague-spreaders', but rather treat them.

Again, Calvin tells Viret a good story about a man who openly made fun of God, a drunkard, quarrelsome and blasphemous. He lived in a hut in the fields, cared for only by his mother and a servant, for his wife and four children had died of the plague which now struck him. While he was lying helpless and hardly able to lift a finger, he was seized by a sort of frenzy, and being possessed he prayed to devils and offered them his soul. Suddenly he leapt up and made a rush for the door where his mother was seated, evading her grasp with such speed that he seemed more swept up by a whirlwind than running. He was carried over a dense thorn hedge and disappeared from sight, leaving nothing but his hat. No matter how much the boatmen dragged the Rhone, they never recovered his body. Since he was certain that the wretched man had been carried away by demons, Calvin saw here a judgment from God, being persuaded that the wretched fellow had been taken away by devils. Some mocked. 'I have said openly,' he writes, 'that if you believe in devils you can clearly see the devil's power in this.' He concludes 'Some only agree outwardly. I do not know if a single one believes it in his heart.'[15] This outlook still medieval in some aspects, however, did not prevent the recent production of a book justly and pertinently entitled, *John Calvin, Contemporary Prophet*.[16]

We have mentioned the Reformer's ill-health, which also explains one trait of his character for which he is often criticised, indeed for which he often criticised himself, namely his extreme irritability. (His friend du Tillet called it his 'impatience-sickness.')[17] Thus he would fly into the most violent rages which often left him completely dejected. For example on one occasion he thought that someone had stolen some papers which he could not find, and flew into such a frenzy of indignation that he was forced to stay in bed the following day.[18] At another time he was so annoyed that the Council of Geneva had censored one of his books that he burst out 'I have a good mind to throw it in the fire!' and he swore that even if he lived a thousand years he would write nothing more in that city.[19] Happily he did not keep that promise. More than once his friends urged him to use moderation in his controversies, and he confessed himself guilty of this testiness and impatience. 'I got out of hand.'[20] 'I was more bitter than I had intended,'[21] 'I admit that I am irritable, and although this vice grieves me, I am not as successful as I would like in correcting it.'[22] On his death-bed he begged the pardon of the City Council for his 'over-vehement expressions, which he regretted'.[23] It is interesting however that Calvin should allow himself a defence for his vehemence and his violent words, and a justification for his attitude against much more bitter and relentless opponents. He felt constrained in spite of himself to use cutting words, 'I feel I deserve some indulgence,' he claims, 'if in defence of the true religion I am forced to attack (*tractus invehor*) such obstinate men as would, I am sure, have received no gentler treatment at the hands of apostles or prophets.'[24] 'You prefer gentleness,' he writes to Zurkinden, 'and indeed I am no enemy to it. If I appear too severe, believe me, I am driven to it out of necessity. On the other hand, does it never strike you how much your "gentleness" actually harms the Church, this "gentleness" which allows the wicked to go on with impunity, which confuses good and evil, and which does not differentiate between black and white. . . . As for me, I would rather be transported with rage than never be angry at all.'[25]

Calvin at work

THE letters also let us see a new facet of this rich personality, Calvin the tireless worker. We stand speechless with admiration in front of the sixty-two large octavo volumes of the *Opera*, some 40,000 pages of them, which flowed from his brain if not from his pen. This herculean task was accomplished day after day in spite of continual suffering. He was constantly interrupted

74

and harrassed by the thousand-and-one unexpected duties of a
very onerous ministry. Calvin writes to a close friend, perhaps
Bucer, 'In the midst of so many interruptions which each
moment tear me this way and that, there is no sort of work
which would not be difficult. I cannot recall two consecutive
hours without interruption. Added to this I have had to finish
the Latin *Institutio*; when it comes out you will see that it cost
not a little perspiration.'[26] In a letter from Strasbourg he gives an
account of what could well be just an ordinary day: 'When the
messenger came to collect the beginning of my book I had to
re-read twenty sheets of printer's proofs. I also had a lecture, a
sermon, four letters to write, a certain dispute to settle, and more
than ten visitors, all of whom required attention.'[27] At Geneva
it was even worse. 'I do not even have one hour free'[28] he
writes. The same day he tells Viret 'I am so weighed down with
endless and urgent correspondence that I am almost weary of
life.'[29] Another time he complains to M. de Falais: 'The difficulty is the vexatious and brain-racking interruptions which
occur twenty or more times even while I am writing one letter.'[30]

The fact was that he was consulted, or rather bothered, and
perhaps that he allowed himself to be bothered, about the most
minute details. For example, he is told of a new kind of stove.
A pharmacist or a student are recommended to him. He is busy
finding a home for some children in Lausanne, or looking for a
servant for his friend Farel, or trying to find a house for his
friend M. de Falais, and this involves visits and negotiations.
People ask him questions, most serious ones about politics, and
most trifling ones about peculiar cases of discipline. Should
one administer communion to two dumb men who come to
church regularly, and who indicate by signs that they would
rather die than go to Mass? He is asked about a young man who
has taken 900 crowns from his father, who would not let him
study. He is asked to arrange marriages, and so on. There is no
service which his friends, or even strangers, will not ask him to
do; each of them requires thought, inquiry, travelling, and always
time. If Calvin managed to accomplish all he did, if he found
the time for everything, his pastoral ministry, his letters, his
theological writing, it was because he was endowed with a prodigious strength of will. Here we see another characteristic of
Calvin, his will-power. In this weak body the will was imperious

75

JOHN CALVIN

and dominant. Emile Faguet says that it was unrivalled by that of the greatest conquerors and emperors. This will dominated the body and explains how in the midst of the most painful physical weakness this prodigious and endless volume of work was accomplished. Calvin has been called a bow always strung, and by that bow we can understand the will. When he could not walk, he was carried in a chair to St. Peter's to preach.[31] When he could not write, he would dictate.[32] If he could scarcely crawl (*reptare*) for pain, he would still continue to go to his lecture, leaning on the arm of a friend.[33]

One example of his indomitable energy triumphing over suffering will suffice. He suffered from a large gall-stone, which he could not eject. On the advice of doctors he rode on horseback in the hope that, once shaken up the stone would be the more easily emitted. On his return from the ride, the only result was a flow of fetid blood.[34] Such unpleasant details are necessary to show the will-power of the man who could stay upright and in the saddle while suffering such agony.

This iron will showed itself on all levels. At Strasbourg Calvin tried to set up a system of church discipline. Listen to his typical answer when the many obstacles were pointed out in an attempt to dissuade him. 'If it is God Who is calling us to this task, and we do not doubt it, then He will bless regardless of the opposition. Let us use every possible means (*remedia omnia*), and if they fail we will continue to our last breath'.[35] To Melanchthon he declares 'Even if the whole world hisses, my soul will not weaken.'[36] Here is a will that is completely unbending, which only death can quell. This will never gives way before obstacles, but rather turns them to advantage, worming round them and always overcoming them. 'If God will not open a door, we must creep in through a window (*reptandum est*), slide in through the narrowest crack, rather than lose the opportunity of doing good.'[37] Calvin was like a rock. The worst difficulties could break over him like the waves of a storm, but he remained unshakeable.

But by one of those contradictions which we have mentioned, this granite-like character had to it a side almost feminine in its sensitivity. 'You well know', he writes to Viret, 'the tenderness, not to say the indulgence of my soul (*mei teneritudinem vel mollitiem potius*).'[38] This sensitivity made him extremely sus-

76

ceptible to emotion. Calvin was upset, wounded by a lack of kindness, and cast down by the least reproach, especially when it came from his friends. One day he received a letter from Bucer. He was so elated that he could not remember, so he states, a happier day for the last three months. After dinner he read the letter, which contained a word of reproach, and he was unable to sleep. 'All night long I was upset: for three days I have not been completely myself.'³⁹ Or again his extreme sensitivity when Farel was lying mortally ill at Neuchâtel. Calvin went to see him, but was so overcome at his old friend's bedside that he could not bear to see him die, and rushed back to Geneva there to spread the news of his end. He confessed when he received the unexpected report of his recovery: 'I wanted to rush away and avoid this suffering which was still to come.'⁴⁰ It is not difficult to understand how a man so impressionable could entertain both the most bitter enmities and the most wonderful friendships.

Calvin the friend

CALVIN'S friendship with Farel seems to have been the strongest and most intimate. Farel had been the colleague of those first days at Geneva and the companion of his exile. He seems to have unburdened himself most easily to him, and not the slightest shadow of a difference ever came between them. From Farel, so vehement, so impulsive, so violent at times, Calvin would take anything. We know that it was the 'thunder' of his friend which compelled him finally to leave Strasbourg for Geneva, just as his thundering eloquence had originally forced him to remain in the city by Lake Leman. When he writes to Farel, Calvin unleashes his pen, which flows along like a torrent bursting its banks, so that he begs pardon for his disorderly (*tumultuarias*) or confused (*turbulentas*) letters.⁴¹ As true friends, they encourage rather than flatter each other. Farel preaches moderation to Calvin, an amazing thing when one recalls the vehemence of this rugged evangelist, but not so surprising when one remembers that of Calvin. 'For the sake of the Churches, and for the peace and edification of all,' he writes, 'we must do and endure much.'⁴² Calvin equally exhorts his old friend to restraint. Suffering from the same 'impatience-sickness' as his friend, he can write—and the delicacy of his terms is striking—'I will not fail to exhort you, to fortify myself with you by the exhortations.'[43] On another occasion Calvin does not hesitate to reproach him for preaching at too great length. 'I am given to understand that your very full sermons are giving some ground for complaint. I beg you most earnestly to restrict yourself, even forcibly if necessary, rather than offer Satan any handle which he will be quick to seize. We do not speak for our own benefit but for that of our people. We must remember proportion in teaching, so that boredom does not give rise to disrespect.' Here one final note softens the apparent harshness of the criticism, 'Do not think that you can expect from everyone an enthusiasm equal to your own'.[44] Yet again he reproaches him for having accepted and passed on false reports without discernment and critical examination.[45] This interchange of advice and encouragement is the stuff of true Christian friendship.

Touching too are the terms Calvin uses of the one who was in some respects the Mentor of his ministry. 'To my dear brother and especial friend. To my very dear and respected friend, one of the most upright, and most cherished (*suavissimo*).' Such friendship can draw together, even unite, hearts and make them beat as one. For Calvin, words addressed to Farel are the same as words addressed to himself, and he begs Farel to accept his advice as such. 'I beg you, my brother, to accept my complaint, my reproach, my accusation, my warning to you as if you were doing it to yourself'.[46] Each is to be in some way the conscience of the other.

His friendship with Viret was of the same order, full of the deepest trust. The two men wrote about everything and anything, about a vacant pastorate or a new book, a domestic difficulty or a health problem. In times of crisis they encouraged each other. In the thick of the fight against the Libertines when Calvin was thinking of leaving Geneva, Viret recalled him to his duty, and reminded him of the sufferings of Christ, of Moses and of Paul. 'Tears and prayers are our weapons. As for the idea of leaving your post, that would be nothing else than kindness to the wolves, and leaving the sheep to the fate the wolves deserve. . . . Courage! Go on as you are doing until the day when you will be glorified with that servant of God whom you now

78

follow and who said, 'I have fought the good fight, I have run the race, I have kept the faith.'[47]

The friendships of these three men, Calvin, Farel and Viret, was so proverbial that Theodore Beza could call them 'le trépied', Dedicating his *Commentary on the Epistle to Titus* to Farel and Viret, Calvin writes 'I am sure that nowhere have friends ever lived in such close fellowship and companionship as we have done in our ministry. . . . It seems as if you and I are just one person.' In the epic struggles of this troubled time such a friendship was for each of the three men an incomparable strength.

Calvin's friendship with Bucer was different. The latter was already at the peak of his career and reputation when he summoned the exiled young Genevan pastor to Strasbourg, and virtually compelled him to remain there. He was eighteen years older than Calvin. The difference in age introduced into the friendship, at least from Calvin's side, a special note of respect and esteem. He lived some three years close to Bucer, and he did not hesitate to borrow certain of his future ecclesiastical ideas from his friend.[48] He had not only a close sympathy with, but also a deep admiration for, his teacher, and speaks of him in the Preface to his *Commentary on the Psalms* as a most faithful teacher of the Church of God. Indeed he goes further and admits that Bucer's work on the Psalms had almost prevented him from writing on the subject.

What little survives of their correspondence to each other brings out this almost father-son relationship, and perhaps suggests the reason why Calvin should be so sensitive to Bucer's slightest rebuke.[49] He is always ready to listen to the advice of the Strasbourg Reformers and trusts them completely. He submits in deference to their views. 'If in any point I do not come up to your expectations, you know that I am in your power. Warn or punish. Do whatever is the right of a father toward his son.'[50] All his life he called Bucer his father, and Bucer responded with touching emotion, 'You are my heart and my soul'.[51]

More surprising was Calvin's friendship with Melanchthon. Emile Doumergue calls their correspondence 'one of those human documents which appeal so much to our age'.[52] Calvin seemed to have an almost incomprehensible indulgence towards Melanchthon. 'I so value your opinion that it would be very painful to think anything which you did not approve',[53] he writes. And while Melanchthon did not share Calvin's ideas on predestination, Calvin, far from being angry, did not hesitate —and the point is worth noting—to have his friend's *Loci* translated into French and then published. He even went further and added a Preface recommending it to French Protestants with the assurance that they would find 'a short summary of those things which a Christian ought to know for his soul's salvation'. Friendship did not however rule out clear-sightedness. We know the weakness of Melanchthon's character, and his timidity first in front of Luther and then when Luther was gone, in front of the ultra-Lutherans. Calvin wanted to inspire him with some of his own strength and boldness. 'Let us follow our course with unswerving mind,'[54] he writes. 'I charge you to your face not to approve those who condemn you behind your back. You know that your own situation is far different from that of most believers. Hesitation in the general or the standard-bearer is far more shameful than is the flight of simple soldiers. . . . In giving way a little you have given rise to more complaints and groans than would have done the open desertion of a hundred ordinary men.'[55]

Sometimes such manly counsels are followed by sentimental outpourings rather surprising in a man like Calvin; they give the lie to the legend of the 'black ghost with the icy countenance'. 'Can we not, as you say, talk more often, if only by letter. The gain would not be yours, but mine, for nothing in the world is more precious than the pleasure I find in reading your charming letters' (*in litterarum tuarum suavitate acquiescere*). 'We have what no distance can take away from us, namely, the glorious hope, as you say in your letter, that one day in heaven we shall live together for ever and enjoy fully this rich friendship (*amore amicitiaque*).'[56]

But this keen sensitivity which we have noticed, at times rendered Calvin terribly open to emotion. Side by side with the most lasting friendships there were also those which were shattered. Such was the case with du Tillet. A Canon and Archdeacon of Angoulême, he had received Calvin into his own home, had put his rich library at his disposal and had finally followed him to Basle and into Italy. He was in Geneva when Calvin was gripped by the charge from Farel, and remained with the Reformer. However the conflicts in which this involved him did not agree with his placid temperament, so he secretly left Geneva and eventually returned to the Roman faith. Calvin never forgave him for this. Doubtless it was difficult, in an age of clearcut and conflicting loyalties, to remain friends with a man of another faith than one's own. It is true that du Tillet had from his own ecclesiastical standpoint questioned Calvin's vocation, and that he had accused him of thrusting himself into the ministry. Calvin appealed to the judgment of God. To that, he said, he appealed against 'the judgment of all the wise people who think that their own word is sufficient for our condemnation.'[57] This was the end of a friendship begun in happier times.

Calvin's friendship with M. de Falais ended even more sadly. Jacques, Seigneur de Falais, had been won for the cause of the Reformation. Immediately suspect and charged before the Emperor, he was forced to leave his home and belongings in order to serve God according to his conscience. It was at this time that Calvin wrote his first letters to him encouraging him in his intentions. The believer cannot live in isolation without harming his spiritual life, and it is vital for him to join with other brethren and 'receive teaching', especially through preaching. The sooner this is done the better, says Calvin, for 'when the Lord gives us an opportunity it is as if He had opened a door for us'. How essential then to 'enter without further delay for fear of the door being shut'.[58]

Leaving his home and his property, M. de Falais went first to Cologne and then to Strasbourg. Calvin encouraged him, reminding him of the shortness of life, and of the need of dying to oneself. Calvin was indeed one of those who weep with them that weep, but never out of a misplaced pity did he put aside or obscure the cross; 'You must now show that when you set out to follow Jesus Christ, you also resolved to follow Him to the Cross, since He does us the honour of being crucified in us so that He may glorify us in Him.'[59] Always Calvin is there to uphold and encourage in his friend that spirit of poverty which refuses to allow him too much regret for the loss of his goods, and that trust which will leave him calm in the midst of the storms. 'We have no other hiding place than God; but when we hide in Him, then we are perfectly safe.'[60]

At length the de Falais family moved to Geneva. Calvin found them a house with a garden, made provision for the wine, had the vines pruned and the wheat sown. Then M. de Falais fell ill. Calvin wrote to his wife to prepare her for any eventuality, urging her to accept the will of God, but the nobleman recovered. The correspondence went on in friendly chatty fashion, discussing the news of the day, outlining projects of marriage, dealing with the printing at Geneva of M. de Falais' *Apology*,[61] talking of theology and politics, always with that note of challenge to constancy, and courage and faithfulness. 'We must use every means God gives us, and press on even when the means seem to be lacking.'[62] Calvin signs himself 'Your humble friend and ever sincere brother'.

Alas! This apparently permanent friendship was doomed to a brutal end. The episode revealed Calvin's whole character, his almost pathological sensitivity of which we have spoken. We know the Reformer's troubles with Bolsec, who had been banished from Geneva for attacking predestination. This Bolsec was a throughly unpleasant character, as he proved by writing—after the Reformer's death—his *Life of Calvin*. This is what can only be called a filthy cesspool in which are found some of the vilest and most defamatory libels ever uttered against the Reformer. It is the quarry from which all those who want to blacken the Reformer's memory come to dig. Now since Bolsec was his doctor, M. de Falais felt deeply indebted to him. He felt that, under God, he owed his very life to him. This gratitude made him take his doctor's side a little too openly and vigorously, and Calvin never forgave him for this. He felt that to take sides with his enemy was the same as condemning both him and his doctrine. So he wrote a last bitter, violent and harsh letter to M. de Falais. 'Since you now want to follow teaching quite contrary to that which I have learnt in the school of my Master (for you say that you are willing to overlook the possible bad in him, while we are told: *Videte canes, observate, notate, fugite, cavete*), I leave you to your pleasures'.[63] We are amazed that after such a long friendship as the one which had united the two men there was on Calvin's side no regret, no word of heart-felt emotion even at the moment of the break. For Calvin, when doctrine was attacked, the honour of God was at stake. In the same letter he writes 'Allow me that I have a duty to maintain the honour of my Master.' There was also a possible explanation for the sharpness in the fact that Calvin was himself ill at the time. 'I write as one who must shortly stand before the God who afflicts me with an illness which is like a reflection of death before my eyes.' But whatever one may say to excuse the Reformer, and while admitting that M. de Falais showed a lack of judgment, concern and tact, it is impossible not to deplore this letter which brought such a long and happy friendship to an end. In it we can sense an 'ego' cruelly hurt, but without any real sadness. But of course all this is very human! Side by side with faithful and enduring friendships we see the sad debris of shattered friendships scattered along life's way.

Calvin the pastor

IF one thing stands out especially from Calvin's letters, it is his concern for souls and their salvation. We would go so far as to suggest that instead of examining Calvin's theology always from an essentially dialectic and intellectual viewpoint, it would be very interesting to consider it sometimes in this pastoral and practical light. Never did his theology lose sight of the needs of godliness and the comfort it could bring to 'troubled consciences'.

It cannot be denied that Calvin's vocation was one thrust upon him from above. It had not sprung up spontaneously from the depths of his being, but rather he had to be taken by force. He was only a pastor by constraint and in spite of himself, and that twice over. First Farel had made him stay in Geneva; and then, driven out of Geneva, Bucer had summoned him to Strasbourg. He would much rather have pursued his studies in some quiet corner, but in the thundering entreaties of Farel as in the urgent pleas of Bucer, who reminded him of the example of Jonah, he believed that he could discern the very voice of God. He thus accepted 'the teaching charge', that is the pastoral ministry. From then on he was a pastor, and having put his hand to the plough, he never looked back.

His former friend, du Tillet, dared, after leaving Geneva, to cast doubt on this vocation. From his point of view no one should put themselves into the ministry without being called by the church and authorised by the sacrament of Orders.

JOHN CALVIN

This was a sore spot, for Calvin had never been 'ordained'. He replied with an impassioned affirmation, a cry of faith. It proved nothing, but demonstrated the sure foundation on which his ministry rested. 'You do not have such strong reasons for impugning my calling as the Lord has provided sure ones for confirming me in it. If for you there is doubt about it, for me it is certain enough.'[64] Du Tillet then accused him of subjectivism. 'You desire us to accept all you say and do as if it were said and done by God . . . as if your judgment can never be other than that of God.'[65] We do not possess Calvin's reply to this letter, but he could only repeat his certainty, incommunicable perhaps, but still unshakeable. Was it possible, as he saw it, that the supernatural force which had on two separate occasions violated his own natural inclinations could not have come from God? Calvin was not in doubt about that. Besides he did not hold simply to his own judgment, but consulted his fellow ministers. 'In such a perplexity I thought it necessary to follow what had been shown me by God's servants.'[66] They all confirmed what his own conscience told him.

He did not fail to extol the greatness of this calling to which he remained faithful to his last breath, 'I would be a most ungrateful wretch, if I did not prefer my present state to all the wealth and honour in the world.'[67]

Spiritual director

CALVIN the pastor is seen in the letters as an excellent spiritual director. The limits we have set ourselves forbid our following through his correspondence with the Duchess of Ferrara, with Admiral Coligny, with D'Andelot, or Mme. de Cany or many another. We can only attempt to portray this spiritual direction, to point out the essential themes in their organic relation.

First, we find as the basic foundation for the whole of Calvin's structure the doctrine of the absolute sovereignty of God. Here is the very heart of Calvinism, the keystone of his theology as of his piety, the central point from which all the rest follows. Here is the rock which underlies the surface everywhere, even if it does not appear to the light of the sun. God is the

84

supreme and final cause, and everything else is secondary. Every event even those least significant in our eyes, as well as the most important, is a manifestation of His eternal plan. Life and death are in the hand of God. He can protect us as we walk along the edge of the grave, and not allow us to fall in 'until it is time'.[68] Healing is His work. 'You must consider that God has not preserved your life in vain'.[69] Death too is his. 'The Lord has taken to Himself the son He gave and committed into your hands.'[70] As for prisoners, it is God 'who put them in the battle', who calls them to witness and perhaps to martyrdom. 'Put yourself in the hands of Him without whose providence nothing takes place, who holds the times and means in His hands'.[71] The Duke of Somerset had been disgraced, but it was God who had purposed to humble him for a little while.[72] Suffering is God's chastening.[73] The Duchess of Ferrara endured cruel trials, but it was God who used such means to test her faith.[74] 'You were going sluggishly. If God gave you a touch of the spur, you should not be surprised'.[75] God, always God, nothing but God. Mortal men, 'these enemies who rage so furiously against us, can do nothing in spite of all their efforts unless God the Sovereign Ruler permits it.'[76] Satan himself is held in check as he tries to hurl himself against believers, and can only go as far as he is permitted by God. He and his demons are held 'bound like wild beasts'.[77] Thus beyond life and death, behind the tumult of history, in the darkness of the dungeon and beyond the flames of the stake, Calvin gazes in adoration at the living God. This great vision lights up all his letters, and he wants to share it with everyone. 'Many', he cries, 'are as dejected as if God were no longer alive.'[78]

In this certainty that God is sovereign, that nothing can take place without His will, the great peace and confidence of the believer reside. By being the herald of the sovereignty of God, Calvin made himself, by the same token, the great preacher of assurance. This is perhaps the most constant theme of his letters. 'Have this point settled in your mind, to leave your cares to the providence of God, trusting that He will provide when it seems impossible to us.'[79] 'God will provide when you do not see how,' writes Calvin to a lady who was hesitating about going into exile from France, 'for this is the way He saves His people, not only from the mouths of wolves but even from the jaws of hell.'[80]

D
85

'Let the confidence that God commands us to have in His grace be an invincible fortress to us'.[81] 'We are told in Scripture that tyrants can do no more to us than God permits. Now in permitting such things, He knows of what we are made, so He will take care of the outcome.'[82] 'So take courage and commit yourselves to Him, for He will show His care for His poor sheep, and it is His bounden duty to preserve them, even in the mouths of wolves'.[83] Everything comes from God; He knows our strength, and proportions our trials to our weakness; the result is a confident assurance. 'If God is going to give you a heavier burden, He will also give you the shoulders on which to carry it'.[84] 'He will either repel the blows, or He will give us the strength necessary to bear them.'[85]

The question of providence never seems to have raised any great intellectual difficulties for Calvin, nor did the problem of evil shake his certainty. He resolutely put doubt on one side. 'It is not for us to inquire why God does this or that. Rather are we to do our duty without further discussion.'[86] It is all the more interesting to discover an occasional word or hint which suggests that this soul had a fierce struggle within itself, which like the temptation to doubt was quickly repressed. We note two examples, taken not from the *Letters*, but from the *Institutio*. 'No one is convinced that God is faithful without a hard and bitter struggle.'[87] Calvin seems to have endured that 'hard and bitter struggle'. Or again 'However much God may display his fatherly goodness towards us, yet a mere contemplation of the world would not convince us that God is our Father'.[88] Looking at the world around would rather make us doubt God's fatherhood and His providence. Our doubts only become resolved in Jesus Christ. Whatever we may say, it seems that questions which bother us most today hardly occurred to the mind of Calvin.

Apart from this confidence, another direct consequence of this principle of God's absolute sovereignty is that man does not belong to himself. God must come first, before everything, before ourselves. Calvin never tires of reminding his correspondents of this: 'When God calls us to Himself, He dedicates us so that our whole life may set forth his honour'.[89] 'God's glory, and everything which belongs to His kingdom must always come first.'[90] 'Above all, glorify God.'[91] In the heat of trials and temptations the thoughts of God's honour ought to encourage us in the fight and lead us to victory. 'No difficulty can serve for an excuse if God's honour is at stake',[92] Calvin wrote to a Piedmont nobleman who was hesitating about professing the Gospel. When he was trying to encourage the King of Navarre not to let himself be hindered by opposition from the enemies of the truth, it was still to the honour of God that he appealed. 'When the honour and service of God are at stake there can be no excuse for timidity.'[93] God's honour must be more precious to us than all the blessings of family life. 'There are no earthly ties which do not deserve to be trodden underfoot to make way for the honour of our sovereign and incomparable Father.'[94] Calvin presses Mme. de Pons to declare her faith in the gospel, especially since God has delivered her from the tyranny of an unfaithful husband. 'I well know that you are concerned for your children, and I am far from saying that this is not entirely correct, so long as you do not leave out of account the sovereign Father both of them and of yourself.'[95] Nothing, even life itself, is too precious to be sacrificed, if necessary, for the glory of God. 'Believe me that your life is precious to me, but it is not for you or me to spare ourselves from preferring to a hundred lives the honour of the One to whom we owe everything.'[96]

God-centred

THE honour of God is more important than our individual salvation. For Calvin the ultimate end of history is not the salvation of man, but the glory of God. Thus he writes to the King of Navarre: 'You will, I am sure Sire, pardon the necessity which causes us to speak thus, that however much we have at heart your salvation, there is something still more worthy and precious which we seek, namely the glory of God and the spread of the kingdom of Jesus Christ, wherein lies the salvation both of yourself and of the whole world.'[97] These lines are characteristic of Calvin's thought. The great preoccupation of the believer in his religion lies not in his own salvation, however legitimate such a concern may be. This would be to put man at the centre and reduce God to a simple means to a personal end. No! The faithful will live for God, for the glory of God; and

87

JOHN CALVIN

because he will be delivered from himself by this great vision of the glory of God and the advancement of the kingdom of Jesus Christ, man will find his own salvation. This surely *is* salvation, to be delivered even in our piety from all egoism, from all ego-centricity, so that we may give to God, in our hearts and in our lives, that place which is His by right, the first place.

We can now see what Calvin means when he speaks of God as glorifying Himself in us. The theme is hardly different, but the form is specifically Calvin's, since it is God who is the subject. It is not man who glorifies God. It is God who glorifies himself in the faithfulness of His servants, and who triumphs in the victory of His elect. 'Our Lord has desired to glorify His Name in you.'[98] 'Have no doubt that He will show Himself victorious in you against His enemies.'[99] There is less concern with exhortation than with the prayer that God will indeed glorify Himself in finishing His work in us. 'I beseech our good Lord to fill you full of all graces, daily to increase His glory in you, and to triumph in your constancy.'[100]

To seek before anything else the honour and the glory of God means to live no more for oneself, to belong no more to oneself. The immediate corollary of the sovereignty of God is the complete renunciation which Christ demanded of each of His disciples. In effect, whatever our favourite idols may be, the real debate, in the final analysis, is between God and us. Either God or myself, His will or my will, His kingdom, His glory, His honour, or my own interest and self-seeking. 'We are not our own.' This is the theme, so magnificently developed in the *Institutio*[101] which reappears constantly in the *Letters*. 'God wants us to be completely His.'[102] 'It is entirely just that we should let ourselves be ruled according to the good will of the One whose we are, and who has all power and authority over us.'[103]

If we are ruled by the will of God, then our whole life must be one of obedience: 'It is entirely just that we should show in our lives that we are His, by submitting everything to Him in genuine obedience.'[104] 'It is not enough to fight manfully in a good cause', Calvin writes to the Prince de Porcien, 'Our Christianity shows in our total submission to the will of Him who has so dearly bought us, so that He may be glorified in our life as in our death'.[105] This obedience may lead to the supreme

88

sacrifice, and then we must 'prefer obedience to Him rather than life for us'.[106]

But Calvin did not ignore the cost of this self-denial, which, whatever the agony, can say 'Not my will but Thine be done'. 'We all know only too well', he cries, 'how hard it is for men to deny themselves.'[107] This is truly to bear one's cross, and this discipline of the cross was one to which Calvin never tired of recalling his correspondents. At first it seems like a completely external resemblance to Jesus Christ. 'Since we seek Christ, we must be ready to find Him crucified wherever we go in the world.'[108] He warns a nobleman against possible illusions he may have in leaving France for Geneva. 'If you will follow Jesus Christ, be ready not to flinch from His cross. You will gain nothing from flight, for the cross will follow you regardless.'[109]

However Calvin goes deeper. This is not merely a superficial conformity to Christ which expresses itself in our suffering. There is also a very intimate relationship which unites us to Him in our death and resurrection with Him. The discipline of the cross becomes a kind of crucifixion for us, preparing and conditioning the new life which springs up in the regenerate soul, the crucifixion of the 'old man' and the stripping-off of all those things which hinder our obedience. Calvin lays emphasis on the fact that we need not only to die, but also to be buried, showing by this that the conflict is life-long. The resurrection is thus no more that newness of life which spreads through the Christian soul, but rather the entrance into that glorious life which is promised beyond the grave. 'Since you have begun to die to the world for love of Him, you must now learn what it is to be buried, for death is nothing without burial. In order to prepare yourselves to endure to the end you must lay hold of the consolation that your cross is much lighter by the price of the Master's cross.'[110]

Union with Christ is thus so intimate that we can at some point 'pass from our being into His'[111] so that ultimately one could say that it is Christ who suffers, is buried and is raised again in us. 'I have been crucified with Christ,' said St. Paul, and Calvin would not hesitate to say also, 'Christ has been crucified in me'. In fact he does so, 'He has done us the honour of being crucified in us so that He may glorify us with Him'.[112] This death, this burial, this resurrection with Christ, which are real-

89

ised by faith and without any confusion of the persons, forms what could be called Calvin's mysticism.

Mystical and yet dynamic was the faith which Calvin sought to communicate to his correspondents. From the doctrine of the absolute sovereignty of God it is possible to draw the conclusion of a complete fatalism which is the conclusion of Islam. Calvin, on the contrary, makes this doctrine into a spur for believers. How so, if it is God who plans and who does everything? No doubt the premise is true, but in the midst of men, God works through the medium of men. There is the famous passage in the *Institutio* 'Since He does not dwell visibly with us, God uses the service of men . . . to do His work through them, just as a craftsman uses his tools'.[113] Thus the believer is an instrument, or even a workman, for God, in whose service he must use all his strength, indeed everything that he has and is. Thus he gives himself to God to ascertain, test and try whether God is willing to use him and work through him. Calvin writes to the Genevan Senate these significant words which bring together and harmonise the sovereignty of God and the activity of man; 'Before returning I very much wanted to test whether God would do a certain thing'.[114] To a foreign church he writes in similar vein, 'Test whether God will be pleased to use me in any way in this place'.[115] He advises M. de Loines, a councillor of the *Parlement* not to leave his post, 'until you have tried the ways by which God may use you'.[116] We must put ourselves completely in the hands of God and remain humble, for we know that whatever we do it is God who works through us. The sovereignty of God and the effort of man are never separated in Calvin's thought, so that he can write those jarringly paradoxical words which are yet so typically Calvinist: 'Act so that God may be the more strong.'[117]

This action on the part of man, which God can use, is basically witness, always a duty, but rendered the more imperative by the circumstances of the time. The open profession of the truth was a necessity in those troubled times. Men had to declare themselves and stand together to avoid being swept away by the storm. This is a duty which Calvin never tires of explaining to everyone. There is perhaps no exhortation in all his correspondence to which he returns more frequently than this. He writes to M. de Falais, who is intending to go to Worms to beg back his property from the Emperor. 'I beg you to think carefully before undertaking this journey. What matters above everything else is that you are resolved to witness for the Saviour openly and without flinching, come what may.'[118] To Mme. de Cany he says, 'If your confession of Christianity means rumours and threats against you, remember that we are called to worship God's Only Son regardless of the world's gainsaying'.[119] 'Since the glory of God must be worth more to us than a thousand lives, we have no excuse, whatever we may say, for not confessing the truth of His Gospel when He has revealed it to us, and like a sacrifice He will require it very exactly of us.'[120] 'We must hold to this point firmly that God has produced you as it were by His hand so that you might be a witness to His truth in a place where witness had been hindered up to then.'[121]

Calvin had also observed, with deep psychological insight, that the faith which did not witness quickly withered and died. 'Faith', he would say, 'cannot stay asleep for long without being extinguished.'[122] As a result it is a fatal mistake to dissimulate or hide one's Evangelical convictions, to be a 'middleman' sitting on the fence, or trying to 'serve God and the devil', so as to avoid professing one's Christian faith. 'When we have reached the extremity of having no other way of escape from the enemies of the truth except by subterfuges which take us far away from the Christian path, there can be no doubt that God is calling us to seal with our blood that confession of faith which we owe Him. . . . If it is a question of refusing to confess the faith this way or that, it is better to die.'[123]

Thus Calvin does not turn the believer back on himself and into the state of his own soul, nor leave him to amuse himself with a faith that stays hidden in the recesses of his heart. On the contrary he hurls him into the conflict like an eager war-horse. 'Those who have the right on their side are like horses with the bit between their teeth,'[124] he writes to Admiral Coligny. The believer is also a witness, and by the same token a soldier. Thus people have been able to call Calvinist piety a militant soldier-piety. Calvin had seen human life, and even more the Christian life, assaulted by all sorts of temptations. The Christian is always being pressed by temptation, and is taking part in a constant battle. 'Satan never rests from starting new conflicts'.[125] 'We cannot serve God without fighting'.[126] 'We must

91

persevere, and not tire of the combat, which is not only a battle of the sword against enemies we can see, but also against everything which hinders or distracts us from the right way'.[127] 'We live in a time of war, and there is no better lot for us than to gather round the standard where we can gain courage to go on fighting until death'.[128] This 'standard', he explains in another letter, is the cross of our Lord Jesus Christ.[129] Elsewhere he speaks of the 'battle of the cross' (*crucis militia*)[130] and of the obligation which that cross lays on us to fight on, whether raising the standard among Christ's enemies by our witness or living ourselves under the discipline of the cross. 'We need to know from experience' he says again, 'that our life in this world is a battle.'[131] So we must be 'good and faithful men-at-arms for Jesus Christ'.[132]

Armed with this great vision of life as a battle, Calvin turns towards believers in an attempt to stiffen their resolve into a heroic and manly attitude. He applies the doctrine of God's absolute sovereignty to give them souls of steel, on which adversity can find no foothold, and then he flings them into battle, transferring a little of his own indomitable spirit, and of his will always tensed for the fray.

He did not just stay, however, in the realm of principles. He was consulted about concrete situations. Should M. de Crussol, Gentleman-in-Waiting to the Queen Mother, accompany her to Mass?[133] Is the Duchess of Ferrara bound by the promise which she made to her husband?[134] (On his death-bed he had made his wife promise not to correspond with the Reformer.) May one help someone to escape by means of skeleton keys or bribery, if the person is imprisoned for his faith?[135] Marital questions were also referred to him. Should a wife leave her immoral husband?[136] May one fly before an outburst of the plague?[137] Textor, his doctor, wanted to know what he should think about the image of the cross.[138] In a very concrete example he was asked whether there were no situations where charity should come before truth.[139] Examples could be multiplied, but we shall cite only a few characteristics of Calvin's spiritual direction.

Biblical counsel

THIS direction was essentially *biblical*. Calvin wanted to be nothing more than the mouthpiece, the trumpet of God. He desired to lead souls in the right way 'which God has shown in His Word'.[140] 'What drives me to speak is that I cannot tolerate the Word of God being hidden, perverted, corrupted and depraved.'[141] He wanted to know nothing apart from the Bible, that source of all true knowledge and standard for all right conduct. Writing to the five prisoners of Lyons, he tells them; 'You know how the Scripture warns us to give us courage as we fight for the cause of the Son of God. Meditate on what you have seen and heard formerly, so that you may put it into practice. Everything that I can ever tell you will not help unless it is drawn from this well.'[142] 'You do not really need my letters so much, for what you hope to learn from me, you can find much nearer to hand if you diligently read God's holy Word.'[143] In fact the Bible itself is the best director of conscience. Calvin would say that it makes all the rest unnecessary. Thus the obedience, on which Calvin insisted so much, is meaningless unless it is obedience to the Bible. Assurance is without an object, unless it is an assurance rooted in the promises of the Bible. It is the promises of God which Calvin uses to strengthen and uphold believers, those promises 'which are intended to be like ladders taking us right up into heaven'.[144] 'Whatever the difficulties, God's promise to protect us and provide for our every need should be amply sufficient to keep us from flinching under trial.'[145] The absolute sovereignty of God is directly linked with the promise. 'When we consider His power, we are thereby to add to His promises a sure and unshakeable faith.'[146]

Since it is biblical, Calvin's direction *respects the individual who is being counselled.* His role is to lead the conscience back to God's will as it is revealed in the Bible. 'Take and read.' It is in this context that, far from calling for a blind faith, he appeals to private judgment. And so we may find in his letters the occasional precise and definite instructions, but there is never any impression of imposing on the individual conscience. Much rather, does he withdraw from view so as to leave the believer alone with God's Word, and with awakened conscience now stirred by God's Word. It is for the individual to judge and decide. He carefully expounds the truth to the Duchess of Ferrara 'so that in the end the decision may be yours'.[147] These words are typical of Calvin's method. He will never so put

93

JOHN CALVIN

himself in the place of those he is directing as to impose a
decision which would be external and alien to their own inner
convictions. He instructs and enlightens them, but then he
leaves them alone face to face with God, for the decision is
theirs alone. Thus his directing is typical too of all Protestant
directing and counselling. The sole aim is so to interpret the
Word of God to those who seek, that when instruction and exhortation is complete, they may be able to 'judge for themselves'.

Founded on the rock of the Word of God, Calvin's direction is
as firm and unyielding as is that Word on which it is based. The
one thing which above all else Calvin feels he owes to those he
counsels is the truth. Thus he will not gloss over errors or faults,
nor will he hide the dangers. 'I do not spare you anything', he
writes to one of his correspondents, 'so that God may spare
you.'[148] 'Do not hope that I will release you from what God
requires of you. Better ask Him for strength for the fight, even
if it be to the death.'[149]

No more than he hid people's faults did Calvin hide the difficulties. Indeed he tore the veil from illusions. 'If you ask me
whether once you have come [to Geneva], you will have lasting
and guaranteed peace, I can only answer, No. While we are in
this world, we must be like birds of passage.'[150] He warned the
Duchess of Ferrara that our faithfulness would often be jarred
by slander and mistrust.[151] He told Mme. de Cany that what she
was enduring was not the end of her sufferings, but that 'God
was trying her very gently and supporting her weakness, so that
she might be the stronger to sustain fresh blows'.[152]

All this may be summed up by saying that Calvin's direction is
as demanding as are the demands of God. It aims to 'take
away all the subterfuges which our flesh[153] puts in the way to turn
us from the path which God shows us'. Everywhere in Calvin's
letters we find stirring injunctions and courageous exhortations,
infinitely modulated variations on the great theme of the cross.
All are aimed at showing in the life of the believer the practical
applications of God's absolute sovereignty.

If it is firm and unyielding, this direction is none the less
human. Calvin shows a real sympathy for those whose faithfulness to God's Word at times led to the most painful sacrifices.
He did not underestimate the weaknesses inherent in what he
calls 'the flesh', and the conflicts necessary if we would truly

94

'follow Christ to the cross'. 'I am not ignorant of the dangers which surround you', he writes to Budé's brothers, 'and I am not so inhuman as not to feel for you.'[154] When he urges those believers who can, to leave France, it is not without understanding, and from his own personal experience, what sufferings are involved and what is the loss as a result of such a decision. Nevertheless if it is the way of duty, his sympathy will not soften his definiteness. He knows, though not this time from experience it is true, all that prisoners endure. When he speaks to them of martyrdom it is with holy fervour as well as with contained emotion. 'Compassion grips me like a vice at seeing you languishing so long',[155] he writes to the prisoners at Chambéry. In a letter to Dymonet, he has a touching phrase which expresses so well that sensitivity which we have already noted. 'I beseech you as if I were a prisoner with you.'[156]

This humanity in Calvin's direction shows especially in his dealings with those who had fallen. It is true that he does not hide from them the gravity of the fault, for each is a victory for Satan and a stumbling-block for believers. 'It is no small nor slight offence to have preferred men before God. God has been dishonoured. . . . The enemies of the truth have had reason for rejoicing. . . . In your very person they feel they have overcome our Lord Jesus Christ.'[157] But while he tries to make those Christians who did not know how to resist feel the gravity of their fall, he never pushes them to despair. He tells them on the contrary—and with great feeling—of the mercy of God. 'Our gracious God is always ready to receive us with mercy, and when we have fallen He stretches out a hand to us so that the fall should not be fatal.'[158]

It is, of course, the future that matters, and Calvin encourages sinners because he can foresee the new attacks which they will have to endure. Their fault may only be an accident, but it must be made good. 'I beseech you, be so unhappy over this recent evil that you will repair the breach by coming back into the way you first walked. . . . Demonstrate from the outcome that while you may have stumbled once, it was not enough to force you out of the right way.'[159] Calvin used every means to revive believers who were in a fallen state. He could not share in their failure, but he urged them, he pressed on them, he besought them to leave the past to God, who would wipe clean the soiled page

95

with His forgiveness, and to face the future with confidence, asking God for His strength.

Calvin's counselling is also human in that he never exhorts to holiness in hard, imperious, reproachful tones. Rather does he encourage not only those who fall, but also those who only plod slowly along the Christian way. Like all good advisers, 'those good husbandmen of the soul', he knew how to bide his time without 'encroaching on providence', to use the words of St. Vincent de Paul. 'Let us each go on in his own little steps', he would say, 'and let us continue in the way we have begun. None of us can travel so meanly that we do not gain a little ground each day. Let us not lose heart, however, if we only travel a little way at a time; we have not wasted our labour if today is an advance on yesterday.'[160] These words from the *Institutio* could easily have come from one of his pastoral letters. Calvin never discourages his correspondents by an exaggerated haste. He knows how to be content with a little progress, so long as it is genuine progress. 'God will need time to strengthen you as much as He thinks necessary, even though His work will not be seen at first.'[161] In almost all his letters we are struck by such expressions as 'more and more'—'serving more and more to the glory of God', and 'to increase in you'—'to increase in you the gifts of His Spirit and the graces which He has put in you', or again, 'always going further on', or 'growing from day to day', etc.

Finally, even when one fails, there is no cause for despair, if the will to do good was there. Calvin has this word so very indulgent and so very human, 'When our aim is right, God will accept the will for the deed.'[162] Thus as long as one tries, and goes on fighting and struggling, and as long as one refuses to give up and admit defeat, whatever battles are lost, one can keep a quiet trust that God is there and that He will not leave us. Is it possible to show more understanding of the weaknesses of us sinners, and more humanity in one direction, without ever hiding the demands of the Gospel?

Conclusion

WE have highlighted certain aspects of this wonderfully rich personality John Calvin, as he shows himself in his Letters.
96

There are of course other aspects. One could speak of the churchman, of his contacts with other Reformers, of his movements towards reconciliation and peace, of the good will and understanding between the Lutherans and the Reformed, and among the Reformed themselves. Everywhere and always Calvin tried to bring peace and to avoid dissension and schism. We ought to speak of the Christian, of his humility, and of his unshakeable faith, even in the worst days. Certainly there were the cries of distress, and he sometimes let slip sighs from his very soul, for death then appeared to him as the great deliverer, but to his dying breath he continued work without weakening.

Whatever else comes out of our study we can at least say that it is impossible to know Calvin truly without reading his letters. In reading the *Institutio*, that great doctrinal treatise, we see the profound and mighty thought of the theologian, and feel the pastoral care for 'troubled consciences'. As we read the *Sermons*, we can visualise the preacher. Based on the adage that 'the style is the man', some have tried to sketch out a portrait of Calvin with the help of certain key-words borrowed from his sermons.[163] All this, however, is insufficient, and indeed fragmentary, revealing only one aspect of the Reformer's personality. It is in his letters that he gives himself freely, not only with the clarity of his mind, but also with all the warmth of his heart. Especially is this so when he is writing to those prisoners called to be martyred for their faith, or to the persecuted believers of the scattered churches in France, to the de Budés or to the de Falais, or to the Duchess of Ferrara, to those whose hesitations and difficulties he understood and whom he wanted to help to a firm resolve to 'follow Christ to the cross'. It is in his letters that he can be seen giving himself to his friends. There his indignation, anger and impatience are uncovered, as also is that 'tenderness of heart'. His other books were written with pen and ink, and we see in them his mind, clear, logical even ruthless perhaps, but we never move out of the realm of the intellect. His letters, however, are written with his heart, sometimes with tears, I was going to say with blood, if one can fairly call tears of sympathy, humiliation and distress tears of blood. It is in his letters, which are moving as is every human document in which we can feel the life throbbing, that he gives himself completely to us. It is here that we must look if we want to

97

find the whole man. It is here too that all those caricatures which have done such outrage to his memory fade and vanish, and Calvin appears in his full stature. A man, a real man, a great man.

NOTES

1. CO Xb–XX. (All references in this chapter are to this edition.)
2. XIV.342.
3. XV.330.
4. XV.894.
5. XII.111–112.
6. Cf. J-D. Benoît, *Calvin directeur d'âmes*, Strasbourg, 1947, pp. 49–61.
7. X.64.
8. XI.43.
9. To Farel, XIII.519.
10. XVII.385.
11. XVIII.14.
12. To Farel, XVI.182.
13. XX.140
14. To Myconius, XII.55.
15. To Viret, XII.413–415.
16. Grand Rapids, 1959.
17. Xb. 292.
18. To Viret, XII.100.
19. To Farel, XVI.535.
20. To Bullinger, XVI.11.
21. To Westphal, IX.250.
22. To Zurkinden, XVII.236.
23. IX.888.
24. To Zurkinden, XVII.239.
25. XVII.465–466.
26. XI.364.
27. To Farel, Xb.337.
28. To Farel, XII.581.
29. XII.579.
30. XII.319.
31. To Beza, XIX.67–68.
32. To Beza, XIX.56.
33. To Bullinger, XIX.99.
34. To Bullinger, XX.53–54.
35. To Farel, X.331.
36. XV.738.
37. To Peter Martyr, XVIII.613.
38. XIII.230.

39. Lost letter, reproduced by Baudouin, *Responsio Altera*, 1562, cf. Doumergue, II.404.
40. XIV.509.
41. Xb.315, 423.
42. XIV.242.
43. Xb.435.
44. XIV.273–274.
45. Xb.431.
46. Xb.10.
47. To Calvin, XII.640–641.
48. Cf. Jacques Courvoisier, *La notion d'Eglise chez Bucer dans son développement historique*, Paris, 1933.
49. Cf. p. 77, lines 11 ff.
50. To Bucer, XI.299.
51. XI.451.
52. Doumergue, II.545.
53. XII.10.
54. XII.100.
55. XIII.594–595.
56. XI.515.
57. To du Tillet, Xb.272.
58. XI.629–630.
59. XII.169.
60. XI.665. The Strasbourg editors read 'Que l'aisle de notre Dieu'. The Amsterdam ed. has 'retraite que *celle* de notre Dieu'.
61. *L'Excuse de Noble Seigneur Jacques de Bourgoigne, S. de Fallez et Bredam: pour se purger vers la M. impériale des calomnnies à luy imposées, en matière de sa Foy, dont il rend confession.* Geneva, 1548.
62. XII.320.
63. 'Beware of the dogs, watch, judge, flee, take care' XIV.449.
64. To du Tillet, Xb.270.
65. Xb.291.
66. To du Tillet, Xb.271.
67. To the Queen of Navarre, XII.67.
68. To M. de Falais XII.128.
69. To Brenz, XIII.98.
70. To M. de Richebourg, XI.190.
71. To a prisoner, XV.346.
72. XIII.530.
73. To Mme. de Grammont, XVII.660.
74. XVII. 260.
75. To Mme. de Cany, XV.193.
76. To the Duchess of Ferrara, XVII.261.
77. To the believers in France, XVII.571.
78. To the believers in France, XVII.682.
79. To a Lady, probably Mme. de Budé, XII.454.
80. To a Lady, XIII.151.
81. To the believers in France, XII.562.

99

82. To the believers in France, XVII.685.
83. To the believers in Poitou, XV.223.
84. To M. de Falais, XII. 86.
85. To the Church in Paris, XVI.630.
86. To M. de Falais, XII.344.
87. *Inst.* III.ii.15.
88. *Inst.*II.vi.1.
89. To Mme. de la Roche-Posay, XII.295.
90. To Admiral Coligny, XVII.320.
91. To the Duke of Somerset, XIII.76.
92. XV.42.
93. XVII.71.
94. To the Duc de Longueville, XVII.606.
95. XIV.669.
96. To Mme. de Rentigny, prisoner for the Faith, XVI.728.
97. XIX.201.
98. To M. de Falais, XII.170.
99. To Le Fèvre, imprisoned for his faith, and due to die at the stake, XIV.19.
100. To Mme. de Falais, XII.174.
101. *Inst.* III.vii.1.
102. To Mme. de Coligny, XVIII.735.
103. To Mme. de Grammont, XVII.660.
104. To M. de Falais, XII.179.
105. XX.11.
106. To the believers in France, XII.562.
107. To the prisoners at Lyon, XIV.562.
108. To M. de Falais, XII.129.
109. To a French Nobleman, XIII.64.
110. To M. de Falais, XII.86.
111. *Comment. on Rom.* 6.5.
112. To M. de Falais, XII.169.
113. *Inst.* IV.iii.1.
114. XI.589.
115. XX.522.
116. XX.183.
117. To Leyner, XIV.348.
118. XII.85–86.
119. XIII.144–145.
120. To the Duc de Longueville, XVII.605.
121. To D'Andelot, XVII.192.
122. To the believers in France, XVII.687.
123. To an imprisoned Lady, XIV.619.
124. XVIII.546.
125. To the Duke of Somerset, XIII.65.
126. To the Queen of Navarre, XIX.347.
127. To the Prince de Porcien, XX.11.
128. To M. de Budé, XII.543.

129. To the believers in France, XII.561.
130. To John Gray, XV.309.
131. To M. de Falais, XII.637.
132. To the believers of an unknown community, XV.811.
133. XX.111–113.
134. To the Duchess of Ferrara, XVIII.147.
135. Xa.257.
136. To Mme. de Grammont, XVII.661.
137. XVIII.105.
138. XI.478. Cf. Xa.195–196.
139. XV.696.
140. To an imprisoned Lady, XIV.618–619.
141. To the Duchess of Ferrara, XI.325.
142. XIV.332.
143. To the believers in the Church at Antwerp, XVI.337.
144. To Mme. de Cany, XIV.557.
145. To Mme. de Coligny, XVII.460.
146. *Sermons on the Book of Job*, XLVI.92.
147. XI.325.
148. XVII.443.
149. To certain women who hold back from supporting the Reformation although they are convinced, XX.429.
150. To Mme. de Budé, XII.453.
151. XVII.262.
152. XIV.557.
153. To a lady who has not yet publicly confessed the Faith, XIII.151.
154. XII.646.
155. XV.809.
156. XIV.467.
157. To D'Andelot, XVII.272.
158. To the Duchess of Ferrara, XV.418.
159. To D'Andelot, XVII.272–273.
160. *Inst.* III.vi.5.
161. To Mme. de Cany, XIV.557.
162. To the Duchess of Ferrara, XVII.261.
163. Doumergue, *Le Caractère de Calvin*, Paris, 1921, pp. 21ff.

5 The History and Development of the *Institutio*: How Calvin Worked

Jean-Daniel Benoît

AT THE BEGINNING it was the Latin *Institutio* of 1536. At the end was the French *Institution* of 1560.

1536 A little booklet, a *libellus* according to Calvin, pocket-size, 10 by 15 centimetres from the press of Platter in Basle, 520 pages in length.

1560 A large octavo volume 20 by 31 centimetres, 684 pages, from the press of Jean Crespin in Geneva.

1536 Six chapters. 1560 Eighty chapters.

1536–1560 Twenty-four years, in the course of which Calvin never stopped revising, reshaping, and developing his book to such an extent that we can say that the *Institutio* is the work of his whole life. And this development was organic, if one can put it thus; it meant the maturing and expansion of thought within the framework which already existed. It was not a case of new chapters being added on one after another like extending a wall, or like the buildings in Calvin's Geneva which went up floor by floor to accommodate the flood of refugees. It was rather the growth of a living entity, the increase of which is at the same time the concern of all the members of the organism.

The Libellus of 1536

THE title, *Institutio Christianae Religionis*, is followed by words which were probably added by the publisher rather than by Calvin himself, for they sound a little too much like publishers' blurb: 'containing almost the whole sum of piety, and everything it is necessary to know in the doctrine of salvation, a work very well worth reading by all those who love piety, and very recently published'. As for the word *Institutio*, we must understand it in its Latin sense of instruction. It can be translated *Manual*, or more exactly *Summary*, according to the publisher's use: *totam fere pietatis Summam*. In brief, a book destined to teach the Christian religion.

Of the six chapters, four were given respectively to the Law, the Creed, the Lord's Prayer, and the sacraments of Baptism and the Lord's Supper. This conformed to the classical pattern of catechism. The last two chapters, in more polemical manner, deal respectively with false sacraments and with Christian liberty. The book was preceded by the *Epistle to the King*, in French, which is to be found without any appreciable change at the head of every subsequent edition. Calvin wished to clear the Evangelicals in France from the charge of rebellion which had been brought against them and by which the persecutions were justified. He demonstrated to Francis I that the faith of the persecuted was that of the Gospel.

The 1539 edition

THIS is a new Latin edition printed at Strasbourg by Wendelin Rihel. The book had been enlarged considerably. It was now seventeen chapters. In it Calvin developed his exposition of the Trinity following his controversies with Caroli, who had suspected his orthodoxy on the point. A new chapter on the agreements between the Old and New Testaments reflected his disputes with the Anabaptists. Two equally new chapters treat repentance and justification by faith, subjects just touched on in 1536. A further chapter was given to the great subject of providence and predestination. Finally, there is the last chapter which underwent no modifications in the course of later editions and was printed on its own in 1545 by the Badius press in Geneva under the title, *Traicté trés excellent de la vie chrestienne*. It was reprinted in 1551.

We know that Calvin, alluding indirectly to the rather pretentious claims in the first edition, could add at the head of this second edition: 'now at last really agreeing with its title'. This second edition already shows the influence of Calvin's days at Strasbourg, though he had only been there a year, and of his close friendship with Bucer. For example in the 1536 *Institutio* Calvin, like Luther, insisted that above all faith was trust and hope. In 1539 he made more of the intellectual nature of faith. Not that one can accuse him of intellectualism, but, in insisting that 'understanding is linked together with faith', he simply meant to reject all confusion with the implicit faith of the schoolmen.

The chapter on providence and predestination sets out in order his views which had matured through his discussions with Bucer and through his study of St. Augustine. His reading as a whole had been wider. Besides Augustine he studied several Greek Fathers, notably Origen. Finally, he seems to have given more attention to Church history, to judge by the frequent mention he makes of Councils.

We can say that the 1539 edition already shows the fundamental theological lines which recur in every later edition of the *Institutio*. This Latin edition Calvin translated into French. That translation appeared in 1541 without the name of the place or the printer, but it was certainly in Geneva. This is the first known French edition.

French translations

THE 1541 French edition is of great importance. First from the point of view of language. With it Calvin is hailed as one of the masters, or rather, one of the creators, of what we can now call modern French. Brunetière does not hesitate to say that it is the first of our books which, by its date, we can call classical. It is the first time that French is used to handle the lofty subjects of philosophy and morality. In this way Calvin helped forge the tool which Pascal and Bossuet were to use after him.

More important still for the destiny of the Reformation in France and French Switzerland was this presentation of the *Institutio* in the common tongue of the people. The Latin *Institutio* was a learned work. The French *Institution* was popular. The Latin *Institutio* addressed itself to the philosophers, the theologians, the learned the world over. The French

Institution was written for the people of France and those in Geneva and its neighbourhood, the humbler people of the 'gens mécaniques', workers, artisans, woolcombers, weavers, even farm labourers, businessmen also and the petty bourgeois, in fact all those who could not cope with Latin.

There are certain distinctive characteristics of this first French edition and of the French editions in general. All the Greek words which Calvin strewed around the Latin *Institutio*, the learned *Institutio*, have disappeared, either translated or paraphrased. Reference to Aristotle is suppressed. The popular *Institution* abounds in repetition, in explanations, superfluous to learned readers of the Latin *Institutio*. Here are some examples of the additions:

Caligula+Roman emperor.
Damasus+Bishop of Rome.
Socrates+Ecclesiastical writer.
Sennacherib+evil and wicked man.
Jehovah+which is the equivalent of one who exists of himself and of his own power.
Mary was the wife of Joseph+and consequently of the race of David.

The explanatory process continues throughout.

Take another matter, Calvin is never afraid of certain strong expressions in popular French: 'ces canailles, ces brouillons, ces fantastiques, ces gaudisseurs, ces chiens mâtins, ces acariâtres, ces opiniâtres', where the Latin has simply *illi*, they. He made use of proverbs and vivid expressions which cannot be translated into Latin: to find the currant in the cake, to be only wind and smoke, to vanish into air (for to disappear), clear as the sun in full midday (Latin: very certain), to live pell-mell 'as rats in straw', to croak like frogs, small fry, etc. . . . He adds incidents to clarify, to explain, to make points more articulate, to give the text a more familiar air: 'And how detestable that is!', 'And that is too great an absurdity', 'To state the matter frankly . . .', etc.

In short, the more popular French text is by itself simpler, more directly accessible and brought within the range of readers who are not by profession intellectuals. For this reason it sometimes appears a little spun out. The Latin text, in contrast, is briefer, more densely packed (Latin being basically more syn-thetic than French). It is also at times clearer, indeed a model of concision itself. Occasionally we have to go back to the Latin text, when that is possible, to determine the exact sense of certain rather diffuse phrases.

Be that as it may, it is by the French *Institution*, widely carried round and distributed by colporteurs, that the thought of Calvin made its impact in French speaking countries. It became the basic doctrinal manual of the Reformed churches. 'It can be affirmed without fear of error', writes Professor Wendel, 'that when these Churches became Calvinist they owed it to the vari-ous French editions of the *Institutes*.'[1]

This 1541 edition is the oldest known French edition, but is it the first that was published? Some have maintained that it was preceded by an earlier translation made from the 1536 Latin edition. It is a question of symmetry. Each subsequent edition had a French sister, so why should 1536 be an exception? This incomplete parellelism has no great value as a proof. All the same more serious arguments exist.

There are as a matter of fact certain passages in the French *Institution*—actually only a few in number—which are a trans-lation not of the 1539 but of the 1536 text. They cannot be accounted for as additions made by Calvin in 1539. From these some have deduced that a French version of the 1536 text ex-isted. The fragments we have mentioned would be the remains of this. To be sure, there are texts, now lost, the existence of which is nevertheless historically attested, but here there has never been the least mention or the slightest trace of such an edition.

We might with greater certainty suppose that Calvin, to meet his occasional needs, had translated certain fragments of the 1536 *Institutio*, and that later he inserted these fragments, al-ready translated, into the 1541 edition, without noticing the minor modifications which he had meanwhile made to his text, or even forgetting that he had made the corrections. Luchesius Smits, in his work on *Saint Augustin dans l'oeuvre de Jean Calvin*, assumes the existence of a complete French translation, not a fragmentary one, of the 1536 *Institutio*. He recognises that this must have remained in manuscript and could never have been published.[2] We might ask in that case why Calvin did not make

106

wider use of it, and how it was discovered again, in 1541, only in such rare fragments.

At the most, it seems we can suppose Calvin intended to translate the 1536 edition into French, and doubtless had begun the work. But rapidly, he must have come to envisage a second edition of the *Institutio*. As his intention was to make considerable improvements, he must have very soon given up his earlier efforts at translation, and have waited to rewrite his book for the French edition. The supposition of a French edition of the 1536 *Institutio*, now entirely lost, is an hypothesis which rests on inadequate foundations.

Further editions

IN 1543 and in 1545 Calvin republished the Latin *Institutio*, the latter being only a reprint of the former. Both came from Wendelin Rihel's press in Strasbourg. Soon afterwards a French translation appeared, the edition of 1545, from Jean Girard's press in Geneva.

These editions scarcely differ from those which immediately preceded them, and together with them they form the same family. The structure is the same. The text has not been modified; it is simply that certain developments occur. The number of chapters is increased from seventeen to twenty-one, less by additions than by the expansion of the chapter on the Creed. Its material was thereafter divided into four chapters.

I have picked out the 1545 additions from the marginal notes of my edition of the 1560 *Institution* [critical edition with introduction and notes by J-D. Benoît, Paris, 1957–1963, 5 vols.]. There are no more than twenty in all. The main one concerns the doctrine of angels; Calvin had said nothing about this in 1541. Another shows a slight difference in Calvin's judgment on images. He notes the religious subjects which can properly be represented. The majority are new quotations; three from St. Paul, two from St. Jerome, one from the ecclesiastical historian Socrates, one from the Council of Elvira, another from the Council of Nicea, and finally six from Augustine.

We can see that Calvin followed up his reading of the Fathers, Augustine in particular. But nothing has been really modified from the preceding edition. It would be pedantic to continue this enquiry into the subsequent books. We should only reach the same conclusions.

Five years passed, and then one on top of another came three Latin editions. 1550 from Girard's press, 1553 from Estienne's, 1554 from the Rivery brothers (this produced the 1551 French editions from Girard), 1553 from Girard again, 1554 from Hamelin. There remains a sixth edition in French (1557) from the press of Bourgeois. It is alone in not having any Latin sister, but it adds virtually nothing to the edition immediately preceding it, that of 1554. It can be considered simply as a new impression of it. It was not cited in the list of French editions which the Strasbourg editors gave. They only discovered it later in the course of their work and were not able to use it.[3] These editions, in Latin and in French, which spread over the years 1550 to 1557, seven in all, form a new family. They all have the same number of chapters—twenty-one, as in the edition of 1545. But there for the first time the chapters are subdivided into paragraphs.

I turn once more to the first book of my edition, where a date in the margin indicates the first appearance of the text. The year 1551 brought some new pages on the authority of the Bible, on *latria* and *dulia*, on the image of God in man. That is about all. But each time there are new quotations, witnessing to the fact that Calvin continued to read ancient literature: one from St. Gregory, one from the Second Council of Nicea, five from St. Augustine. Here again I have only followed this enquiry through the first book of the *Institutio*. In continuing it through the subsequent books, one would only be convinced, as in Book I, of the smallness of the additions brought to this family of the *Institutio*. In the volume of Tables and References, which contain a synoptic view of the different editions [vol. 5 of my ed.], the successive increases appear clearly.

The final editions

AND so we reach the two editions (Latin 1559 and French 1560) which terminate the changes in the *Institutio*, and constitute the crown of the work. This time, there is a complete recasting, an entirely new plan, considerable additions, so much so that Calvin can write in the subtitle: '*The Institutio Christianae Religionis* newly put out in four books, and divided into chapters, according to a proper order and method. Also enlarged by so much new material, that you can almost call it a new work.'

Changes in structure

IN place of the twenty-one chapters in the previous editions since 1545, there are now four books and eighty chapters. The plan is different. It no longer follows the first edition of 1536, which was more or less preserved in the course of the subsequent editions, the classical plan of catechisms: Decalogue, Apostles' Creed, The Lord's Prayer, the Sacraments. Calvin recast his work and rearranged his material. This time he followed the Apostles' Creed: God, Jesus Christ, Holy Spirit, in his intimate work within a man to bring him to faith and the appropriation of salvation. Finally, the Church and the Sacraments. This parallelism between the plan of the Creed and that of the last *Institutio* edition is only relative. Calvin, for example, speaks of the resurrection in Book III before speaking of the church in Book IV.

Above all, he does not make forgiveness of sins depend on faith in the church, as one might—strictly—suspect that the Creed does: 'I believe in the holy catholic church, the communion of saints, the forgiveness of sins.' He attaches the forgiveness of sins not to the church but to the Holy Spirit in us and to faith in Jesus Christ, and by that he excludes all specifically Roman interpretations of the Creed. These readjustments lead to others. We shall single out three of the most important:

(1) Up to 1559 the doctrine of providence and predestination were treated as a single whole. That chapter was placed in the exposition of the Creed. Thereafter the doctrine of providence is treated in Book I where it is a question of God; the doctrine of predestination in Book III where it is a question of salvation.

(2) All that in previous editions was said of the church and of ecclesiastical power was said as in the Creed's exposition, under the heading of faith. In 1559–1560 one finds it in Book IV, where it is treated alongside the church. This appears more rational.

JOHN CALVIN

(3) Finally, the chapter on the Christian life, which had hitherto formed the conclusion of the *Institutio*, is placed in Book III
and seen as a manifestation of the work of the Spirit in us.

THEY are considerable, since this last edition was increased
more than four times by comparison with the preceding edition.
Several of these additions were given over to refuting opponents.
They originated in controversies which the Reformer had kept
up against the Anabaptists, against Socinius, against Osiander,
against Servetus, and finally against the Papists (as he calls
them). They allow Calvin to articulate and develop his own position. But these are not the only additions.

New chapters appear, for example chapter vi of Book II,
where the doctrine of redemption in Jesus Christ is developed.
Chapter ix in the same book on the revelation in the Old and
New Testaments, and chapter xvii of the same book, where
Calvin returns with a more thorough treatment of the fact
'That only Jesus Christ has truly merited for us the grace of
God and salvation. . . .' Let us not make the mistake of supposing that because the book grew from twenty-one to eighty
chapters, Calvin had just added about sixty chapters to the
Institutio. More often he has subdivided one that was rather too
long into several chapters. For example, the last chapter of the
previous editions, the one on the Christian life, made five chapters (vi-x) in the final Book III.

If the *Institutio* grew, it was less by the addition of new chapters than by the insertion of new developments, often new paragraphs put into the body of an older text. Calvin foresaw an
objection. 'Someone will say . . . Someone will answer . . .'
Or else he takes an exposition already made under another
form: 'The whole comes to this . . . The complete sum is that . . .
Yet I would again mention this point. . . . We must note here
again. . . .' The quotations multiply from the Scriptures, from
the Fathers, from the Councils. We sense a mind that has reached
its full maturity and whose thought is the complete master of
itself.[4]

110

How did Calvin work?

(1) He never let anything be wasted, once it had been written. He might rearrange his material or he might keep it intact. At the very most we can find four or five pages from previous editions which do not appear in the last edition.

(2) Sometimes he rewrote certain parts of the earlier text for greater accuracy, for greater clarity, or because he retranslated directly from the Latin. As a result there were a great many variant readings, but these variants do not generally show a different orientation of the thought. For the most part they are purely formal. I have selected one, which, interestingly enough, shows in Calvin, contrary to what we might expect, a softening of his earlier harshness, perhaps even a change of heart—I am thinking of Servetus. The magnificent passage on the ministers of the Word of God which is found already in the 1537 *Confession de Foi de L'Eglise de Genève*, is well known: 'Let them boldly venture all things by the Word of God, let them feed the sheep, kill the wolves, instruct and exhort the teachable, rebuke and confute the rebellious, but all by the Word of God.' Calvin reproduced this passage in every edition of the *Institutio*, with slight modifications. But whereas in 1559 he wrote, let them kill (*interficiant*) the wolves (and we can think of all the death-sentences pronounced for the crime of heresy) in the last edition he wrote, *qu'ils exterminent* (Latin *profligent*) the wolves. But, in the language of the sixteenth century, *exterminer* does not mean kill or put to death, but to drive out over the boundaries, beyond the limits of the fold, *ex terminis*, and consequently to banish, or simply to excommunicate. This sense is not open to doubt. It is actually found, and it is stated precisely in the *Institutio*; 'Those who falsely pretend the faith of Christ . . . ought to be driven out and banished (*exterminés et chassés*) from before the people of God.' Here is a real mitigation, a humane softening of attitude which is worth noting.

(3) Calvin, as we have seen, expanded his book by inserting fresh developments in the midst of the earlier text. So by reading in the margins the date when the text first appears, we find for example: 1541 . . . 1545 . . . 1551 . . . 1560 . . . And after a final addition in 1560 Calvin resumed the 1541 text at the exact spot

111

where he had left off. The overall plan is relatively simple, but some parts of it are more complicated. Here is one—I have not invented it, I found it in Book I: 1541 . . . 1545 . . . 1551 . . . 1545 . . . 1551 . . . 1545 . . . 1551 . . . 1560 . . . And all that in forty-two lines! Sometimes these additions are quite important, occasionally several paragraphs; sometimes it is a question of an image, a quotation, a single phrase, or even an incident.

On occasions Calvin completely breaks up his earlier text to reassemble the constituent pieces in a different order. Here is, for example, a passage from 1541, broken up as one might say into four pieces: a, b, c, d. Calvin does not let anything get lost, but he puts them together in another order and this is the scheme we have: 1541-b . . . 1545 . . . 1541-d . . . 1545 . . . 1541-c . . . 1560 . . . 1541-a . . .

We can understand the inextricable confusion presented by a manuscript composed of such a multitude of pieces. For Calvin did not copy everything out again. He took a sample from the previous edition, which he sacrificed. He broke up the binding and inserted the interpolated pages; sometimes he cut the old text into pieces, I imagine with a pair of scissors; he regrouped these pieces in a new order and pasted up the whole; he stuffed his text with *addenda*, and loaded it with corrections and reference marks showing where fresh changes had been inserted. He wrote in the margins, and tacked on more pieces of paper. As a consequence the difficulties at the printing stage are considerable. Sometimes certain additional phrases have not been inserted by the printer in the right place; they have to be shifted to give the right text. Fragments which we find in the Latin edition and in the earlier French editions fall out, we don't know why. They have to be reinstated. Some passages, by contrast, appear twice in almost identical form. These blots are more or less inevitable, once granted the manner in which Calvin proceeded. It is astonishing they are not much more numerous.

(4) What adds to the difficulty is that Calvin was in the habit of dictating. 'So little life being left,' said Beza, 'he used to sleep very little, and for most of his time he was forced to warm himself on his bed, from which he dictated most of his books, engaging continually and very happily in mental work.'[5] But how could he have done otherwise? He prepared the de-

finitive edition of his *Institutio* during the winter of 1558–1559. On 2 May 1559 his brother Antoine asked the Council for a three year license to print the *Institutio* of M. Calvin, his brother, both in Latin and in French, 'which he has renovated, corrected and expanded so that it is an excellent work, and of which his aforesaid brother has given him the copies.'[6]

But during this winter, Calvin had been constantly ill, and obliged for several months to keep to his room. From the month of October he had violent attacks of malaria, an unrelenting cough, violent pains in his leg (rheumatism? sciatica? gout?), haemorrhoids the pains from which frequently racked his whole body. When once again in the month of July he could resume his preaching in St. Peter's, he had to be carried there on a chair or go on a horse. We could imagine him reclining or seated on his bed, 'with someone who used to write under his supervision', that is to say a secretary. He used to dictate passages which he would augment or modify. As a result certain mistakes were repeated from one edition to the next. They are very obviously errors of hearing for example, *Pères* for *Perses*, *imite* for *limite*, *voilent* for *voisent* (subjunctive of *je vais*, old French: *je vois*), *fait* for *paix*, etc.

This is no romancing. That his manuscript has constituted a veritable puzzle which gave the typographers a field-day, his printer, Jean Crespin, bears witness. He excuses the inevitable mistakes which he had made. At the end of the 1560 edition he inserted an announcement to the reader: 'Because the copy of the present *Institutio* is difficult and hard to follow in view of the hand-written additions, some in the margin of the book, others on separate paper, it may be there are others which we had not noticed, and that some mistakes and omissions have remained, which you will therefore excuse and correct.' There follow some errata.

Completing the final editions

BESIDES, there exist still more precise details on Calvin's method of working. When Colladon had been charged with republishing the *Institutio* at Lausanne in 1576, he wrote a Foreword in Latin in which he related how he had been led to look at the manuscript prepared for the 1560 edition again. We know it is the French edition which he used.

> As he [Calvin] was preparing the French version of his *Institutio* he dictated a crowd of things as much to his brother Antoine as to a manservant doing the office of secretary. He inserted in many places pages pulled out of a French copy which had been recently printed. Also he often had to hand his papers over to be bound (*glutinatoribus sane ei saepe utendum fuit*). But in the end it was absolutely necessary for someone to revise the work. Indeed there had been considerable changes in a very great number of passages; erasings and additions were littered in confusion from one end of the text to the other, making it difficult to read, often faulty, more especially as the secretaries did not always understand the words dictated to them. Then at the request of Antoine, at whose expense the French edition was soon to be printed by Jean Crespin, I re-examined all these rough copies, Latin and French, all that were among the author's papers. And I was instructed to read them again, correct and collate them, to make the end-product more certain, more clear, more easy and less cluttered for the printing.

The manuscript is as we have described it, complete with its printed fragments belonging to earlier editions, its additions in the margins, its erasings, its corrections, its loose leaves for insertion, everything summarily tied up and 'glued down', simply to hold them together. We can understand how, in sorting out such a tangle, the printer let a certain number of mistakes through. Taking them all together, they are relatively few and far between.

All this constitutes, it seems to me, a decisive argument against the view of the Strasbourg editors, followed here by Pannier. They assure us that 'the French translation of the *Institutio*, in its definitive and received form, in leaving out the parts of the old editing, has been worked over with a certain carelessness, by hands less able and lacking the author's supervision'.[7]

Indeed the whole work of which we have just spoken could not have been produced by others than Calvin himself, even though he may have been helped. To presuppose the existence of a Latin manuscript, well finished, accurate in detail, well polished and one for which scribes would only have had to translate the new parts, is a piece of pure imagination. The mistakes which we can pick out in the French 1560 translation

114

Marmelstein has shown to be minimal mistakes, copyists' or correctors' errors, obvious verbal confusions. In the final reckoning they are no more numerous than those which we can pick out of the 1541 edition which one does not hesitate to attribute them to Calvin himself.[8]

Besides we have at this point two testimonies which are in my judgment sufficient to settle the question. First that of Beza: 'In the year 1559,' he writes, 'being attacked and vigorously oppressed with a quartan fever, he [Calvin] nevertheless constructed his final Christian *Institutio* when the sickness was at its strongest, and, what is more, he translated it into French from beginning to end.'[9] It is certainly Calvin, Beza affirms, who has constructed (*basti*) his *Institutio*. We note on the one hand the suitability of the word *batir* for the method of work which we have described, and on the other hand, the abrupt affirmation that the translation was from beginning to end the work of Calvin. But Théodore de Bèze was in Geneva from the month of September 1558 onwards. He lived in close relationship with Calvin during the course of the winter 1558–1559, when he 'constructed' his *Institutio*, enjoying familiar conversation with him almost every day. He saw him preparing his last edition, both Latin and French. What he said of it, he said on good authority.

The other testimony, still more direct, is that of Calvin himself. In the announcement to the reader in the 1560 edition he wrote: 'During the next winter [the one just passed], when the quartan fever was threatening me with death, and more especially as the disease pressed me, I did not spare myself until I had completed the book. It would survive after my death and show how much I desire to satisfy those who have already profited by it and how much I desire to help them still further.' So the question appears to us settled; it is certainly Calvin who constructed the 1560 *Institutio*, who 'completed the book'. In the course of the winter (1558–1559), without allowing disease to stop him, Calvin devoted himself to this task with all the more speed, because he kept asking himself if death would leave him time to finish the job properly.

How did Calvin work? We have seen what we may call his technical methods. We have pointed out the prodigious energy with which he gave himself to his work, even in the midst of disease and suffering. He worked conscientiously, keeping up his reading without fail and yet, for twenty-four years, never satisfied with the results obtained. He worked not selfishly, for his own glory, for the satisfaction of his intellectual tastes, but with a desire to serve his fellow countrymen and to meet spiritual needs. That was for him to work 'to the honour and glory of God'.

For us, four centuries later, Calvin provides an enduring example of faithfulness, courage, and integrity.

NOTES

1. Wendel, p. 116.
2. Vol. I. 51.
3. CO IV, pp. vii, viii.
4. Can one characterise in a particular manner each of the successive *Institutio* editions as Luchesius Smits tries to do in the work we have cited *Saint Augustin dans l'Oeuvre de Jean Calvin*? The first edition, that of 1536, appears to him as the *Institutio* of the sacraments, in view of the space devoted by Calvin to the doctrine of Baptism and of the Lord's Supper (I. pp. 47, 64). He thinks the second (1539) to be that of depravity of human nature (p. 47) or that of sin and grace (p. 64). He sees in the *Institutio* of 1545 the *Institutio* of the church. He does not dare to call the 1551 edition that *Institutio* of the Holy Scriptures despite the attention which he gives to the Scripture (p. 82). Finally, the 1559–1560 edition is for him the *Institutio* of the Lord's Supper and of predestination (p. 109).

These distinctions appear a bit artificial. Doubtless the doctrine of the sin of man and of the fall are more accentuated in the 1539 edition than in 1536, but in the latter sin and the depravity of human nature are far from absent. Doubtless the developments on the church are more considerable in 1545, but the essentials were already there in 1539. Doubtless too, the chapter on predestination is detached in 1559, and related to salvation, but the doctrine is seen, equally stressed, in the chapter on providence in the previous editions. In a word, the distinctions which Smits proposes seem forced. We do not consider this view acceptable, despite the mental satisfaction it would give if such a classification were really justified.

5. CO XXI.35.
6. CO XXI.715.
7. CO III. xxvii.
The legends have certainly died hard. With regard to a difficult passage in the *Institutio*: priests who 'know neither how to act or to speak', Doumergue writes: 'It is nonsense which the translation of 1560 wrongly attributes to Calvin', in such a way that he is convicted of 'negligence', lack of care and trouble over this translation (V.90, n. 6). However, Dou-

mergue has not noticed that if this is a mistake, the mistake is already present in the 1541 edition, which is the same here as the text of 1560. No one has ever doubted that coming from the hand of Calvin himself.

8. J. W. Marmelstein, *Etude Comparative des Textes Latins et Français de l'Institution*, Groningen, 1923.

9. CO XXI.33.

6 Calvin and the Union of the Churches

Jean Cadier

CALVIN, AN ADVOCATE OF UNION! This description
may sound like a paradox, a difficult assertion to vouch for.
Calvin the arch-fanatic, that hot-headed man, who if he was not
the first to declare the breach with Rome, at all events stoutly
reinforced it, Calvin the man who brought Servetus to the stake,
how could he be an advocate of union and not a promoter of
schism? To speak in this way is to see only that picture of Calvin which has been deliberately distorted by centuries of slander.
But anyone who rejects this picture and goes back to the writings of the Reformer will find on the contrary a desire for
reconciliation which shows a disposition to seek the via media
if we may accept the testimony of recent scholars.[1]

Yet we must make it plain from the outset that Calvin's
position vis-à-vis Rome was quite distinctly a position of separation. A theologian of the second generation of the Reformation,
Calvin broke with Rome and joined a movement which had
already been in existence more than fifteen years, and had already made Europe heave with its ground swell, to use Luther's
bold phrase. We must also remember that the monk of Wittenburg did not break away from Rome, but was rather driven out.
He was excommunicated after being called upon to retract. He
was rejected after making a confident appeal to the Pope. Calvin, who began writing nearly twenty years after, did not have to
face the question of separation; for separation, the breach, was
a fact. He simply knew that Rome persecuted 'Lutherans', that
she handed them over to the secular arm to be burned, that she
118

accused them falsely of subversion. From then on he took sides, he spoke of Roman doctrine as of a deep slough from which he had been drawn by divine grace. He writes in impassioned terms to Cardinal Sadoleto:

> Now, therefore, if you will accept and submit to a truer definition of the Church than yours, call it henceforth the assembly of all the saints, spread over the whole world, dispersed in every age, yet bound together by one doctrine of Christ and by one Spirit of Christ, holding and maintaining the unity of the faith with a brotherly concord and charity. Now we deny that we are at variance with this Church; rather, honouring her as our mother, we wish to remain in her embrace.[2]

The church

FOR Calvin then there is a *true* church and a *false* church. The true church is that which has at all times been faithful to the Word. 'You well know, Sadoleto, that we are more consistent with antiquity than you are. You know also that the only thing we ask is that the ancient face of the church should be restored and made whole, that face which has been distorted and soiled by unlearned men, and almost obliterated by the Pope and his faction.'[3] Calvin did not wish to found another church. He wished to restore to the church its apostolic character, to recover the ancient state of which the Fathers speak, to raise up the ruins, 'to restore to their primitive splendour things which have been depraved and dissipated in the church'. Calvin wanted the Reformation of the church, her renewal, and not a deep division. He wanted a purified church, not a new church. This hope was frustrated. Positions became hardened. On the Roman side the Council of Trent, which has been called the Council of the Counter-Reformation, was held at the same time as the Reformation was being organised at Geneva (1546–1563). In 1547 Calvin wrote his treatise *Les Actes du Concile de Trente avec le remède contre la poison*,[4] a work of extreme severity. We do well to realise that the Reformer waged a very bitter struggle against the Roman Church in the name of the Word of God. But at the same time he spoke of the Church of Christ, of the universal body of the church, and he taught the conditions of its unity.

119

The first chapter of the fourth book of the *Institutio* bears this significant title: 'Concerning the true church, with which we must maintain unity because it is the mother of all the faithful.' At the beginning of this chapter, taking up Cyprian's words (*On Christian Unity*, ch. VI), he declares: 'It is not lawful to separate these two things which God has joined together; namely that the Church should be the mother of all those of whom he is the Father.' (IV. i. 1.) 'We must understand a unity of the church of such a kind that we are persuaded of being truly grafted into it; for if we are not bound to all the other members under the common head, who is Jesus Christ, we can have no hope of the inheritance to come. This is why the church is called *catholic* or *universal*, since there could not be two or three churches without tearing Christ asunder, which cannot be.' (IV. i. 2.) Outside the bosom of this church, there is no hope of the remission of sins, nor of any salvation (IV. i. 4). It is a dangerous and deadly thing to withdraw or separate from the church (IV. i. 4).

> Wherever the preaching of the Gospel is reverently heard and the sacraments are not neglected, there for a time a certain form of church is to be found, and it may not be held in doubt. Its authority may not be lawfully despised, nor its admonitions scorned, nor its counsel rejected, nor its rebukes ridiculed. Much less is it lawful to secede from it or to break its unity. For God values so highly the fellowship of his church that he holds as a traitor and an apostate from Christianity a man who separates himself from any Christian company in which the ministry of his Word and of his sacraments is to be found. . . . It follows that whoever secedes from the church denies God and Jesus Christ. We must all the more therefore keep ourselves from the enormity of such a breach, which is an attempt, so far as we have it in our power, to destroy the truth of God, and for which we deserve to be struck down with all the violence of his anger and brought to ruin. (IV. i.10.)

'If we are divided one from another we are estranged from God.'[5]

The texts which we have just cited are of such force that it will be asked, 'Why did Calvin separate himself from the church which existed in his day with sixteen centuries of history behind it? Why did he break that unity which he said it was unlawful to break? Did he not condemn himself by his own words?' We can guess the tension in a mind at once so lucid and so courageous, the deep struggles in which he engaged within himself before coming to a conclusion. But the reason that he did so was that the Church of Rome was not in the sixteenth century the church where the Word of God was preached and heard in its purity and the sacraments appointed according to Christ's institution, in keeping with the definition that he gave of the marks of the true church (IV. i. 9). It was the church which burned at the stake those who wished to return to the purity of preaching. It was the church where the service of God was disfigured by various forms of superstition. 'So we must not fear that we are breaking away from the church of God by withdrawing from participation in these sacrileges. The fellowship of the church was not instituted with the intention that it should be a fetter to bind us to idolatry, ungodliness, ignorance of God and other kinds of wickedness, but rather to keep us in the fear of God and in obedience to his truth.' (IV. ii. 2.) His purpose was to maintain the preaching of the gospel of salvation by the grace of God alone, and so to magnify the glory of God who alone saves, and who requires of those whom he saves only faith in his work. He had therefore to break away from the Church of the Papacy. It was certainly not without much grief.

Conferences with Roman Catholics

BUT seeing that the principle of the unity of the church of Christ was laid down, and since Calvin asserted that it must be sought for with the greatest care, how did he in fact endeavour to show this concern for unity; in what way was he a promoter of union?

Let it be said, first of all, that Calvin joined in the Conferences which took place in 1540 and 1541 between Roman Catholics and Protestants for an attempt at reconciliation, before positions became too entrenched. These conferences are of great interest for the history of the Reformation. They show that these men were not obstinate and hostile from the outset to any attempt at coming to terms. Amongst these peace-makers two men, Melanchthon and Bucer, had a great influence, both of them men of great theological learning and brotherly disposition. Now Calvin, still very young compared with them (he was hardly thirty), quickly became friends with them and took his place by their side in the great quest for the unity of the church. We must of course recognise that these conversations had a political background. The emperor Charles V wanted a peaceful Germany, and he wanted to be strong for his struggle with the Turks. Furthermore, these encounters ended in failure. But at least Calvin was present at them, and he played an important part. This is how he introduces the Acts of the Conference of Ratisbon (1541):

> There are many holy persons in all nations, true lovers of the truth of God and desirous of the advancement of his kingdom. They wait from day to day for the time when the Lord will be pleased to set his church in order again, and have their ears open listening continuously for news that some overture has been made for putting the church in a better state. But there are also many weak people throughout the world, who dare not decide what path they must follow until there is a reformation brought about by the combined authority of those to whom God has given the rule and government of Christendom. I thought therefore that it would be a useful task, and one profitable for all Christians, to set in order the sum of what has lately been treated of amongst all the States of the Empire at the conference of Ratisbon, touching differences in Religion. My purpose is that the former may have reason to be comforted and to rejoice in our Lord, seeing that the truth of the gospel, though assailed by the devil, has not been suppressed and vanquished, but rather set forward; and that the latter may realise, from the proceedings which took place there, that it is time wasted to rely upon men, as they will easily see; and that they may accept the light of God when it is offered to them, without looking this way and that to see which way the wind is blowing.

This passage takes us back to the situation of those times, the situation of men with their ears open, ready to receive any overture made to them in the interests of the Gospel, but at the same time entertaining no false hopes.

In these conversations, Calvin met Melanchthon who struck up a firm friendship with him, and Bucer from Strasbourg from whom he had received so much in previous years. He met also the Roman Catholic doctors, Pighius who was afterwards to attack him in his writings, and Cardinal Contarini the Papal legate, a man of moderation.

Protestant divisions

BUT the attempt at reconciliation failed not only between the newly formed Reformation and the Roman Church, resulting in continued separation. It failed also within the newly formed Reformation itself, where distinct churches were being founded, divided on points of doctrine and already contending one against another. In 1522 it was the 'ultra-spirituals', the Anabaptists, the 'prophets'. They declared that Luther had not gone far enough in his reformation, that it was necessary to give oneself up to the directions of the Spirit, to establish a new social order, to establish a Christian communism. Carlstadt, one of the Wittenburg theologians, joined their movement and gave them his support. Realising the danger that threatened the early advances of the Reformation, Luther left his refuge in the Wartburg, at the risk of his life, went back to Wittenburg and preached the Word, calmly and powerfully. But this Anabaptist movement continued, to end in 1535 with the siege of Münster. This was the first sectarian manifestation. Calvin made efforts to reduce it. He won back to the Reformed church a great number of Anabaptists at Strasbourg, and married an Anabaptist's widow, Idelette de Bure.

In 1529 a new division became evident. A colloquy took place at Marburg on the question of the Lord's Supper. It was between Luther and his friends, Melanchthon, Jonas, Osiander, Brenz and others on the one side, and Zwingli, Oecolampadius, Bucer and Hedio on the other. The difference turned on the mode of the presence of Christ in the sacrament of the eucharist. Luther did not admit the Roman dogma of transubstantiation, which teaches that at the moment of the consecration of the elements the substance of the bread is replaced by the substance of the body of Christ. But he maintained the rather similar doctrine of consubstantiation, which says that the substance of the bread and the substance of the body of Christ coexist in the bread and are both present. Zwingli and his friends rejected this substantialism and saw in the sacrament a spiritual presence, taking their stand on the word of Christ (Jn. 6. 63): 'It is the spirit which makes alive, the flesh is of no profit.' The conference was distressing and ended in failure. Luther refused to hold out to Zwingli the hand of fellowship, and declared: 'We are not of the same spirit.' The new-born Reformation was divided. The Church of Wittenburg and the Church of Zürich were separated. This failure of the Colloquy of Marburg produced a painful impression.

Calvin relates himself that he knew of it when in 1529 he began to be interested in the evangelical movement, but that these discussions tended rather to abate his eagerness. Twelve years later, Calvin took up the question again in his *Petit Traité de la Sainte-Cène*, published at Geneva in 1541. He states that this dispute between the two great men of the Reformation was an occasion of confusion. It was however inevitable, for they were still at that stage faltering in their attempt to find expression for their thought. With a remarkable sureness Calvin shows that the notion of substance must be abandoned to the schoolmen. Instead one must speak of the person of Christ. He leaves the static field of definitions and looks for the true meaning of the Supper in the dynamic nature of the meeting between Christ and the believer in the emblem of the sacred meal through the action of the Holy Spirit. The prophetic value of this thought of Calvin's deserves emphasis. In our day the notion of substance has disappeared from theological thought, carried away, like matter itself, in new physical theories which teach us that everything is movement. The notions of the sixteenth century are outworn, and the terms of transubstantiation and consubstantiation belong to another age. The notion of substance must be replaced by that of presence. Calvin, in affirming the presence of the living Christ in the sacrament of the Lord's Supper by the action of the Holy Spirit, is modern in his dynamic conception of the sacrament.

We must be satisfied, he says, that there is brotherhood and fellowship between the churches, and that all are in agreement in so far as it is necessary in order to be united according to God's commandment. We all confess then with one mouth that in receiving the sacrament by faith according to the Lord's ordinance we participate truly in the very substance of the body and blood of the Lord. (The word substance is still used, but it is illuminated by the use of the word participation, which denotes the action of encounter with Christ in his person, flesh and blood denoting the human reality of that person.) How this happens, some can better deduce and more clearly expound than others. Suffice it to say that in order to exclude all mistaken earthly notions we must lift up our hearts to heaven, not imagining that the Lord Jesus is abased to the point of being enclosed in a few tangible elements. On the other hand, so as not to underestimate the efficacy of this holy mystery, we must realise that it takes place by the secret and miraculous power [French *vertu* = Latin *virtus*] of God, and that the Spirit of God is the bond of this participation, which for this reason is described as spiritual.[6]

Luther read this treatise and declared: 'If Oecolampadius and Zwingli had treated the question like Calvin, the dispute would have been neither so long nor so bitter.' But although there were fresh matters for discussion, and new men to discuss them with, he did nothing to resume a conference which might have restored the broken unity.

Calvin's ecumenism

THIS, however, is what Calvin attempted. Three churches faced each other in the Reformation: Wittenburg, Zürich and Geneva. Since the death of Zwingli on the battle-field of Cappel in 1535, the church at Zürich had been directed by Henry Bullinger. It was to him that Calvin turned to establish an agreement on the Lord's Supper. This agreement was reached and its importance is considerable. The document of the agreement is significant. It is the *Accord de Zürich*, in Latin *Consensus Tigurinus*—of 1549. One thing strikes us on reading it. Though an agreement on the meaning of the Lord's Supper, out of its twenty-six articles only seven speak of this sacrament. The first nineteen expound the doctrine of Christ, the eternal Son of God, the source of all life. This life 'is the spiritual intercourse which we have with the Son of God, when, living in us by His Spirit, He makes us share in all the benefits that are in Him. In order to bear witness to this He has ordained both the preaching of the Gospel and the use of the sacraments, namely Baptism and the Lord's Supper'.

This method employed by Calvin, of laying first the foundation which is Christ, the source of all life, the fountain of all blessings, and of examining afterwards particular points, is a true method of unity. For if we are united in acknowledging Christ, we shall be united on matters of detail. Division arises because we stress secondary points, which then assume such importance that they obscure the essential, on which we should be united.

Calvin hoped that the Zürich Agreement would be extended to other churches, and that the Lutherans would accept it. His hope was disappointed. In fact, article 24 contained a small phrase which roused the opposition of Luther's disciples, Luther himself having died some years previously (1546). These were the words: 'Now we do not consider it any less an absurdity that Jesus should be enclosed in the bread or joined to the bread than that the bread should be transubstantiated into his body.' The quarrel rebounded in the writings of the partisans of consubstantiation. It was interminable. Between Joachim Westphal and Calvin uncomplimentary tracts followed one after another, widening the gulf between Lutherans and Calvinists—a gulf which has still not been filled in. May we hope that it soon will be, forgetting a quarrel which modern concepts have made totally unreal? We pray for the establishment of a united Evangelical church, bringing together in France and elsewhere all those who acclaim in Jesus Christ, God's Son, the source of life, and who receive him as food for their souls, as well in the testimony of the Word as in that of the sacraments.

Calvin did not limit himself to an attempt to establish links with the followers of Zwingli. He thought also of the Anglican Church. After the breach achieved by Henry VIII around 1540, it rapidly took shape, theologically speaking, with a leaning towards Calvin's teaching. Numerous continental theologians, driven out by persecutions in Europe, took refuge in England and exerted a great influence there: Peter Martyr Vermigli and Ochino in 1547, à Lasco in 1548, Bucer in 1549.

From a letter that Calvin wrote to Archbishop Cranmer in April 1552 we extract these lines:

God grant that there may be brought about in some place a meeting of learned and serious men from the principal churches, to define the main points of the faith, and to hand down to posterity a solid, scriptural doctrine framed by common counsel. Amongst the greatest evils of our century must be counted the fact that the churches are so divided one from another that there is scarcely even a human relationship between us; at all events there is not the shining light of that holy fellowship of the members of Christ, of which many boast in word, but which few seek sincerely in deed. In consequence, because the members are torn apart, the body of the church lies wounded and bleeding. So far as I have it in my power, if I am thought to be of any service, I shall not be afraid to cross ten seas for this purpose, if that should be necessary.[7]

The desired meeting did not take place. There never was at Cranmer's summons what Calvin calls elsewhere 'a holy banding together (in Latin *syncretismus*) of the children of God, to fight together under Christ's banner against their common enemy'.[8] But Calvin would have feared nothing to make his way to such a meeting, so necessary did he consider it to be, and so grievous to him was the vision of the torn body of Christ.

'*Adiaphora*'

HOW in practice did he envisage the possibility of a unified church? We discover this from a distinction which was especially dear to him, that between *fundamental* and *secondary* matters.

All points of the doctrine of God are not of the same order. There are some, the knowledge of which is so necessary that no man may question them, for they are fundamental pronouncements and principles of Christianity: as for example that there is one God, that Jesus Christ is God and God's Son, that our salvation rests on his mercy alone, and other such doctrines. But there are others which are disputed among the churches, and yet do not break their unity. To give an example: suppose one church happened to maintain that the soul upon leaving the body is carried at once to heaven and another church believed simply that the soul lives in God, without venturing to define the place; if this difference of opinion were held without contention and obstinacy, why should the two churches separate? The words of the apostle are that if we will be perfect we must be of one mind; moreover that if we think differently, God will reveal it to us (Phil. 3.15). Does this not show that if Christians have any disagreement over matters which are not essential, this must not cause disorders and rebellions amongst them? . . . I do not intend by this to support certain errors, not even the slightest ones, and I would not have them fostered by covering them up or indulging them. But I say that it is wrong to leave a church inconsiderately, on the grounds of a disagreement,

127

when that church maintains in its integrity the principal doctrine of our salvation, and the sacraments as our Lord appointed them.[9]

This is an excellent principle, and ought to put an end to the temptation which so often besets the sects, to draw Christians away from the church on points of detail, as they do from time to time. The difficulty lies in defining principal points, for one regards as essential what others regard as subordinate, for example healing, speaking in tongues, etc. . . . But the fact remains that the very possibility of establishing a distinction between principal and secondary matters betokens a great breadth of mind and a great desire for unity.

There is one point in particular which Calvin regards as secondary—that of ritual, ceremonies. Now this is one of the most frequent causes of remaining apart. In fact, many churches have the same doctrine and remain divided on questions of rites, which are very difficult to abandon. Calvin shows here a great breadth of outlook. We have a proof of it in his letter to the faithful at Wesel. Driven out of England by the persecution of Mary Tudor, numerous people of Reformed beliefs had taken refuge in the churches of the Low Countries and Germany. Several came to Wesel in 1554 and experienced difficulties in identifying themselves with the Lutheran churches of the country. They wrote about this to Calvin, who in his letter of 1554 replied to them especially:

> As you are only a particular member [viz. of the body, and not the whole body], you not only may but also must bear and put up with defects which it is not in your power to correct. We do not think that lighted candles at the Lord's Supper, or figured bread, are matters of indifference to be consented to and approved, but we have to accommodate ourselves to the use already accepted. . . . Nobody of our number would wish to separate himself from the body of Christ, and so deprive himself of the use of the Lord's Supper, out of resentment against a candle or chasuble. We must take care not to offend [Fr. *scandaliser*] those who are still held in such infirmities, not appearing to condemn them upon inadequate grounds.[10]

Calvin had a very firm vision of the unity of the church. In our day he would certainly have been on the side of the movement towards the uniting of the churches, the Ecumenical

CALVIN AND THE UNION OF THE CHURCHES

Movement; not the ecumenism of Roman Catholicism which he would abhor, and which is unthinkable for a son of the Reformation, for it consists in a return to a church in which the power of the Papacy has hardened still more than in the sixteenth century; but non-Roman ecumenism, that of the World Council of Churches, in which the Reformed Churches hold an important place because of their faithfulness to the will for reunion which they derive from their founder.[11]

NOTES

1. Otto Weber, *Die Einheit der Kirche bei Calvin* in *Calvin Studien* 1959, Neukirchen, 1960, p. 131. He quotes Bohatec who calls Calvin *ein Theologe der Diagonale, ein Theologe des Kompromisses.* See also G. Reichel: *Calvin als Unionsmann,* Tübingen, 1909.
2. *Epître à Sadolet* in *Trois Traités,* ed. Je sers, 1934, Paris, p. 52.
3. *ibid.* p. 53.
4. *Opuscules* 1566, pp. 880 to 1009.
5. *Comment. on Eph.* Sermon 22, CO LI.520.
6. *Traité de la Sainte-Cène* in *Trois Traités,* p. 141.
7. Calvin to Cranmer, Letter no. 1619, CO XIV.313.
8. *Comment. on Acts* 4.23.
9. *Inst.* IV.i.12.
10. Calvin: *Lettres françaises* ed. Jules Bonnet, 1854, I. 420.
11. A few texts on the unity of Christians in Calvin's commentary on the fourth chapter of the Epistle to the Ephesians.

By bearing with our brothers we maintain unity, which would otherwise be broken a hundred times a day. Let us remember that the starting point in maintaining brotherly concord is humility. Where do pride and arrogance come from, and outrages against brothers? What is the origin of disorders, scoffing, reproaches, if it is not that each man loves and pleases himself too much. . . .

V.4: We are all called to one life and one inheritance. So it follows that we cannot enjoy eternal life except by living in this world in love and concord with one another. For this reason God invites all men by the same summons, so that being joined together by the same consent of faith they may endeavour to support one another. Now if this thought were deeply rooted in our hearts, that . . . the children of God can no more disagree amongst themselves than the Kingdom of Heaven can be divided, how much more diligent and careful should we be to maintain brotherly peace and union among us? In what horror we should hold all rancour, if we remembered that all those who separate from their brothers are estranged also from the Kingdom of God. But I do not know how it happens that we boldly glory in being God's children, while forgetting that mutual

129

brotherhood which we should have among us. Let us learn from St. Paul that we cannot enjoy the same inheritance if we are not one body and one spirit.

V.5: . . . Christ cannot be divided, the faith cannot be split in two. There are not various baptisms, but one only which is common to all. God cannot be dismembered into different parts. So we must safeguard among us that holy unity, which is held together by so many bonds. . . . God is not discordant within himself, so he must necessarily join us in one.

7 The Lord's Supper in the Theology and Practice of Calvin

G. S. M. Walker

THE REGISTERS OF the Venerable Company, now in process of publication,[1] illustrate amongst much else a continuing concern for the Lord's Supper. In a period (1546–1553) almost dominated by the affair of Bolsec and other disciplinary matters, there is none the less a transcription of the *Ordonnances* of 1541, recommending frequent celebration; there are the regulations, accepted six years later, for the country parishes, with a strict injunction that intending communicants must first attend the sermon; there is a copy of the *Consensus Tigurinus*, which concludes with a letter from Zürich commending Calvin's zeal for unity; there are twenty articles of similar import on the sacraments, sent to Berne in 1549, with interesting corrections by Calvin himself; there is the stirring record of Berthelier's excommunication; and in an appendix of theological propositions maintained by various ministers, while there is much on grace, freewill and faith, there is one concluding proposition which asserts that 'by believing we eat the flesh of Christ in reality'.[2] All this, culled from a chance period of seven years, is characteristic of Geneva under Calvin. For to him the Lord's Supper was central[3] in the church's life, and up to the last edition of the *Institutio* he pleaded for its weekly celebration.

In his practice of worship, as in his theology of the sacraments, Calvin followed the teaching of Scripture and the tradition of the early Church. His liturgy of 1542 is qualified by the phrase 'selon la coustume de l'Eglise ancienne'. His theological writings are studded with references to the Fathers; and

131

although the name of St. Augustine predominates, it must be remembered that Calvin was willing also to learn from those with whose sacramental doctrine he disagreed. Thus Niesel[4] has demonstrated that his conception of the Holy Spirit, as the *vinculum* or *canalis* of our communion with Christ, is derived from a sermon attributed to St. John Chrysostom which Erasmus published in 1530. Equally significant, but less easy to explain, are Calvin's points of contact with writers of the Carolingian period. Like Alcuin and Erigena,[5] he believes that Abraham's faith in God was increased by astronomical observation. Like Ratramnus and in opposition to Paschasius,[6] he thinks that in the sacraments of the Old Testament, no less than in those of the New, the flesh of Christ was really given. This is a striking parallel, because the common patristic view, represented for example by St. Augustine,[7] distinguished sharply between the spiritual value of the two dispensations. Paschasius had been published by the Lutheran Job Gast in 1528, as a counterblast to Zwinglian doctrine and in preparation for the Marburg Colloquy; the first edition of Ratramnus followed in 1531. Calvin does not refer to either writer by name,[8] but he seems to be well aware of the points in dispute[9] between them.

Calvin's doctrine

FOR his own doctrine of the Lord's Supper we have a number of systematic statements, including the short *Confessio Fidei de Eucharistia* of 1537, and the *Petit Traité de la Sainte Cène* of 1541. Successive editions of the *Institutio* dealt with the subject in growing detail, and there are also the three treatises in which he defended himself against the Lutheran Joachim Westphal: the *Defensio* (1555), *Secunda defensio* (1556) and *Ultima admonitio* (1557). The *Consensus Tigurinus* should not be quoted in evidence of Calvin's own views, for it represents the extreme limit which he was prepared to concede in the cause of unity. Much additional material can be found scattered in commentaries, sermons and tracts; of this the collection made by R. S. Wallace[10] is the fullest available in English.

Although he discoursed on the subject at great length, Calvin considered that the doctrine of the Lord's Supper was basically

132

very simple. As Hunter[11] writes, 'he believed that the simpler the view taken of the sacrament, consistent with the significance attributed to it by Christ and his Apostles, the greater would be its potency, the more would it be a real means of grace; also, the more likelihood would there be of general agreement'. His own simplest statement is the *Confessio* of 1537, drawn up at the Synod of Berne in order to reconcile Lutherans and Zwinglians by omitting the distinctive extremes on either side. It is a characteristic document, both in purpose and content, and sufficiently short to be reproduced here in full:[12]

> We confess that the spiritual life, which Christ bestows on us, does not consist simply in the fact that he quickens us by his Spirit, but also that through the power of his Spirit he makes us participate in his life-giving flesh, and by this participation we are nourished for life eternal. Therefore, when we speak of the communion which believers enjoy with Christ, we understand them to communicate no less in his flesh and blood than in his Spirit, so that they thus possess the whole Christ. For when Scripture openly declares that Christ's flesh is indeed food for us, and his blood drink indeed, it is clear that we must be nourished by these things if we seek for life in Christ. The apostle teaches nothing mean or common when he asserts that we are flesh of Christ's flesh and bone of his bones; but he thus indicates the great mystery of our communion with his body, a mystery so profound that none can explain it adequately in words. But it is no contradiction to this teaching that our Lord, ascended into heaven, has deprived us of the local presence of his body, which in this case is by no means required. For although in this mortal pilgrimage we are not shut up or enclosed in the same space as he is, yet his Spirit's efficacy is not restrained by any limits from the power of joining and uniting things that are separate in their localities. Thus we recognise that his Spirit is the bond of our participation with him, in such a way that he truly feeds us on the substance of our Lord's flesh and blood, to give us by sharing in them life and immortality. This communion of his flesh and blood Christ offers in his holy supper under the symbols of bread and wine, and he presents[13] this to all who celebrate it duly in accordance with his lawful institution.

Here as elsewhere Calvin asserts two paradoxes: although communion is a spiritual act, it involves an actual sharing in Christ's

133

flesh and blood, and although his body has now ascended physically into heaven, we are none the less able to make contact with it through the Spirit. How these things can be remains a mystery, to be treated with reverence and accepted in faith. The emphatic reference to 'the substance of our Lord's flesh and blood' raises the question of precisely what Calvin meant by the term *substantia*. Gollwitzer[14] attempts to distinguish three different senses of the word in his writings: (1) the corporeal nature of the physical body, (2) Christ's person as the reality of the sacrament, and (3) the spiritual power of the benefits received from him. From the outset, Calvin had denied[15] that the sacrament conveys Christ's body in the first sense, and the dynamism of the third sense is the conception which he most commonly employs. 'He conceives of the essence of "substance" as consisting in its "power", so that wherever anything acts, there it is.'[16] The presence is not static but dynamic; it is God and not man who takes the initiative in, and retains control of, the sacramental encounter.

It was either in the same year 1537, or more probably during his Strasbourg exile,[17] that Calvin composed the *Petit Traité de la Sainte Cène*. Here the Roman doctrines of propitiatory sacrifice[18] and transubstantiation[19] in the Mass are condemned; but both Luther and Zwingli have also erred, in attempting to rectify the Roman errors, and Calvin seeks to find a genuinely middle way.[20] Although spiritual food is distributed through the Word of the Lord, the Supper has also been instituted to sign and seal the Gospel promises, to awaken our gratitude, and to teach us holiness of life.[21] It is a mirror[22] of Christ crucified.

> Because the good things of Jesus Christ do not belong to us at all, unless He first of all is ours, it is needful that in the first place He should be given to us in the Supper, in order that what we have described should be truly accomplished in us. For this reason I am accustomed to say that the matter or substance of the sacraments is the Lord Jesus; their effects are the graces and benedictions which we have through Him.[23]

And Calvin continues[24] that Jesus Christ is 'the substance and foundation' of the whole Supper, while bread and wine are the 'instruments' through which he distributes his body and his blood.

134

CALVIN AND THE LORD'S SUPPER

The Institutio

THE *Institutio* in its finished form devotes six chapters to the subject of the sacraments, of which one (IV. xvii) relates especially to the Lord's Supper, and another (IV. xiv) to sacraments in general. Calvin defines[25] a sacrament as 'an outward symbol by which the Lord seals on our consciences the promises of his goodwill toward us, to maintain the weakness of our faith, and we in turn attest our devotion to him in the presence of God, angels and men'. In this definition he expressly claims to be following St. Augustine, but he amplifies for greater clarity. There can be no sacrament unless it is instituted by a specific divine promise, to which it is joined as a seal and confirmation[26] suitable to our human state. Hence the sacrament is made up of two parts, word and external sign. 'With the outward and visible symbol is also joined the Word. This is the source from which the sacraments derive their strength; not that the efficacy of the Spirit is confined within the Word which sounds in the ear, but because the effect of all the things which believers receive from the sacraments depends on the testimony of the Word.'[27] When the Word is removed the entire power of the sacraments is lost,[28] and therefore 'as soon as the sign itself meets our eyes, the Word ought to sound in our ears'.[29] Here Calvin is referring to the whole 'word of faith' which is embraced in the preaching of the Gospel, and not to any mere formula of consecration which is used like a magical charm. 'Calvin is concerned' writes Hunter,[30] 'to make it plain that the sacraments are not the cause of anything. There is nothing of magical efficacy or potency in them to effectuate what they symbolise. . . . It is by the will of God expressed in the words of institution that they occupy a primary place in the life of the Christian.' Nevertheless they do depict[31] the promises in lively pictorial fashion, so that they can be reckoned as 'nothing else than a visible word, or sculpture and image of that grace of God which the word more fully illustrates'.[32] Their value lies in making explicit and bringing home the message of the Gospel, but they have no independent status because they require the word to give them meaning and purpose.

They also require the grace of the Holy Spirit to make them efficacious,[33] since God works through the sign in such a way

135

that its entire efficacy depends upon his Spirit.[34] This personal mode of operation ensures that there is nothing mechanical in the reception of sacramental grace. Calvin ridicules the 'absurd definition of grace given by the schoolmen'[35] that it is a *qualitatem hominum cordibus infusam*, and he insists that grace is not a quality or substance 'but the personal presence of Christ offering men a personal relationship even in uniting them to himself'.[36] In a letter to Bullinger[37] Calvin does not object to the idea that in some sense grace is contained or conferred in the sacraments, but in the *Institutio*[38] he insists that they are only pledges (*tesserae*), with which grace is not necessarily bound or included. The reality is indeed offered along with the sign,[39] and the bread is named body because it not only represents but also presents it to us.[40] But whether or not we receive the gift depends upon our faith. Just as the Gospel can be spurned without ceasing to be in fact the Word of God, so the sacraments,[41] though truly offering Christ, may fail to take effect because of the recipient's unworthiness. On the other hand the faithful, even apart from the sacraments, enjoy a permanent communion; 'the mystical union subsisting between Christ and his members should be a matter of reflection not only when we sit at the Lord's table, but at all other times'.[42]

Thus the sacraments must be neither overvalued nor undervalued. They are particularly vivid tokens of God's merciful understanding of our nature. 'In the human word of preaching God condescends to us sinners' writes Niesel,[43] 'in the Eucharist his merciful condescension to the measure of our everyday realities attains its utmost extent.' He confronts us here through inescapably tangible media. But apart from faith they are utterly destructive to the church,[44] for she is lost as soon as she places her confidence in the outward symbol alone. As Augustine often pointed out,[45] the reality which is apprehended by faith must be distinguished from the sign which all can see. Christ is the matter or substance of all sacraments,[46] and He is offered to us in word and sacrament alike[47]; but He is received only by the faithful, and since faith is itself the gift of God to His elect, both the power and the effect depend in the last resort on His electing grace.

Where the divine promise is granted, anything may acquire a sacramental meaning. The tree of life and the rainbow[48] served as sacraments to Adam and to Noah, and being given of God they were effectual means of grace. Under the Old Testament, the substance of Christ's body was ministered no less than under the New,[49] but the old dispensation has now been abrogated, so that baptism and communion[50] remain as the only normal sacraments possessing a divine institution and promise. They serve especially to maintain the corporate fellowship of the church, as a pardoned and redeemed community.

When he turns, in the seventeenth chapter of Book IV of the *Institutio*, to deal specifically with the Lord's Supper, Calvin divides his material into two principal parts: first he gives a general account[51] of the nature and reception of this sacrament, and secondly he refutes the various errors of the different theological schools. There is also a short concluding section on liturgical rites and the frequency of communion.

As a wise and loving parent, God has not only adopted us into his family, but also continually feeds us with the 'spiritual banquet' of his Son. Because this 'great mystery' and 'inestimable treasure' of the church has been perverted by the delusive arguments of Satan, it is necessary to state that bread and wine are signs, representing the invisible food which we receive from Christ's flesh and blood. He is the only sustenance[52] of our souls, and the secret union subsisting between him and his members is depicted in the sacrament, in such a way that by partaking of it, we actually receive[53] the body that was once offered for our salvation.[54] There is thus a 'wondrous exchange' between Christ and us; he takes our manhood, with its mortality, weakness, poverty and unrighteousness, to give us[55] the status of sonship, entrance into heaven, and all the riches of his power (2). Of this exchange or sharing or communion, the sacrament is a witness,[56] because we see that as the body is nourished by bread, so the soul is quickened by Christ; further, 'He is as truly offered to us here, as if He were present to our eyes and handled with our hands' (3). The truth of this depends upon His own promise, ratified at Calvary and apprehended in faith (4). Christ with His benefits is 'applied' to the faithful both by the Gospel and by the eucharist; but the latter brings Him to us 'more clearly', because it inwardly fulfils what is otherwise outwardly declared. Having once given himself for the redemption of the world, Christ is at all times the bread of life, being received

137

everywhere by faith;[57] but He is received with particular certainty in the faithful reception of the sacrament, which He has himself instituted to confirm His promise (5).

Two battles

CALVIN is very conscious of fighting a battle on two fronts. He thinks that Lutherans and Romanists attribute more to the eucharist than Scripture will properly allow. At the same time, he is anxious to show that it is something higher than a mere 'badge of outward profession' (6), and he argues from the scriptural texts that communion is not merely in the spirit but also in the body[58] of Christ. Lacking adequate means of expression, he feels obliged to 'break forth in wonder at that mystery which neither the mind can adequately suffice to meditate, nor the tongue to explain' (7).

From all eternity, Christ as the Father's quickening Word was the fountain and source of life for all things; but it was only at the Incarnation that His life was visibly bestowed, when coming down from heaven He gave His flesh (8). Although by nature subject to mortality, that flesh has obtained the life-giving power of God, and it is by communion with it alone that man can aspire to the life of heaven (9). Despite the vast distance of space between us and the ascended Christ, we are united with Him through the hidden power (*arcana virtus*) of the Holy Spirit,[59] so that when we communicate in His body and blood He pours His life into us, and the sacramental signs, so far from being naked and bare, are accompanied by the veritable presence of the things signified (10). The spiritual reality is not only depicted but also bestowed[60] through the symbols; while the evangelical promises declare the meaning of the sacrament, its 'matter or substance' (*materiam aut substantiam*) is Christ with His death and resurrection; and its effects are the blessings of redemption and eternal life. Thus by the signs of bread and wine, Christ's body and blood are truly given[61] to us, when we receive the mystery of the Supper with faith (11). For this a local presence in the elements is not required, since the bond of union is provided by the Spirit (12).

The scholastic teaching, with its emphasis on a corporeal presence, is without scriptural foundation and contrary to the

138

writers of the ancient church. Logical absurdity, coupled with theological ignorance, produced the doctrine of transubstantiation, which destroys the essence of a sacrament, and implies deceit on the part of God (13–14). A change does take place in the elements, but it is dynamic, a change of use and not of nature, concerning the recipients rather than the elements themselves (15).

Consubstantiation is an attempt to preserve the distinction between symbol and reality; Calvin would accept it if it meant simply that delivering of the bread is accompanied by that of the body;[62] but he is obliged to criticise it because it involves a localisation of Christ's presence and a certain ubiquity of His glorified manhood (16). To assert that Christ as man was or became omnipresent, is in fact to revive the docetic heresy of Marcion (17). It is essential for His work of salvation that His humanity should be and remain of like nature with ours.

The presence

IN order to reach a true doctrine of the Supper, we must remember that Christ cannot be tied to or confined in any material objects, since He has now ascended into heavenly glory with the genuine manhood which He assumed (19). The words of institution of the sacrament do not state that bread is converted into the body, or that the body is in, with and under the bread (20); on the contrary, the use of the term 'is' in this context can only be figurative or metaphorical, although it is based on a real analogy between the sign and the thing signified (21). At this point, Calvin pauses to insist that he is not seeking to limit the power of God by rationalistic arguments, but is merely providing a faithful exegesis of Scripture (24–25), in which the fact of the ascension[63] is given its due place. Locally, Christ is now seated at God's right hand; dynamically, He is present on earth, as St. Augustine says, through His majesty, providence and grace (26). Scripture provides no warrant for supposing that the glorified body of Christ is invisible (29) or omnipresent (30); on the contrary, to assert such ideas is to renew the heresies of Eutyches[64] and Servetus, according to whom Christ's humanity has been lost and absorbed in his Godhead.

On the other hand, Christ is really present in the Supper,[65] through the power of the Spirit, who raises us up to Him in the heavenly places (31). The manner[66] of this presence is inexplicable by human reason (32), and subtle attempts at theorising are only productive of heresy. As has been said, 'Christ Himself is the substance of the Supper'; but 'men do not receive more from the sacrament than they gather with the vessel of faith' (33), so that in fact the wicked fail to receive the Christ who is there present.[67] Calvin here devotes some space (34) to showing that the idea of a spiritual manducation, by faith alone, agrees with the teaching of St. Augustine, and further that the sacraments are efficacious only in the elect, who alone exercise saving faith.

Since the presence of Christ, though real, is spiritual, He cannot and must not be adored in the sacramental elements (35–37). The Lord's Supper is given to be received, not worshipped, and such superstitious worship is contrary to the teaching of Scripture and the practice of the early church. *Sursum corda* in the liturgy is intended to remind us that Christ is not here, but risen, and the purpose of the sacrament is that our faith may ascend[68] to Him.

A final purpose, for which the sacrament was instituted, is to encourage unity and love among Christian people. The church is in a sense constituted by the sacrament[69] because, by partaking in Christ's one body, His members are themselves made one (38). Since this involves a personal relationship, it cannot be achieved by the 'dumb action' (39) of mechanical ceremonies, but it requires the living power of the Word for its true ministration. And because of this close connexion between word and sacrament, because the sacramental service is incomplete without a sermon, it is useless to reserve the elements for communion of the sick.[70] Although there is great danger in communicating unworthily (40), we must not fall into the Roman error (41) of demanding that communicants should be in a state of sinless perfection; on the contrary, to those who are humbly penitent, the sacrament is intended to provide medicine and comfort (42). In the outward forms of administering the rite, considerable liberty[71] is allowed to the church (43); but it should be celebrated frequently, not once a year (44–46), and the people should receive the cup as well as the bread (47–50).

Such, in broad outline, is the teaching of Calvin on the Lord's Supper. It suffers from a number of obscurities and apparent contradictions, for which a reason is probably to be sought in the conflicting claims[72] of piety and doctrine. Calvin himself regarded clarity[73] as one of the virtues of his exposition; but one cannot help feeling that it is involved in paradox, and that it rightly preserves an essential element of mystery. The confusion of his language appears in such a passage as the following:[74] 'though I confess that our souls are truly fed by the *substance* of Christ's flesh, I certainly do this day, not less than formerly, repudiate the *substantial* presence . . . this fiction of *transfusion* being taken out of the way . . . nor will I ever hesitate to acknowledge that, by the secret virtue of the Holy Spirit, life is *infused* into us from the *substance* of his flesh. . . .' Here the meaning of key-words undoubtedly varies from one sentence to another.

Nothing fresh is added by the controversial writings against the Lutheran Joachim Westphal, but they underline a number of points in the argument. Thus Calvin makes it clear[75] that he always felt more sympathy for Luther than for Zwingli, because of his conviction that the sacraments are something more than bare and empty signs, and he expresses[76] his cordial agreement with the Augsburg Confession. However, he is determined to maintain the truth of the ascension, and the distinction between Christ's divine and human natures. 'Though I have classed among opinions to be rejected the idea that the body of Christ is really and substantially present in the Supper, this is not at all repugnant to a true and real communion, which consists in our ascent to heaven, and requires no other descent in Christ than that of spiritual grace.'[77] 'The simple argument of our party is that Augustine plainly asserts that our Saviour, in respect of His human nature, is in heaven, whence He will come at the last day . . . . that if we take away locality from bodies they will be situated nowhere, and consequently not exist; that Christ is everywhere present as God, but in respect of the nature of a real body occupies some place in heaven.'[78] 'For we deny not that the flesh and blood of Christ are communicated to us. We only explain the mode, lest carnal eating should either derogate in any respect from the heavenly glory of Christ, or overthrow the reality of His human nature.'[79]

Practical outworking

IN the course of this argument with the Lutherans, Calvin remarks[80] that 'the utility of private absolution it is not my purpose to deny'; and the phrase may serve to introduce the practical matters[81] with which he deals in regard to the celebration of the liturgy. By way of 'private absolution', when in exile at Strasbourg he demanded that his people should consult with him individually before communicating, and he told Farel that he thought it undesirable to abolish the confessional unless it were replaced by some such practice, 'in order that the ignorant... might be better prepared, that those who needed a special admonition might receive it, in short that those who were tormented by an anxiety of conscience might be consoled.'[82] A vestige of this practice survives in the Prayer Book rubric which requires intending communicants to signify their names to the curate 'at least some time the day before'. In lieu of confirmation, Calvin thought it would be 'a fitting climax to the catechism' if 'children or young people, after making their profession of faith, should be dedicated to God by the laying on of hands'.[83] This would indeed, as Bucer thought, go some way towards meeting Anabaptist objections to the automatic way in which children were received into the church. In order to regulate admission to the sacrament, Calvin instituted the use of communion tokens,[84] which were already being employed in some Roman Catholic circles.

He suggests the outlines of a typical order of communion in *Institutio* IV. xvii. 43. There should be the normal service of public prayer with sermon;[85] then the minister, with wine and bread placed on the table, reads the institution narrative of the Supper; having explained the promises which are there given, he fences the table against all those whom the Lord prohibits; prayer is offered for grace to make the communicants fit; while the ministers break and distribute the elements in due order, psalms are sung or lessons read; there is an exhortation to faith, love and Christian living; and the service concludes with a prayer of thanksgiving and the singing of praise to God. All this is extremely simple, and Calvin makes a point of stating, at the start of the chapter, that details of administration are unimportant. He had used a formula of absolution at Stras-

142

bourg, but suppressed this[86] on his return to Geneva, together with the chanting of the decalogue, in conformity with local usage. His personal preference was for kneeling at prayer, and a written liturgy with considerable freedom in its use,[87] but he turned none of these points into a shibboleth. When he described[88] the Anglican service as containing *multas tolerabiles ineptias*, his emphasis lay on the adjective rather than the noun; and in writing to the church at Wesel,[89] he insisted that such trivialities as chasubles and candles must not be made an occasion for disunity. The most surprising feature of his liturgy, as described in the *Institutio*, is the absence of any prayer of consecration or thanksgiving over the communion elements. This omission is supplied[90] in the Genevan liturgy of 1542, which is much fuller and more traditional in form. Indeed, Lecerf has pointed out[91] that behind the stark simplicity of the Genevan rite, there is a genuine feeling for liturgical tradition and propriety; the fencing of the tables, for example, can be regarded as an elaboration of the *sancta sanctis*, and the *sursum corda* makes its appearance in a slightly amplified phraseology. But there are no sacramental formulae from the Roman canon, and Calvin always stresses the action to be done, rather than the forms to be recited, in celebration of the Supper. 'His test of true religion is spiritual reality,' writes J. S. Whale;[92] 'the only acceptable worship of God is from the heart, and since this inward attitude alone determines real devotion to God and His will, worship becomes relatively independent of given forms.' But what was lost in outward magnificence was more than regained in passionate intensity; 'those who were present at the services have told us that often they could not keep back the tears of their emotion and joy'.[93]

With a vernacular service followed at every point by the people, Calvin had restored the primitive pattern of corporate, congregational communion. It is, however, a tragedy that for his spiritual descendants, no less than for himself, the scriptural ideal of weekly celebration has not yet been adequately realised; the result has been an unnatural divorce between word and sacrament to which the whole theology of Calvin is opposed.

JOHN CALVIN

NOTES

1. J-F. Bergier (ed.) *Registres de la Compagnie des Pasteurs de Genève*, vol. I, Geneva, 1964.

2. *op. cit.*, 182.

3. 'The focus of church life, that upon which the act of worship depends, is not simply the Word of God proceeding from human lips, but also and above all the sacrament in its objective reality independent of man' (W. Niesel *The Theology of Calvin*, ET 1956, 212).

4. W. Niesel *Calvins Lehre von Abendmahl*, Munich, 1935, 92. See Calvin *Confessio Fidei de Eucharistia* (1537) in OS I. 435, and *Inst.* IV. xvii. 12; the sermon is not printed by Migne, but appears in the Basle edition of Chrysostom (1530) V. 379.

5. Alcuin *Epist.* 83 (PL 100, 272A), Erigena *De div. nat.* 3.23 (PL 122, 689C); cf. Calvin *Comment. on Gen.* 15. 4. Here, if it is not coincidence, there is probably a common patristic source, although a certain amount of search has so far failed to disclose it.

6. Ratramnus *De corp. et sang. Dom.* xx–xxv (ed. van den Brink 38-40), Paschasius *De corp. et sang. Dom.* V 1 (PL 120, 1280ABC); cf. Calvin *Comment. on I Cor.* 10. 3-4 (ET J. W. Fraser, 1960, 203–205).

7. Augustine *Enarrationes in Psalmos* 73.2 (PL 36, 930): non sunt eadem sacramenta, nec eadem promissa . . . sacramenta novi testamenti dant salutem, sacramenta veteris testamenti promiserunt salvatorem. In the *Last Admonition to Joachim Westphal* (*Tracts* CTS II.391) Calvin claims that Augustine is really on his side here, but he quotes nothing to support his own strong statement that the O.T. saints ate the as yet un-created flesh of Christ (*Comment. on I Cor.* 10.4; Fraser 205).

8. He refers on several occasions to Berengarius; e.g. *Second Defence* against Westphal, *Tracts*, CTS II. 260.

9. It is important for the history of eucharistic doctrine that even Paschasius (PL 120, 1282CD) believes the virtue of the sacrament to be withdrawn from the unworthy, so that they do not spiritually eat the flesh of Christ; in the later *Epist. ad Frudegard.* (1356B) he takes a slightly more static view of the sacramental presence. Ratramnus was rejected by Lutherans and Roman Catholics; but Dom Mabillon regarded him as orthodox, and if this is correct, Calvin is certainly orthodox too.

10. R. S. Wallace *Calvin's Doctrine of the Word and Sacrament*, 1953; see the footnotes to chaps. XI–XVIII.

11. A. Mitchell Hunter *The Teaching of Calvin*, 1950, 167.

12. I translate from the Latin text in OS I. 435.

13. *exhibet*; 'Calvin uses the verb *exhibere* . . . more in the sense of "to present in reality" or even "to convey", rather than in the sense of "to show" ' (R. S. Wallace *op. cit.*, 159 note 4).

14. H. Gollwitzer *Coena Domini*, Munich, 1937, 120 ff.

15. See for example his *Epistola de fugiendis impiorum illicitis sacris* (1537) with its strictures on the Mass as *summum illud abominationum omnium caput* (OS I. 289).

16. A. M. Hunter, *op. cit.*, 185. Ratramnus makes a similar equation

144

CALVIN AND THE LORD'S SUPPER

between *substantia* and *potentia De corp. et sang. Dom.* xlix (Brink, 46).
17. See OS I. 500; the text of the treatise follows at 503–530.
18. *ibid.*, 517 ff.; (cf. *Inst.* IV. xviii.3).
19. *ibid.*, 520 ff.
20. *ibid.*, 527 ff.; cf. *Comment. on I Cor.* 10.3 (Fraser 203), 'papists confound the reality and the sign; unbelievers . . . separate the signs from the realities; let us preserve a middle position (*nos mediocritatem servemus*)'.
21. OS I. 505.
22. *ibid.*, 506.
23. *ibid.*, 507.
24. *ibid.*, 508.
25. IV. xiv. 1; cf. *Comment. on Ezek.* 20.12 (CTS II. 302–303), 'there is a mutual agreement in the sacraments, by which God binds us to himself, and we mutually pledge our faith'.
26. IV. xiv. 3; cf. *Comment. on Acts* 2.42 (CTS I. 128), 'the Supper is added unto doctrine instead of (*vice*) a confirmation'.
27. *Comment. on Jn.* 20.22 (ET T. H. L. Parker, 1961, 205–206); cf. *Inst.* IV. xiv.4.
28. 'Verbo sublato perit tota vis sacramentorum' (*Comment. on Eph.* 5.26).
29. *Comment. on Gen.* 17.9 (CTS I. 452); without the word, the sacrament is 'mortuum et inane spectrum'.
30. A. M. Hunter, *op. cit.*, 167.
31. IV. xiv. 5; cf. *Comment. on Acts* 7.30 (CTS I. 277), 'God doth apply the signs unto the things by a certain likelihood (*similitudine*) and this is almost the common order and way of the sacraments'.
32. *Comment. on Gen.* 17.9 (CTS I. 451); cf. *Inst.* IV. xiv, 6.
33. *Inst.* IV. xiv. 9, 17.
34. 'Nam ita Deus per signum agit, ut tota signi efficacia nihilominus a spiritu suo pendeat' (*Comment, on Eph.* 5.26; CO 51. 223); 'the Lord . . . performs inwardly by his Spirit that which the sacraments figure to the eye' (*Second Defence* against Westphal, CTS II. 274).
35. *Comment. on Rom.* 5.15 (ET R. Mackenzie, 1961, 115).
36. R. S. Wallace, *op. cit.*, 154.
37. CO 12. 483; cf. J. Beckmann *Vom Sakrament bei Calvin*, Tübingen, 1926, p. 37.
38. IV. xv. 4.
39. '. . . in sacramentis rem nobis cum signo exhiberi' (*Comment. on Is.* 6, 7; CO 36. 133).
40. *Petit Traité* (OS I. 509).
41. IV xiv, 7 and xiv. 16; cf. *Second Defence* against Westphal (CTS II. 303), 'the unbelief of men does not overthrow the faith of God, because the sacraments always retain their virtue . . . thus, on the part of God, nothing is changed, whereas in regard to men, everyone receives according to the measure of his faith'.
42. *Comment. on Ps.* 63, 2 (CTS II. 435).
43. W. Niesel, *The Theology of Calvin*, 214.
44. IV. xiv. 14.

45. IV. xiv. 15.

46. IV. xiv. 16.

47. IV. xiv. 17.

48. IV. xiv. 18.

49. IV. xiv. 23.

50. IV. xviii. 19; ordination can be regarded as a sacrament, but it is not a normal one, because it is not intended for all Christians (IV. xiv. 20). See IV. xix. on the five false sacraments of Rome.

51. His thought is more original on the Lord's Supper than it is on Baptism; see Wendel, 329. Apart from Scripture, the chief influences are those of St. Augustine and of Bucer (*ibid.* 332).

52. 'When we receive the Supper, He shows us that He is our food' (Sermon on Deut. 7. 19–24); cf. *Inst.* IV. xviii. 19 ('coena vero assiduum velut alimentum').

53. 'It is as clear as day to me that here the reality is joined to the sign; in other words, we really do become sharers in the body of Christ, so far as spiritual power is concerned, just as much as we eat the bread' (*Comment. on I Cor.* 11. 24; Fraser 245).

54. *Inst.* IV. xvii. 1; subsequent references to this chapter will be noted in the text by the number of the section alone.

55. The gift is sealed in the sacrament because 'the Supper is the pledge of a perfect atonement' (*Comment. on Jn.* 19. 34–35; Parker 186).

56. In the Supper 'we are ingrafted into the body of the Lord' (*Comment. on I Cor.* 10. 15; Fraser 215); cf. *Sermon on Tit.* 1.7–9, 'when we come to this holy table, we must know that our Lord Jesus Christ presents himself to confirm us in the unity which we have already received by the faith of the gospel, that we may be grafted into his body . . .'

57. Cf. 'the continual communication . . . the perpetual eating of faith' (*Comment. on Jn.* 6. 53–4; Parker 169–170).

58. 'The spiritual union which we have with Christ is not a matter of the soul alone, but of the body also, so that we are flesh of His flesh etc. (Eph. 5. 30). The hope of the resurrection would be faint, if our union with Him were not complete and total like that' (*Comment. on I Cor.* 6. 15; Fraser 130).

59. 'Christ overcomes the distance of space by employing the agency of his spirit to inspire life into us from his flesh' (*Second Defence* against Westphal, CTS II. 287).

60. 'Christ does not offer us only the benefit of His death and resurrection, but the self-same body in which He suffered and rose again. My conclusion is that the body of Christ is really (*realiter*) . . . i.e. truly (*vere*) given to us in the Supper . . . or, what amounts to the same thing, that a life-giving power from the flesh of Christ is poured into us through the medium of the Spirit, even although it is at a great distance from us and is not mixed with us (*Comment. on I Cor.* 11. 14; Fraser 246).

61. 'The gift of the Lord's Supper is not therefore the spirit of Christ or His divine nature. Nor does it consist in His human nature as such, but in His humanity in so far as it was given over to death for our sakes. There lies the crux of the matter' (W. Niesel, *op. cit.*, 219).

146

62. At the same time as we receive the outward signs, we are truly given what the words of institution promise; but the material elements must be carefully distinguished from the body and blood of Christ (Wendel, 258).

63. 'The ascension of Jesus is thus, for Calvin, decisive in illuminating the meaning of the sacraments' (R. S. Wallace, *op. cit.*, 227).

64. The same point is made in the preface to the *Comment. on Jeremiah*.

65. 'This also is the reason why the holy table is prepared for us: that we may know that the Lord Jesus, having descended here below and emptied Himself of all things, yet has not separated Himself from us, when He ascended in His heavenly glory' (*Sermon on Lk.* 2. 1–14).

66. 'Modus autem praesentiae, quam Dominus suis promittit, spiritualiter intelligi debet' (*Comment. on Matt.* 28, 20; CO 45. 826).

67. 'The Lord offers what the sign represents to worthy and unworthy alike, but everyone is not capable of enjoying it' (*Comment. on I Cor.* 10. 5; Fraser 206).

68. 'We must ascend unless we want to be separated from Him' (*Comment. on Jn.* 20, 18: Parker 200).

69. 'Calvin regards the Church as essentially a eucharistic fellowship' (W. Niesel, *op cit.*, 212); sacraments, equally with the word, are a necessary mark of the church.

70. Calvin had no objection to communion of the sick at home, provided there was a congregation, however small, and an adequate ministry of the word; see A. M. Hunter, *op. cit.*, 190.

71. 'The Lord allows us freedom in regard to outward rites, in order that we may not think that His worship is confined to those things . . . however . . . He has restricted the freedom . . . in such a way that it is only from His Word that we can make up our minds about what is right' (*Comment. on I Cor.* 14, 40; Fraser 310).

72. Wendel, 354.

73. Cf. R. S. Wallace, *op. cit.*, 217–218; he also points out (*ibid.*, 167–168) that in some sense the whole mystery of the Incarnation is involved.

74. *Second Defence* against Westphal (CTS II. 277), italics mine; Wendel (p. 350) remarks that Calvin makes two apparently contradictory assertions (that the body of Christ is present in the Supper, and that it has no local connexion with the communion elements), and reconciles them by invoking the bond of the Holy Spirit; I should myself prefer to say that he locates the presence in the action rather than the elements.

75. *Second Defence* (CTS II. 252).

76. *ibid.*, 306.

77. *ibid.*, 281.

78. *Last Admonition* (CTS II.382); the resurrection appearances were not due to Christ's ubiquity, but to His 'divine energy' (*ibid.*, 380).

79. *ibid.*, 411.

80. *Second Defence* (CTS II. 321).

81. His long struggle to secure for the church the right of excommunication belongs to the subject of ecclesiastical discipline, and cannot be considered here.

JOHN CALVIN

82. See Doumergue II. 412–413.

83. *ibid.*, V. 364.

84. A. M. Hunter *op. cit.*, 190 and note 130.

85. In his summary, A. Dakin (*Calvinism*, 1940, 125) strangely omits the sermon.

86. Doumergue II. 498; for the wording of the formula see OS II. 19.

87. A. M. Hunter, *op. cit.*, 213–214.

88. CO XV. 394.

89. *ibid.*, XV. 79–80.

90. There is a convenient tabular summary of Calvin's liturgies compared with Bucer's in W. D. Maxwell, *Outline of Christian Worship*, 1949, 114–115.

91. A. Lecerf, *Etudes Calvinistes*, Neuchâtel, 1949, 46–48.

92. J. S. Whale in N. Micklem (ed.) *Christian Worship*, 1936, 161.

93. Doumergue V. 504.

8 Calvin the Theologian

J. I. Packer

'THE THEOLOGIAN' was the affectionate and admiring phrase by which Philip Melanchthon, Professor of Greek at Wittenberg University and leader of the German reformation after Luther's death, regularly referred to his twelve-years-younger contemporary, the senior pastor in the Swiss city of Geneva. 'Minister of the Word of God' was the only title to which John Calvin himself laid claim. Yet he would have agreed that in this capacity he could not help being a theologian of some sort. For to him the word 'theologian' denoted, not just a member of the church's academic élite, but anyone who ventured to make statements about God.

Calvin's Calvinism

WHAT sort of theologian was Calvin? Not the sort that he is often thought to have been. It is depressing to observe how, despite all the disciplined Calvin-research of the past sixty years, the old hostile misrepresentations persist. Thus, many still think that the main mark of Calvin's theology, so far as it was distinctive, was audacity of speculative logic, especially regarding predestination—though in fact, as has often been shown, all his teaching was conscientiously biblical, and on predestination in particular he declined to go a hair's breadth beyond what he understood Scripture actually to say. Many still take his doctrine of sin (later called 'total depravity') to mean, not just that no man is at any point as good as he should be,

but that every man is at every point as bad as he can be—
though Calvin explicitly taught that a kindly providence (later
called 'common grace') operated through conscience, law,
custom, and example, to restrain the full outworking of inborn
perversity and to move even ungodly men to ethical and cultural achievements of abiding worth. Many still equate Calvin's
faith in divine sovereignty with physical or metaphysical determinism (with which it had nothing to do), and on the moral
level with fatalism—though Calvin always stressed that man is
responsible to God for his choices, and that God's will is done
by means of intelligent, calculated action on man's part, and
that God's ordering of our circumstances is for ethical ends, to
wean us from sin and to train us in faith, patience, and love.

In recent years, Calvinism has been seriously construed as a
psychopathic phenomenon, a projection of sublimated cruelty,
or disgust at human life, or an inferiority complex, or some
other neurotic disorder, into a malevolent 'anti-gospel' whose
main point was that God is fierce, and most men are irremedi-
ably damned; and many who would not go so far still think of
Calvinism as inimical to evangelism, and as narrowing the
bounds of God's mercy—though Calvin held that in the Gospel
Christ is offered to all, and spent his whole working life seeking
to spread the Gospel throughout Europe by praying, writing,
advising, and training leaders. Many still see Calvin as a theological iconoclast who swept aside the post-apostolic Christian
heritage as so much useless lumber—though the Anabaptists,
who actually were iconoclasts of this kind, had no sterner foe
than John Calvin, nor in the Reformation era did the Fathers
have a more diligent student. The popular idea of him is still of a
chilly, arrogant intellectualist—though in fact no Reformation
leader was more consistently practical in his teaching, or more
humble and adoring in his thoughts of God. Yet all serious
Calvin-scholars now know that the Calvin of legend—the slob-
bering ogre, the egoistical fanatic, the doctrinaire misanthrope,
the inhuman dictator with a devilish God—is a figure of fancy,
not of fact.[1] The real Calvin was not like that, nor was his theology the monstrous and mis-shapen thing that the legendary
image would suggest.

Not that all ever accepted this image, or that Calvin ever
lacked partisans. In each century from his day to ours, self-

styled 'Calvinists' have claimed him as their patron. But it would not always be safe to judge of his theology by theirs. The 'five points of Calvinism' formulated at the Synod of Dort—total depravity, unconditional election, particular redemption, irresistible grace (better, effectual calling), and the preservation of the saints—do indeed proclaim the sovereignty of grace in a way Calvin would have endorsed. Four of these 'points' he insisted on himself, and there is little doubt that the Dort formula of particular redemption states what he would have said had he faced the developed Arminian thesis.[2] But other 'Calvinistic' developments have involved a certain shift from Calvin's view of things. Examples are the divine-right Presbyterianism of Beza, Gillespie, and the Westminster Confession; the Puritan treatment of assurance as the main problem of religion; and the scholastic custom of setting the Gospel promise in the context of the double decree, rather than, as in Calvin's definitive (1559) *Institutio* and Paul's epistle to the Romans, vice versa. Whether these developments be seen as the perfecting of Calvinism or the distorting of it, at all events they should not be read back into Calvin himself, any more than the 'Christomonism' of Karl Barth should be, or the 'hyper-Calvinism' classically voiced in old Mr. Ryland's shout from the chair when William Carey mooted a missionary society—'Sit down, young man: when God pleases to convert the heathen He will do it without your aid or mine.' (Calvin, who himself sent out, to an island off Brazil, the first Protestant foreign missionaries in history, would not have approved of that!) If we would know Calvin the theologian, we must do more than study the 'Calvinists'; we must go to the man himself.

The Institutio

THIS prospect, however, appears at first sight somewhat daunting. For Calvin's output was huge. His first theological work (*Psychopannychia*, a refutation of the Anabaptist belief in soul-sleep) was written in 1534, when he was twenty-five. Between then and his death thirty years later, he developed his *Institutio Christianae Religionis* from its original pocket-book size into a folio of eighty chapters and half a million words; wrote commentaries or preached expositions, later published,

151

on all the major books of the Bible;[3] and composed controversial treatises on all the main doctrines of the faith against Romans, Lutherans, and Anabaptists, not to mention Socinus and the heady pantheist Servetus. His works fill fifty-nine thick volumes of the *Corpus Reformatorum*. Nor is there much padding in them; apart from his homiletic and satiric excursions, Calvin's thought moved fast, and his style was accordingly compressed. (He claimed to love brevity!) Confronted with so much material, the student might well quail. Yet two facts make it possible to grasp the substance of Calvin's theology with less labour than might have been expected. The first is his consistency; the second is the comprehensiveness of his *magnum opus*.

His consistency is remarkable. All that he wrote was homogeneous. He never changed his mind on any doctrinal issue. The only alteration in his published views that has been demonstrated to date is that whereas in *Psychopannychia* and the 1536 *Institutio* he ascribed the apocryphal book of Baruch to Baruch, he later concluded it to be pseudonymous.[4] Apart from this detail of criticism—not strictly biblical criticism, at that, and of no theological significance—all his opinions remained identical. 'Though he is of the number of those who grow old learning every day,' wrote Beza towards the end of Calvin's life, 'from the very beginning up to now, in all his many laborious writings, he has never set before the church one dogma about which he needed to alter his mind and part company with himself.'[5] Unlike Luther and Melanchthon, his contemporaries, and Augustine before him and Karl Barth after him, his outlook was fully formed before his literary career began, and though as time went on he was able to amplify and augment, he never needed to correct or retract. Among creative theologians there is hardly a parallel, save, perhaps, on a smaller scale, Athanasius. Thus, any statement of view in any of Calvin's writings, early or late, may be taken as integral to his thought throughout. Those scholars who study particular themes in Calvin cross-sectionally have no need to raise questions of changing opinions from one work to another. No such changes took place. Calvin's theology, first to last, was a great tapestry of biblical strands of thought, masterfully woven, and all of a piece.

The second fact which simplifies the task of grasping Calvin's point of view is the comprehensiveness of the 1559 *Institutio*.

This quality is explained by the book's history. Calvin's *Institutio* (the word means 'principles', 'basic instruction') was first conceived as a vest-pocket-companion for Reformed Christians and an apologia for them against their detractors. The original (1536) edition contained only six chapters, on the Law, the Creed, the Lord's Prayer, the dominical sacraments, the five false sacraments of Rome, and Christian liberty. The first four of these chapters had links with Luther's catechetical writings, and both Calvin and his publishers (Platter and Lasius, of Basle) called the book a catechism, though it was not written in question-and-answer form. For preface, it carried a letter to the French king, Francis I, explaining that Reformed Christians were not, as some supposed, disloyal citizens. Its title, considering its limited size and scope, was, to say the least, grandiloquent: *Basic Instruction* (institutio) *in the Christian Religion, containing virtually the whole sum of godliness* (pietatis) *and all that needs to be known in the doctrine of salvation: a work very well worth reading for all Christians with a zeal for godliness.* It sold out within nine months, and a new edition was called for. Startled, as well as pleased, by its success, and uneasily conscious that it had not been all that its title claimed, Calvin set himself to revise and amplify, and the 1539 *Institutio* was almost three times as long as the first edition. In a new preface, Calvin explained that part of his aim in enlarging it had been, first, to provide a text-book for theological students (apart from Melanchthon's *Loci Communes* and Zwingli's less systematic *Commentarius de Vera et Falsa Religione* none such existed as yet on the Protestant side), and, second, to display the system of thought that would underlie the commentaries he proposed to write. With a clear allusion to the fulsome 'trailer' of the 1536 title-page, Calvin named the enlarged volume *Basic Instruction in the Christian Religion, now at last truly answering to its description* (nunc vere demum suo titulo respondens). The work still sold, and grew through further editions, till Calvin gave it final form in 1559. The 1559 title ran thus: *Basic Instruction in the Christian Religion now first arranged in four books, and divided into particular chapters, according to the fittest method* (ad aptissimam methodum) *and so greatly augmented that it can almost be regarded as a new work.* The *Institutio* was now five times its original length. Its four books were headed: (i) The knowledge of

153

God the Creator; (ii) The knowledge of God the Redeemer in Christ; (iii) The way of coming to know the grace of Christ, and the benefits which thence derive to us, and the effects that follow; (iv) The external means or helps by which God calls us into the fellowship of His Son and keeps us there. The themes of this fourth book were the church, the sacraments, and civil government, all being regarded as means of grace. Thus Calvin's new arrangement (which, interestingly enough, was an almost point-for-point return to that of his first catechetical booklet, the 1537 *Instruction in Faith*) reproduced the order of the main topics in the Apostles' Creed—'I believe (i) in God the Father, maker of heaven and earth; and (ii) in Jesus Christ . . . ; (iii) I believe in the Holy Ghost; (iv) the holy catholic church. . . .' Under these headings Calvin set out a complete statement of Christian truth as he understood it, and a full defence of it against Roman and Anabaptist alternatives.[6]

Calvin's *magnum opus*, therefore, came before the world as a Reformed *summa theologica* and *summa pietatis* in one. Calvin himself saw it as the centre-piece of his life's work. He laboured at the definitive edition of 1559 at a time of extreme bad health, but the prospect of imminent death only spurred him to flog himself harder, in order to complete the task before life ended. He put into it all that he knew. Accordingly, it is supremely from the *Institutio* that we may, and should, take his measure as a theologian. Much is said today of the danger of over-simplifying and over-petrifying Calvin's thought if one reads the *Institutio* in isolation from his commentaries and catechisms, where polemics are not so obtrusive. The point is no doubt valid. Yet the heart of Calvin is in the *Institutio*, more than in any of his other works. The harsh controversial passages, which cause modern readers much offence, are actually essential to its design. Just as the Bible, being the proclamation of God's truth to an intellectually warped world, is necessarily polemical at point after point, so Calvin, as a Christian and a minister, could not but be a fighting man, and the Reformation, as a renewal of biblical faith amid ecclesiastical paganism, could not but be a fighting movement, and the *Institutio*, as a Reformation manifesto and apologia, could not but be a fighting book. John Calvin was a peace-loving person who found controversy a tedious burden, and who worked tirelessly to bring Protestants together, yet
154

any account of him which minimised the intensity of his commitment to the conflict of God's Word with human error, as well as sin, would be an injustice. We may not dismiss Calvin's polemics as mere appendages to his positive teaching, as unnecessary as they were unpleasant. Rather, we must reckon with Calvin's insistence that some notions ought to be fought to the death.

The knowledge of God

THE layout of the 1559 *Institutio* shows us at once its scope and range. As the opening chapter, dating from 1539, explains, it is a treatise on the knowledge of God, and the knowledge of ourselves which is bound up with it. As in Scripture, so in Calvin, 'knowledge of God' is a concept which unifies belief, experience, and conduct. It embraces both the knowing of God, which is religion, and what is known of, or about, God, which is theology. It denotes an apprehension of God, not merely as existing but as being 'for us' in grace, and of ourselves as being 'for Him' in worship and service. 'Properly speaking, we cannot say that God is known where there is no religion or piety.' 'The effect of our knowledge (of God) ought to be, first, to teach us reverence and fear; and, second, to induce us, under its guidance and teaching, to ask every good thing from Him, and, when it is received, to ascribe it to Him.' 'The knowledge of God does not consist in cold (*frigida*) speculation, but carries along with it worship.' 'We are summoned to a knowledge of God which does not just flutter in the brain, satisfied with empty speculation, but to one which will prove firm and fruitful when it is duly grasped by us and takes root in our hearts.'[7]

In making the knowledge of God his central theme, and presenting the reformed faith as a recovery of this knowledge—a truly religious theology, and a truly theological religion—Calvin was picking up Luther's early polemic against the scholastics, mystics, and merit-mongers, who thought to know God without knowing Jesus Christ. With Luther, Calvin insisted that we only know God as we listen to the Scriptures, and learn Christ from the Scriptures. The *Institutio* assumes throughout the basic correlations by which Luther had maintained this thesis. These were as follows. The first was the correlation between

155

revelation and Scripture, in the name of which Luther had attacked transubstantiation, the Mass-sacrifice, meritorious works, purgatory, and current ideas of Papal and conciliar authority, and had anathematised all traditional tenets that lacked biblical support. The second was the correlation between *the Spirit and the Word,* in the name of which Luther had attacked Anabaptist illuminism and anathematised all 'spiritual' teaching that diverged from the written Word, and its witness to Jesus Christ. The third was the correlation between *the Word and faith,* in the name of which Luther had attacked as superstitious all religious attitudes which did not take the form of response to biblical truth and to the Christ of Scripture, the incarnate Son of God who in His humanity and humiliation not merely spoke, but was, God's word of grace to man. The fourth was the correlation between *faith and works,* in the name of which Luther had insisted that there was no true knowledge of God where there was not also active discipleship of Christ— that is, faith spontaneously working in love to God and men, and in obedience to the law. Calvin reproduced all these points.

Three questions may be asked to clarify Calvin's concept of the knowledge of God. First: what does it mean to know God? To this question the *Institutio* replies, in effect, that it means acknowledging Him as Scripture reveals Him, abasing oneself before Him as a sinful creature, learning from His Word the law and the Gospel, believing the promise that He is our reconciled Father through the mediation and blood-shedding of Jesus Christ, rejoicing in the reality of redemption, pardon, and sonship, hoping in the promise of preservation and reward that God makes to all who are Christ's, delighting in the prospect of a joyful resurrection, loving God for all His love and mercy, obeying His law, practising daily self-denial, loving others for His sake and seeking their good, submitting to His providential ordering of things, maintaining dependence on Him by prayer and thanksgiving, and seeking to honour Him in all commerce with the created order and all human relationships. Calvin stresses that this knowledge of God as our God is His gift to us and the work of His Spirit within us, and that it is itself correlative to that union with Christ which is the means of our salvation. 'Christ, when he produces faith in us by the agency of

His Spirit, at the same time ingrafts us into His body, that we may become partakers of all blessings.'[8]

Second, we may ask: what is the intellectual basis of this knowledge—what, in other words, can be known about God by those who know Him? To this question the *Institutio* offers its whole eighty chapters as a reply. They are arranged as a theology of the Gospel, in an order evidently reflecting the structure of the epistle to the Romans, which Calvin, like Luther, regarded as the key to Scripture. Justification by faith stands at the centre of the *Institutio*, spatially as well as theologically; it occupies chapters xi-xviii of Book III. Calvin introduces it in a way which makes plain its central importance. 'We must now discuss justification thoroughly,' he writes, 'bearing in mind that it is *the mainstay for upholding religion*, and so giving it the more care and attention.'[9] Justification is in fact the focal centre of the *Institutio*. What precedes it is a survey of things that must first be known before we can grasp it—namely, that we gain true knowledge of God only from Scripture (I. i-ix); that God is Triune, Creator, and Sovereign, lord of history and disposer of all things (I. x-xviii); that godliness means humble love, reverence, submission, and dependence God-ward (I. ii); that we are by nature guilty, blind, and helpless in sin (II. i-v); that Jesus Christ, the divine-human mediator, has procured salvation for us, and that both Testaments proclaim Him to us (II. vi-xvii); what the law requires (II. viii); what faith is (III. ii); how God gives faith (III. i), and how faith begets repentence (III. iii-v) and a Christian life (III. vi-x). What comes after the section on justification is an account of what more the justified man needs to know to keep his faith in healthy exercise and to serve his God aright—namely, that his freedom from the law is not for lawlessness, but for free obedience (III. xix); that he must always pray (III. xx); that God's free election and gracious sovereignty guarantee his final salvation; that he has a hope of resurrection in glory (III. xxv); that he must wait on the ministry of word and sacrament in the church for his soul's good (IV. i-xix); and that he must be a loyal citizen, inasmuch as civil government exists to protect the church (IV. xx).[10]

The *Institutio*, however, like the epistle to the Romans, is a many-sided book, and no one analysis can do justice to its total thrust. That given in the last paragraph brings out its practical, catechetical framework, but a further review is needed to set Calvin's pastoral concern in the perspective of his basic theocentrism. His concern that men should know grace was rooted in a deeper concern, that men should glorify God. As Christian, pastor, and theologian, Calvin's ruling passion was that God, the source, stay, and end of all things, should receive the glory that was His due. What this meant positively was that men should live their lives in a spirit of adoring worship, conscious of the wonder of all God's work in creation, providence, and grace, bowing to His authority in every sphere of life, and sanctifying the secular by taking His thoughts as the rule of truth, His will as the rule of right, and His approval as the standard of value. What the glorifying of God meant negatively was that men must neither cast off His rule nor intrude into His work. The slogans which served to circumscribe the understanding of Christianity for which Calvin and his fellow-reformers stood— *sola Scriptura; solo Christo; sola fide; sola gratia; soli Deo gloria!*—point to the radical self-denial to which we sinners are at this point called. Knowledge of God as Creator and Redeemer, holy, just, wise, and good, comes to us by Scripture *alone*, not by our own speculation. The benefits of redemption—reconciliation, righteousness, sonship, regeneration, glory—come to us by Christ *alone*, not by any fancied personal merit or any priestly mediation by the church. Christ and reconciliation are received by faith *alone*, not earned by works and effort; and that very faith is given to us and kept alive in us by grace *alone*, so that our own contribution to our salvation is precisely nil, and all the glory for it must therefore go to God *alone*, and none to ourselves. As in the *Institutio* Calvin controverts misconceptions of various kinds—idolatry, anti-Trinitarianism, illuminism, antinomianism, autosoterism, sacerdotalism, the mass-doctrine, Papal supremacy, the finality of conciliar decisions, and so forth —his polemic is constantly spurred forward by the sense that these things dishonour God, and rob Him of His glory and praise.

It is already clear that the focal centre of Calvin's concern with the intellectual structure of the knowledge of God was his anxiety that men should think biblically of Christ, and of grace. Like Luther, he stressed that Christ is the *scopus* of Scripture, the 'goal' to which it all points, and that grace is the uniting theme which binds the two Testaments together. Calvin, indeed, made more of the gracious covenantal basis of Old Testament legislation than ever Luther did. We may pin-point Calvin's aim exactly by saying that he wanted men to know the grace of God in Christ as it is set forth in the epistle to the Romans. And here lies the explanation of some features in his treatment of sin and salvation which are not always rightly understood.

No reader of the *Institutio* can fail to be struck by the intensity of Calvin's stress on the wretchedness of fallen man—corrupt, demented, defiled, beastly, vile, full of rottenness (these are his regular epithets). Why such violent denigration? we ask. We can dismiss the naïve idea that Calvin's natural outlook was so jaundiced as to make all human life appear to him brutish and nasty. Everything we know about Calvin refutes that. Nor are the true reasons for this language far to seek. They are not psychological, but theological. In the first place, writing against a humanistic background—we must remember that he was a child of the Renaissance before he became a son of the Reformation—Calvin wished to convey the sense which Scripture had given him of the tragic quality of the human predicament. Here was the noblest of this world's occupants, a creature made for fellowship with God and given great intellectual and moral potentialities, now spiritually ruined; he had lost his *rectitudo* (uprightness), the image of God in which he was made, and had been banished from God's favour; and yet in this condition he was so perverse as to be proud, and vain-glorious, and self-satisfied! Calvin wished to bring out the tragic folly of the universal human attitude. And then, in the second place, he wished to make men see and feel their own spiritual extemity. He knew that fallen man, just because sin has darkened his mind on moral and spiritual issues, is disinclined to take his fallen state seriously, and he knew too that shallow views of sin are a barrier to true faith. He who thinks himself still good at heart, still free to do good and please God, will trust in his own works for salvation, and never learn to look to Christ as his righteousness. So Calvin laboured the bondage of man to sin, and the vileness of man in sin, in order that his readers might learn to be realistic about themselves, and in self-despair go out of themselves to find peace with God through trusting the blood of Christ. In other words, his motive was to lead men from Romans

1. 18 ff. through to Romans 3. 21 ff. This was not misanthropy, but pastoral evangelism.

The main thrust of Calvin's treatment of salvation in Books II and III of the *Institutio*—a more thorough and systematic treatment than any previous theologian had written—is against the false gospel of synergism and self-help. Fallen men are spiritually helpless, Calvin insists; not only can they not obey God's truth, they cannot even properly understand it in their natural state; and the work of saving them must therefore be God's work entirely. We can sum up his contention thus: *God* (alone) *saves sinners* (however bad) *in and through Jesus Christ*.

God saves *sinners*. Here is the *wonder* of grace. Like Romans, the *Institutio* is dominated by the biblical thought of the judgment-seat of God, and of God Himself as set to judge mankind retributively, giving evidence of personal pleasure or anger (as judges in Bible times were expected to do) according to the desert of the various parties before Him. As in Romans 1–3, the present wrath of the Judge against all sin, and the coming day of reckoning for every man, appear in the *Institutio* as vivid realities, constantly to be kept in view. But if God is set to judge, what hope can any of us have? for we are all sinners. We have hope, says Calvin, because God has freely and undeservedly set His love upon us, and reconciled us to Himself by propitiating His own wrath through the atoning sacrifice of His Son. 'Of His mere good-pleasure He appointed a mediator to purchase salvation for us.' 'Christ . . . was destined to appease the wrath of God by His sacrifice.' Calvin quotes John 3. 16 and I John 4. 10, and comments on the latter as follows: 'There is great force in this word *propitiation*; for in a manner which cannot be expressed (*ineffabili quodam modo*) God, at the very time when He loved us, was hostile to us until reconciled in Christ.'[11] Here is the mystery of God's free grace—a wonder, not to be pried into by speculation, but to be reverently adored.

God saves sinners *through Jesus Christ*—that is, through His cross. Jesus is the *mediator* of grace, the God-man, who took our place before God, bore the penalty of our sins, and by His resurrection conquered death on our behalf. Against the background of his doctrine of judgment, Calvin interpreted the atonement transactionally, in terms of penal substitution. Whereas Anselm

160

had taught satisfaction for sin by, in effect, compensation, Calvin, following Luther, taught satisfaction by substitutionary punishment, the one suffering what the many deserved. Though Calvin stressed the unity of will and affection between the Father and the Son in carrying out the atonement, yet with Luther he held that on the cross Christ 'bore in His soul the dreadful torments of a condemned and lost man',[12] and identified this with His descent into hell. Hasty criticism here will be unwise; Calvin was only seeking to spell out a divine mystery in terms of the biblical witness to it.[13]

God saves sinners *in Jesus Christ*—that is, by uniting them to Him in His risen glory through the secret work of the Holy Spirit. Still following the sequence of Romans, Calvin adds to the thought of Christ *for* us (Romans 3–5) that of Christ *in* us (Romans 6–8). Through our incorporation into Him, to which the sacraments point and the gift of faith is correlative, the benefits which he won for us are conveyed to us. This is the *method* of grace. In Christ we are justified (pardoned and accepted), adopted, given access to our heavenly Father, and progressively changed into Christ's image through self-denial and works of love. In Christ we have our hope of glory.

So God *saves* sinners. First to last, salvation is of the Lord. He who began the work by election, redemption, and the gift of faith, can be trusted to complete it for all believers. Here is the *stability* of grace, and also the point at which knowledge of God's election brings comfort and strength. Why in the *Institutio* did Calvin treat of predestination and election, not in Book I, where he handled divine sovereignty in creation and providence, but late on in Book III, after dealing with the Gospel and the Christian life? The reason seems to be that he wanted the theme to appear in the same evangelical context in which it appears in Romans. There it first enters in 8.29 f., not for any controversial purpose, but to encourage the people of God by assuring them that as their justification and calling sprang from free grace, so God's gracious purpose will stand, and they will be preserved to the end. If God resolved to save them, and gave His Son to that end, before ever they turned to Him, He will certainly not abandon them now that they have turned to Him. This is the 'unspeakable comfort' which the doctrine of election brings in Romans 8.29–38; and it was in order that it might bring the

161

same comfort to his readers that Calvin held it back till he could
set it in an equivalent context in the *Institutio*.

Calvin and Scripture

THE third question to be asked concerning Calvin's view of the
knowledge of God is: by what means is this knowledge brought
to us? Calvin's answer to this question, as we have seen, was: by
Scripture alone. He did not deny that the whole natural order
reveals God (though only as Creator, not as Redeemer), but he
insisted that so far as this revelation is concerned sinful man is
purblind: he may have an inkling that there is something—
or Someone—there, but he cannot 'see' God revealed in creation till he has, as it were, put on the 'spectacles' of Holy
Scripture (it is Calvin's own illustration)[14] and learned of God
from the written Word. Scripture functions as 'spectacles' in
this way by reason of both the content of its teaching and the
ministry of the Spirit in connection with it. Here several questions arise.

   First, how did Calvin regard Holy Scripture? As *Institutio*
I. vi-ix and IV. viii-ix show, his concept of Scripture focused on
two related ideas. The first is *os Dei*, 'the mouth of God'—that
is, God's use of human language to address us. The second is
doctrina, 'teaching'—that is, instruction conveyed by God's
verbal utterances. 'Teaching from the mouth of God', or, more
simply and dynamically, 'God *speaking*'—'God *teaching*'—
'God *preaching*'—this is the essence of Calvin's view of Scripture.
'Whoever wishes to profit in the Scriptures,' he wrote, comment-
ing on II Timothy 3.16, 'let him first of all lay down as a settled
point this—that the law and the prophecies are not teaching
(*doctrinam*) delivered by the will of men, but dictated (*dictatam*)
by the Holy Ghost . . . Moses and the prophets . . . testified, as
was actually the case, that it was the mouth of the Lord that
spoke (*os Domini loquutum esse*) . . . we owe to the Scripture the
same reverence which we owe to God, because it has proceeded
from Him alone, and has nothing of man mixed with it.' Compare these sentences from the *Institutio*:

   The full authority which they [the Scriptures] obtain with the faithful proceeds from no other consideration than that they are per-

suaded that they proceeded from heaven, as if God had been heard giving utterance to them . . . . Clear signs that God is its speaker (*manifesta signa loquentis Dei*) are seen in Scripture, from which it is plain that its teaching (*doctrinam*) is heavenly. . . . Being enlightened by [the Spirit] . . . we are made absolutely certain . . . that [the Scripture] has come to us by the ministry of men from God's very mouth (*ab ipsissimo Dei ore*). The apostles were the certain and authentic amanuenses of the Holy Spirit and therefore their writings are to be received as oracles of God, but others have no other office than to teach what is revealed and deposited in Holy Scripture.[15]

Calvin's thought is clear. The historic phenomenon of prophecy is the paradigm of all Scripture. All of it has the same unique character as did the original 'oracles . . . consigned . . . to public records' (see *Inst.* I. vi. 2) which formed its nucleus. The prophets prefaced their oracles by 'thus saith the Lord', and the words they spoke were words from God: what came from their mouths actually issued from God's mouth, nor did it cease to be God's message when they wrote it down. In Calvin's view all Scripture, whatever its literary character, has the same double authorship: it all consists of words of men which are also words of God, and it is all God's *doctrina*, for our learning.

Calvin's reference to the Holy Spirit 'dictating' Scripture (a frequent phrase with him), and to the apostles as His 'amanuenses', does not, of course, imply anything as to the psychology of inspiration. Warfield, Doumergue, and others have shown that this is simply a theological metaphor conveying the thought that what is written in Scripture bears the same relation to the mind of God which was its source as a letter written by a good secretary bears to the mind of the man who dictated it—a relation, that is, of complete correspondence, and thus of absolute authenticity.[16]

It would have been strange indeed had this concept of Scripture not led Calvin to believe that everything laid down in Scripture is true, or, putting it negatively, inerrant. It is true that he never discussed this question directly; but he had no need to, for it was a matter of general agreement in his day. We cannot, therefore, deduce from his lack of emphasis on the point that he was either unclear about it or indifferent to it. Many since Doumergue have sought to find room in Calvin's thought for the possibility that biblical assertions may err in detail; but the evidence adduced proves the reverse—namely, that there was no such room.

The handful of passages in Calvin's commentaries which have sometimes been treated as admissions that biblical writers were astray in their teaching appear on inspection to fall into the following categories.

(1) Some observe that at certain points God has accommodated Himself to rough-and-ready forms of human speech, and tell us that in these cases God is evidently not concerned to speak with a kind or degree of accuracy beyond what such forms of speech would naturally convey. Thus, Calvin warns us not to expect to learn natural science (he specifies astronomy) from Genesis 1.

(2) Others tell us that by absolute biblical standards particular sentiments of inspired authors are deficient. The sentiments of Psalm 88.5, for instance, are 'apparently harsh and improper', 'unadvised words' which 'the prophet . . . spoke less advisedly than he ought to have done'. But this created no difficulty for Calvin, for he did not regard the psalmist's prayer as didactic in intention. (What prayer, we may ask, ever was?) Calvin defined the Spirit's purpose of instruction in this psalm as, not to teach the doctrine of the after-life, but to give universal expression to the desperate feelings which men in spiritual distress actually have, and so to furnish 'a form of prayer for encouraging all the afflicted who are, as it were, on the brink of despair, to come to Himself'.[17] Calvin would clearly have told us that to equate the Spirit's accommodation to the realities of human experience with false instruction was to fail to take seriously the fact that this was a prayer. It is not the purpose of prayers to give exact definitions of the faith.

(3) Others note that particular texts show signs of scribal error in transmission. Thus, for instance, Calvin tells us that 'by mistake' Jeremiah's name has somehow 'crept in' (*obrepserit*, Calvin's regular word for unauthentic textual intrusions) in Matthew 27.9. There is a similar comment on 'Abraham' and the seventy-five souls in Acts 7.14–16. Elsewhere he writes that no 'reverence' prevents us from opining that 'a wrong number may have crept in from the carelessness of scribes'.[18] He was willing to consider the possibility of mistakes in all extant manuscripts.

(4) Others deal with cases where apostolic writers quote Old Testament texts loosely. Calvin's point in this group of comments is always that the apostles quote paraphrastically in order to bring out the true sense and application—a contention strikingly supported by modern discoveries about the *pesher* quotation-method of New Testament times.

(5) Others deal with a few points of what we might call formal inaccuracy by suggesting that in these cases no assertion was intended, and therefore no error can fairly be said to have been made. One example of this is Calvin's denial that the evangelists meant at every point to write a chronologically accurate narrative. Since on occasion they preferred a topical or theological principle of arrangement, Calvin argues, they cannot be held to contradict each other when they narrate the same events in a different sequence. Another example is Calvin's suggestion that in Acts 7.14 (the seventy-five souls) and Hebrews 9.21 (Jacob's staff) the writer may have chosen to leave the Septuagint's mistranslation uncorrected, rather than risk distracting his readers from the point he was making. In these cases, Calvin implies, to allude to the incidents in the familiar words of the Greek Bible would not involve asserting either that the Septuagint translation was correct or that it expressed the true facts at the point where it parted company with the Hebrew. On neither issue would the New Testament writer himself be asserting anything, and consequently his formal inaccuracy in echoing the substantial inaccuracy of the Septuagint would not amount to error (false assertion) on his part.

Whatever be thought of Calvin's positions in the various passages cited, it seems clear that his basic assumption throughout is that Scripture, rightly interpreted, will not be found to make false assertions. This was the presupposition of all his exegesis. It is also clear that his concept of divine accommodation in Scripture was flexible enough amply to safeguard the full humanity of the inspired writings.

Calvin assumes without discussion that objectively the authority of Holy Scripture, that is, its claim to be believed and obeyed, rests on the fact of its inspiration. 'We owe to the Scripture the same reverence which we owe to God, because it has proceeded from Him alone.' To acknowledge biblical authority is a way of confessing that the teaching of God's prophetic and apostolic spokesmen, and that alone, should rule the mind of His church. The only question in this field that he discusses in detail is of the subjective ground on which our acknowledgment of biblical authority rests. Rejecting both the Roman contention that Scripture is to be received as authoritative on the church's authority, and with it the idea that Scripture could be proved divinely authoritative by rational argument alone, Calvin affirms Scripture to be self-authenticating through the inner witness of the Holy Spirit. What is this 'inner witness'? Not a special quality of experience, nor a new, private revelation, nor an existential 'decision', but a work of enlightenment whereby, through the medium of verbal testimony, the blind eyes of the spirit are opened, and divine realities come to be recognised and embraced for what they are. This recognition, Calvin says, is as immediate and unanalysable as the perceiving of a colour, or a taste, by physical sense—an event about which no more can be said than that when appropriate stimuli were present it happened, and when it had happened we knew it had happened. Through this inward enlightenment we perceive the truth of the deity and mediation of Jesus, as set forth in the Gospel, and receive Him as the Saviour of our souls; and through it we also recognise the divinity of the Scriptures, and receive them as the Word of the speaking God, still spoken to ourselves today. The proof that the 'inner witness' is a reality is that these transforming spiritual certainties really do dawn and abide, even against opposition, in human hearts. Of Christian certainty regarding the Scriptures, Calvin wrote, in words partly quoted already: 'Enlightened by Him (the Spirit), we no longer believe that Scripture is from God either on our own judgment or on that of others; but, in a way that surpasses human judgment, we are made absolutely certain, just as if we beheld there the majesty (*numen*) of God Himself, that it has come to us by the ministry of men from God's very mouth.'[19] 'I say nothing more than every believer experiences in himself,' Calvin adds, 'though my words fall far short of the reality.'

Authentication, as described, is the first part of the Spirit's ministry to the people of God in connection with the Scriptures; *interpretation* is the second. Calvin's approach to biblical interpretation may be summed up as follows. Being as truly human as it is divine, the Bible must be understood literally—that is, in

166

the plain natural sense intended by its human writers. It is by getting into their minds that we get into the mind of God. But to get into their minds requires more than skill in grammar and logic and cultural forms; it requires some acquaintance with the God of whom they spoke, the spiritual realities with which they dealt, and the Christ to whom, in one way or another, their witness relates. This the Spirit alone can give. Moreover, when we have grasped the meaning of each passage for its author and first readers, we still have to ask what application it has to ourselves and our own situation, and what effect God means it to have on us here and now. Here, again, it is only the interpreting Spirit who enables us to discern the application, and thus effectively to learn God's will from His Word.

By this means, according to Calvin, the private reading and public exposition of inspired Scripture, through the attendant ministry of the Holy Spirit, conveys knowledge of God to sinful men.

Calvin's theological stature

CALVIN'S theological achievement was not to innovate, but to integrate. His mind, though independent, was not original; nor in any case was originality his aim. As a second-generation reformer, his object was to conserve and confirm the gains of his predecessors, Luther and Bucer (whom he admired greatly), Melanchthon (whom he valued as a friend rather than a mentor), and Zwingli (whom privately, however, he regarded as rather second-rate).[20] 'The system of doctrine taught by Calvin is just the Augustinianism common to the whole body of the Reformers,' wrote Warfield. 'And this Augustinianism is taught by him . . . fundamentally as he learned it from Luther, whose fertile conceptions he completely assimilated, and most directly from Martin Bucer, into whose practical, ethical point of view he perfectly entered. Many of the forms of statement most characteristic of Calvin—on such topics as predestination, faith, the stages of salvation, the church, the sacraments—only reproduce, though of course with that clearness and religious depth peculiar to Calvin, the precise teachings of Bucer, who was above all others, accordingly, Calvin's master in theology.'[21] But Calvin was able repeatedly to synthesise the ideas of his predecessors, and draw out their implications, with a systematic precision which in the world of Reformation theology was entirely new, and proved extraordinarily fruitful. It was no accident that the *Institutio* became the fountain-head of a great theological tradition. The major clarifications which Calvin achieved were perhaps the following.

He was the first to display the unity of the work of Christ under the rubric of His threefold office, as prophet, priest, and king. Earlier theologians from Eusebius on had mentioned these offices, sometimes all three together, but (in Calvin's view) 'frigidly and with no great profit, due to ignorance of what each title comprehends'.[22] Luther had made some use of the thought of Christ as priest and as king, but it was left to Calvin to see that the third office must be added to show the full range of Christ's mediatorial ministry. All the Reformers had insisted that I am saved, not by my own works, nor by what the Church does for me, but by Christ alone. But it was Calvin who first perceived that the best and most biblical way to make this point was to present Christ as *prophet*, teaching His people by His word and Spirit; *priest*, securing their salvation by His blood-shedding and intercession; and *king*, ruling not them only, but all creation for their sake; thus, by His threefold ministry, compassing their whole salvation.

Also, Calvin was the first to offer a unified account of the work of the Holy Spirit. Warfield hails him as 'the theologian of the Holy Spirit', and regards this as his foremost contribution.

> In the same sense in which we may say that the doctrine of sin and grace dates from Augustine, the doctrine of satisfaction from Anselm, the doctrine of justification by faith from Luther—we must say that the doctrine of the work of the Holy Spirit is a gift from Calvin to the Church. It was he who first related the whole experience of salvation specifically to the working of the Holy Spirit, worked it out into its details, and contemplated its several steps and stages in orderly progress as the product of the Holy Spirit's specific work in applying salvation to the soul. . . . What Calvin did was, specifically, to replace the doctrine of the Church as sole source of assured knowledge of God and sole institute of salvation, by the Holy Spirit. Previously, men had looked to the Church for all the trustworthy knowledge of God obtainable, as well as for all the communications of grace accessible. Calvin taught them that neither function had been committed to the Church, but

God the Holy Spirit had retained both in His own hands and confers both knowledge of God and communion with God on whom He will. The *Institutes* is, accordingly, just a treatise on the work of God the Holy Spirit in making God savingly known to sinful man. . . . Therefore it opens with the great doctrine of the *testimonium Spiritus Sancti*— . . . that the only vital and vitalizing knowledge of God which a sinner can attain, is communicated to him through the inner working of the Spirit of God in his heart. . . . And therefore it centres in the great doctrine of Regeneration—the term is broad enough in Calvin to cover the whole process of the subjective recovery of man to God—in which he teaches that the only power which can ever awaken in a sinful heart the motions of a living faith, is the power of the same Spirit of God moving with a truly creative operation on the deadened soul.[23]

This testimony, provided it be read Christocentrically (in terms, that is, of the fact that the Holy Spirit is Christ's Spirit, sent by Him to bear witness of Him and unite men to Him), is true. Luther had at least adumbrated all the main points in Calvin's statement (those who doubt this should read Regin Prenter's *Spiritus Creator*), but it was Calvin who welded Luther's insights into a whole and clarified their polemical thrust against the many-sided Roman claim that the church is the object and ground of faith—a claim which, at each point where it emerged, offered, as Calvin said, 'great insult to the Holy Ghost'.[24]

Again, Calvin was the first to bring out the Trinitarian character of the work of salvation, which Paul's epistles and John's Gospel make so plain. On the basis of a sharp insistence on the full co-equality of the three Persons in the Godhead—an insistence which Warfield thought epoch-making in itself[25]—Calvin displays the saving of sinners as a single complex divine work in which all three Persons share, the Father choosing men to save and His Son to save them, the Son doing the Father's will in redeeming them, and the Spirit executing the will of both Father and Son in renewing them. This organic character of God's saving work was stressed more strongly and polemically by Calvin's successors in the Arminian controversy, but it is already explicit in Calvin's soteriology in *Institutio* II and III, which inspired the later development.

Then, too, Calvin brought clarity to the Protestant understanding of the Lord's Supper, which had become clouded

169

through the Lutheran-Zwinglian debates. Calvin thought that both Luther and Zwingli had argued lop-sidedly. Luther had held that the eucharistic bread actually contains Christ's body, thus seeming to identify our receiving of Christ at the Supper with the act of eating—one of Rome's mistakes. Zwingli had insisted that Christ's body, now glorified, is in heaven, not in the bread, and the eucharist is primarily a memorial of His death; thus seeming to imply that we do not receive Christ in His Supper at all. Calvin agreed that Christ's glorified body, being in heaven, is not physically and substantially in the sacramental elements, but maintained that in the Supper Christ, by His 'virtue'—that is, the Holy Spirit—communicates His 'flesh'— that is, Himself, in the unity of His divine-human person and the power of His atonement—to all who receive the outward signs with faith in Him whom they signify. By his method of integrating the idea of sacramental communion into the more basic concept of faith-union with Christ through Word and Spirit, Calvin blazed the trail later followed by Cranmer and Peter Martyr, and established among non-Lutheran Protestants lines of thought which have controlled their eucharistic theology ever since. Much work remains to be done on the eucharistic teaching of the Reformation, but it is unlikely that Calvin's pre-eminence in this field will be seriously challenged.

Calvin also clarified the idea of the church as a self-governing body, subject directly to Christ through His Word. Luther and Zwingli had been content, in effect, to reverse the medieval subordination of the state to the church; having defined the church as a company of believers, inwardly ruled by Christ, they had left the regulating of its outward life to the civil government. Calvin, by contrast, stressed that the church must fix its faith, order its life, and administer its discipline (with Bucer, Calvin held church discipline to be part of the cure of souls), through its own appointed officers. Magistrates, Calvin held, were not called of God to rule the church, but rather to maintain the church's right to rule itself. Of the way this principle kept the Reformed churches from falling prey to Erastianism, and of its later influence, both within and outside Presbyterianism, up to modern times, it is needless to speak.

Moreover, Calvin wrote what was in effect the first-ever theological study of the Christian life, the little treatise in *Institutio*
170

III. vi-x. 'These chapters', writes Schmidt, 'have had an influence on men of the Reformed faith more living, direct, and lasting than any other part of Calvin's writings.'[26] They view the life of the Christian pilgrim in terms of God's call (to holiness and good works) and God's ways (of discipline, through providential pressures). The main themes developed are self-denial, cross-bearing, 'meditation on the life to come' (the practice of hope— Quistorp calls Calvin 'the theologian of hope'),[27] the right use of earthly pleasures, and the serving of God in secular vocations. Schmidt characterises Calvin's ideal as 'an austere and moderate asceticism, tempered by an underlying humanism'—'mortified cheerfulness'.[28] These chapters, with the rest of the material on the doctrine and life of faith which *Institutio* III contains, became the fountain-head of the massive and in many ways classical developments in the fields of ethics and sanctification which occupied Reformed theologians, particularly English-speaking ones, for a century after Calvin's death.

As for the doctrine of predestination, where Calvin is supposed to have surpassed his fellow-Reformers in boldness of speculation, the unexpected truth is that he stated it more cautiously, biblically, and devotionally, than either Luther or Zwingli had done—or, at any rate, had consistently done. All three (and all their colleagues with them till the later period of Melanchthon) followed in Augustine's footsteps and maintained in some form double predestination (to life, and to condemnation). But Zwingli handled the theme speculatively, and Luther paradoxically, and it was left to Calvin to treat it in a consistently scriptural and pastoral way. His vigour of assertion and debate on this issue must not blind us to the essential sobriety of his exposition. As we have already hinted, Calvin taught the *decretum horribile* (the adjective means 'awesome' not 'repulsive') for the purpose for which, as he believed, God had revealed it—namely, to gladden and strengthen the Christian, and with that to humble the proud and alarm the self-reliant, in order to bring them through self-despair to faith in Christ. Predestination, the eternal purpose of God concerning grace, is not, as used to be thought, the focal theme of Calvin's theology; rather, it is the undergirding of the Gospel, the ultimate explanation of why the Son of God became by incarnation Jesus the Christ, and whence it is that some who hear the Word come to faith, and how it is that Christians have a sure hope of heaven. Predestination, as Calvin treats it, is merely a spelling out of the basic thesis about God in the epistle to the Romans, that 'in Him, and through Him, and to Him, are all things: to whom be glory for ever. Amen.' We only understand Calvin's predestinarianism when we see its evangelical significance and motivation, as finally establishing the *sola gratia* and thus compelling the *soli Deo gloria*.

Consistency

THE main aim of this chapter has been, not so much to catalogue Calvin's tenets as to point out the structural principles of his thought. For Calvinism must be understood as a way of thinking before it can be effectively estimated as a set of beliefs. Calvin, who did not distinguish the theologian's task from the preacher's, composed his *Institutio* in the same way that he prepared his sermons—namely, by disciplining himself to echo and apply what he found taught in the inspired Scriptures, and to exclude all lines of thought which, however attractive otherwise, lacked biblical sanction. To him, the *doctrina* of the Bible was the self-testimony of God, the Word of the Creator delineating Himself to sinful men as their Redeemer through Jesus Christ, and teaching them how to acknowledge and serve Him in His dual capacity. The *Institutio*, which sets out and safeguards this knowledge, should accordingly be read as a vast expository sermon with the whole Bible as its text, a systematic confession of divine mysteries learned from God's own mouth. Its analytical structure, its sustained theocentrism, and its leading themes—the unacknowledged majesty of the Creator; God's judgment-seat; the shame of sin; the quenching of God's wrath by the blood of Christ; the knowledge of God in Christ as a reconciled Father; the life of faith as the work in us of the Holy Spirit; the believer's hardships and hopes; predestination as guaranteeing glory; the church as the ministering fellowship of elect believers; the state as a servant of God; the unity of both Testaments in their witness to Christ—are sufficiently accounted for by reference to Calvin's key to Scripture, the epistle to the Romans. The Calvin-critic's first task is to grasp Calvin's theological method, and to learn to see his tenets as its products.

172

Failing this, our praise and blame of Calvin will inform men, not about him, but merely about ourselves. It is good that this century should be seeing the emergence of a better Calvin-criticism than that which, by its use of irrelevant non-theological criteria, has for so long obscured the true stature of 'the theologian'.

Such then, was Melanchthon's friend, 'the theologian'. Bible-centred in his method, God-centred in his outlook, Christ-centred in his message, he was controlled throughout by a vision of God on the throne and a passion that God should be glorified. His theological aim in the last analysis was to declare his vision, as he had received it from the Scriptures, in order that God might receive praise thereby. Warfield wrote:

> The Calvinist is the man who has seen God, and who, having seen God in His glory, is filled on the one hand, with a sense of his own unworthiness to stand in God's sight as a creature, and much more as a sinner, and on the other hand, with adoring wonder that nevertheless this is a God who receives sinners. He who believes in God without reserve and is determined that God shall be God to him, in all his thinking, feeling, willing—in the entire compass of his life activities, intellectual, moral, spiritual— . . . is . . . a Calvinist. . . . The Calvinist is the man who sees God behind all phenomena, and in all that occurs recognises the hand of God . . . ; who makes the attitude of the soul to God in prayer the permanent attitude. . .; and who casts himself on the grace of God alone, excluding every trace of dependence on self from the whole work of his salvation.[29]

Such a Calvinist was John Calvin. He lived as he preached and wrote, for the glory of God. Good theologians are not always good men, nor vice versa, but Calvin's life and theology were all of a piece. Consistency was his hallmark, both as a thinker and as a man.

NOTES

1. Modern books which show this include T. H. L. Parker, *Portrait of Calvin*, London, 1954; J. Cadier, *The Man God Mastered*, London, 1960; A-M. Schmidt, *Calvin and the Calvinistic Tradition*, London, 1960; F. Wendel, *Calvin*, London, 1963; Doumergue's *Jean Calvin* was the pioneer work rehabilitating Calvin; it remains indispensable for the serious student.

JOHN CALVIN

2. On the grounds of this judgment, see W. Cunningham, *The Reformers and the Theology of the Reformation*, Edinburgh, 1862, pp. 395–402. This is not, however, to say that he would have acquitted of the charge of speculation the developed supralapsarian scheme against which Arminianism was a reaction, and on the basis of which the Synod of Dort conducted its deliberations. Wendel notes (*op. cit.*, p. 129) that in Calvin redemption is 'logically subordinated' to election: he suggests that this shows dependence on Scotus, but since Calvin never makes Scotus' nominalist point, that Christ's sacrifice has no value other than that which God chooses to set on it, this must be held doubtful.

3. Only the Solomonic writings, Judges, Ruth, Kings, Chronicles, Ezra, Nehemiah, Revelation (which Calvin professed not to understand), and II and III John, were omitted. Calvin preached through Judges in 1561 and Kings in 1563–1564, but the sermons have not survived. See T. H. L. Parker, *The Oracles of God*, London, 1947, pp. 162, 164.

4. B. B. Warfield, *Calvin and Calvinism*, New York, 1931, p. 389, n. 21.

5. Beza, *Abstersio Calumniarum*, p. 263.

6. On the growth of the *Institutio* from the first edition to its final form, see Wendel, *Calvin*, pp. 112 ff.; Warfield, *op. cit.*, pp. 373 ff.

7. *Inst.* I. ii. 1; I. ii. 2; I. xii. 2; I. v. 9.

8. *Inst.* III. ii. 35.

9. *Inst.* III. xi. 1; my italics.

10. The practical bearing of each of these topics on Christian living is indicated in the paragraphs which introduce them: cf. *Inst.* III. xix. 1, xx. 1–2, xxi. 1, xxv. 1, IV. i. 1, xiv. 1, xx. 1.

11. *Inst.* II. xvii. 1, 2. Cf. Inst. II. xvi. 4: 'in a wondrous divine way He loved us even when He hated us'.

12. *Inst.* II. xvi. 10.

13. For a full analysis of Calvin on the atonement, see P. van Buren, *Christ in our Place: the substitutionary character of Calvin's doctrine of reconciliation*, Edinburgh, 1957.

14. *Inst.* I. vi. 1. Chapters iii–vi deal with this whole subject.

15. *Inst.* I. vii. 1, 4, 5, IV. viii. 9. Scripture is an 'official record (*consignatio:* almost, "affidavit") of heavenly *doctrine*' (*Inst.* I. vi. 3).

16. Cf. Warfield, *Calvin and Augustine*, Philadelphia, 1956, pp. 62 ff.; Doumergue, III. 725, IV. 73 ff.; R. E. Davies, *The Problem of Authority in the Continental Reformers*, London, 1946, pp. 114 ff.; E. A. Dowey, *The Knowledge of God in Calvin's Theology*, New York, 1952, pp. 101 ff.; K. S. Kantzer, 'Calvin and the Holy Scriptures', in *Inspiration and Interpretation*, Grand Rapids, 1957, pp. 137 ff. There is a valuable review of evidence, and of scholars' readings of it, in J. K. S. Reid, *The Authority of Scripture*, London, 1957, pp. 29–55. Reid would apparently regard our view of Calvin's teaching on the Bible as an oversimplification. But his argument that because Calvin did not identify the Spirit with the Word, or Christ with the Scriptures, therefore he did not accept 'the theory of verbal inspiration' (pp. 48, 54) gives the latter phrase a decidedly Pickwickian (Barthian!) sense.

17. *Commentary on the Psalms* (CTS III. 410 f., 407). Calvin comments

similarly on Psalm 39.13: 'he errs . . . his mind was so affected with the bitterness of his grief that he could not present a prayer pure and well seasoned with the sweetness of faith . . . he could not lift up his heart with so much cheerfulness as it behoved him . . . the desires of the flesh . . . forced him to exceed the proper limits in his grief' (*Commentary* . . . , II. 88).

18. *Harmony of the Pentateuch* (CTS II. 304).

19. *Inst.* I. vii. 5; see the whole chapter.

20. Wendel, p. 136.

21. Warfield, *Calvin and Augustine*, p. 22. On the details of Calvin's debt to Bucer, which Warfield, writing in 1909, perhaps slightly exaggerated, see Wendel, pp. 137–144. On Calvin's debt to Luther, Wendel quotes A. Lang and J. Koestlin. Lang wrote: 'In the first edition of the *Institutes* [Calvin] seems almost to be a Lutheran of southern Germany. But afterwards too, Calvin was entirely in agreement with Luther with regard to all the fundamental doctrines bearing upon justification, upon the total perversion of sinful man, upon sinning and original sin, upon Christ the unique Saviour and mediator, upon the appropriation of salvation through the Holy Spirit, the Word and the sacraments. We have even authority to claim that the central teaching of Luther on the justification of faith and regeneration by faith was preserved more faithfully and expressed more forcibly by Calvin than by any other dogmatician of the Reform.' Koestlin wrote: 'In the developments (in the 1536 *Institutio*) concerning the Christ who made himself wholly one of us, who overcame death, who interceded for us with his whole person and his entire work, by his obedience and by the fact that he took his (?) sins upon himself, one perceives an intimate relatedness to Luther . . . Upon the subject of predestination, one would discover nothing that Luther might not have written at the epoch' (Wendel, p. 133). One could also add that Calvin reproduced Luther's teaching on the threefold use of the law, and his distinction between spiritual and temporal government (inward, by Christ, in the conscience, and outward by the magistrate), and also that, like Luther, and unlike Zwingli, Calvin would not justify active resistance to the civil power.

22. *Inst.* II. xv. 1. For the history of the three-office formula before Calvin, see J. F. Jansen, *Calvin's Doctrine of the Work of Christ*, London, 1956, pp. 23 ff.

23. Warfield, *Calvin and Augustine*, pp. 485 f.

24. *Inst.* I. vii. 1.

25. See 'Calvin's Doctrine of the Trinity', *op. cit.*, pp. 189 ff.

26. Schmidt, *Calvin* . . . , p. 115.

27. H. Quistorp, *Calvin's Doctrine of the Last Things*, London, 1955, p. 15.

28. Schmidt, *loc. cit.*

29. Warfield, *op. cit.*, pp. 491 f.

9 Calvin the Biblical Expositor

T. H. L. Parker

ONE OF THE MOST VALUABLE early reviews of Calvin's work is to be read in the Ecclesiastical Polity of Richard Hooker (Preface, ch. ii.8). On his writings he says: 'Two things of principal moment there are which have deservedly procured him honour throughout the world: the one his exceeding pains in composing the *Institutions of the Christian religion*; the other his no less industrious travails for exposition of holy Scripture according unto the same Institutions.' This is a judicious assessment and may serve us as a text throughout our essay. For we may need the help of Hooker in persuading the reader that Calvin the expositor is as important and worthy to be studied as Calvin the dogmatician and that his commentaries are as authoritative for the understanding of his theology as the *Institutio*. Not every scholar would agree with our judgment. The learned Dr. Luchesius Smits, for example, has no qualms in introducing his book with the blatant sentence: '*Calvin fut l'homme d'un seul livre.*'[1] He justifies his assertion by saying that in this early writing Calvin gave a summary of Reformed teaching, that he went on correcting and enriching it all his life and that it represents one of the most remarkable of all Protestant syntheses of theology. His is an extreme view. Very few scholars would care to crawl so far along the limb. But the fact that many books have been written on the *Institutio* but none on the Commentaries[2] shows that in practice the 'one book' has been regarded as infinitely more important, that the *Institutio* is definitive and the Commentaries at most illustrative of Calvin's thought, in brief, that the *Institutio* was Calvin's life-work, the Commentaries merely incidental.

176

It is not the purpose of this essay to minimise the *Institutio*—an exercise as obviously ridiculous as Smits' isolating of it. Nor do we wish to overpraise the Commentaries as the only part of Calvin's work worthy of attention. But the Commentaries are, as Richard Hooker perceived, an integral part of Calvin's theological activity. Take them away and we are left, not merely with a poorer and weaker Calvin, but with something that is not Calvin at all. We may be bolder and say that Calvin saw himself primarily, not as a systematic but a biblical theologian. Moreover, once we accept this view, it is clear that we have confirmation from his career. However, the case remains to be proved.

Biblical expositor

WE will begin by establishing that Calvin regarded himself primarily as a biblical expositor. He does not often allow us into the deeper places of his mind and will, at any rate respecting particularities; but there is a passage in his dedicatory epistle of the Catholic Epistles to Edward VI of England where he quite specifically states his aims. Most of the dedication has consisted of an attack on the Council of Trent, by then well established in its course. The basis of the errors of Rome he regards as a refusal of the Scriptures; the teaching of their church is their criterion, they only pretend to revere Scripture. It is therefore necessary that scholars should do all they can to remove the erroneous glosses that obscure Scripture and to 're-store its brightness'. One scholar, at least, will devote his life to this work; 'I have determined to give the rest of my life, however much may still remain to me, chiefly to this study, if I can find leisure and freedom for it. The first fruit of this work, the church to which I am committed shall receive, that it may last the longer. For although I have little time left after carrying out my duties, I have determined to give it, however short it may be, to this kind of writing.'[3] These duties to which he refers were primarily his daily work as a minister in Geneva.

The quotation we have given needs no elaboration or further explanation. It establishes certainly what Calvin intended to make his main work from 1551 onwards. The objection might be raised that this represents a new departure in his purpose.

But the dedicatory preface to the 1539 *Institutio* also shows that Calvin had set out on this course by then. He promises not only the commentary on Romans, which he was now writing or had perhaps finished, but also forecasts commentaries in the plural. 'And so I have, as it were, paved the way, and if I shall hereafter publish any commentaries on Scripture, I shall always condense them. . . . The Commentary on the Epistle to the Romans will furnish an example of my intention.'[4] The doubt implied by 'if I shall' is explained by the French translation: 'If hereafter our Lord gives me means and opportunity to compose some commentaries.'[5] This is equivalent to the doubt in the preface to the Catholic Epistles: 'If I can find leisure and freedom for it.' Given the time and opportunity he will write commentaries.

His first commentary appeared in 1540, when he was thirty-one years old. This seems, at first sight, rather late for the man who had published his earliest book eight years before and who already had the first edition of the *Institutio* and some shorter treatises to his credit. It was, moreover, six years before he published another commentary (excepting the little expositions of Jude in 1542 and of I and II Peter in French in 1545). But in fact his biblical work was not an inspiration of 1538 or 1539 but must be pushed back still further. Already in 1535 he was asked to revise Olivétan's French Bible. Robert Olivétan, Calvin's cousin,[6] was commissioned by the Waldensian Church to translate the Bible into French. This appeared in 1535 with a Latin preface by Calvin. That he had no part in the translation, however, E. Reuss (one of the editors of *Corpus Reformatorum*) wrote an essay to prove,[7] and apparently with success. It must be pointed out, though, that his case rests to no small degree on the dating of a letter in September 1535 instead of 1534. If Reuss should perhaps have been mistaken (and it may be time his essay was re-examined), then, in spite of other problems that still remain, Calvin helped in the translation of the first edition. But if Reuss is right, it is the second edition that he worked on (though his revisions were not necessarily used).

The letter in question shows Calvin already engaged in responsible biblical scholarship in 1535. (We cannot accept Reuss's explanation that he was asked to help because he was known to be a good classical scholar. It is far more probable that he was asked because he was known to be a good biblical scholar.) We give the letter in our own translation, as it is somewhat mangled in the Edinburgh edition:

> When our Olivétan had told me in the letter he wrote about the time he left that he had postponed his intended publication of the New Testament, I saw that I could make my promised revision at my leisure and keep it also until another time. Meanwhile I gave myself to other studies and thought no more about it, or rather, sank into my usual laziness. As yet, I have hardly started work on it. And in any case the volume that I used for the collation has not yet been put together (*concinnatum est*), although it was brought three months ago. This has not happened through my indifference, but partly through the slackness of the binder (even though we have visited him every day), and partly because when it was first brought to me, six sheets were missing which could not be immediately supplied. But from now on I shall set aside an hour a day for the work. And if I accumulate any criticisms, I will send them only to you—unless, of course, Olivétan should return first.'[8]

Moreover, although the commentary on Romans was not published until 1540 and was written sometime before the date of the dedication, 18 October 1539, this same dedication tells us that Calvin had at least been intending to attempt a commentary and had been pondering the problems of methods since 1536. From February 1535 until early in 1536 Calvin lived in Basle and became intimate with many of the scholarly Reformers there—Münster the Hebraist, Capito, Simon Grynaeus the friend of Erasmus. It is to Grynaeus that he dedicates Romans: 'I remember that three years ago we were discussing between ourselves the best way of interpreting Scripture. What pleased you the most seemed best to me too; for we both felt that the chief virtue of an expositor lay in clear brevity.'[9] Nevertheless, he was deterred from taking up this formidable task by the thought of how many commentaries had been written, not only by the early fathers but even in his own day. To name no others, Melanchthon, Bullinger, and Bucer had written on Romans; what remained to be said? How could he write anything fresh? Would it not be regarded as arrogance to enter into competition with them, and especially with Bucer? He was therefore undecided for a time whether he would not be doing more good if he were to publish selections from these great men for readers

179

who were too busy to read the originals (for it has to be conceded that, good as they were, their writings were too prolix—again, especially Bucer). He seems to have had in mind a sort of up-to-date *Glossa ordinaria*. 'I hesitated for some time whether to gather some gleanings following them and others which I judged would help those who were not scholars (*mediocria ingenia*), or whether to compose a full commentary (*perpetuum commentarium*).'[10] The fact that they differed among themselves at last decided him to write his *perpetuum commentarium*.

It was impossible to start work yet, however, even had his mind been clear. There was *Psychopannychia* to revise drastically, after it had been strongly criticised by Capito; the first edition of the *Institutio* was being finished and printed; there followed the visit to Italy, the weeks in France to clear up family business, and then for two years the torture chamber of Geneva when his writing as good as went by the board.

Exile from Geneva in 1538 and sojourn in congenial Strasbourg gave him the opportunity to start again where he had left off. He not only wrote the commentary on Romans but enlarged his purpose to take in all the Pauline epistles. He was at this time extremely poor and seems to have been in some disorder in his affairs. The Basle printer, Wendelin Rihel, came to his help both with a generous gift or loan and by straightening out the whole business. Whether this help was given on condition that Calvin published with him or whether, as is more probable, it was gratuitous and laid him simply under a moral obligation, is not clear. But he certainly felt himself bound, not only to publish Romans with him, but also to offer him later commentaries. He wrote to Farel in 1546: 'I have now set myself in earnest to the Epistle to the Galatians. I am not free in the matter of publication, so far at least as the epistles of Paul are concerned.' He then recounts his debt to Rihel and repeats: 'I am therefore now not at liberty to refuse him the epistles.'[11] In the event, Rihel printed only I Corinthians and that he seems to have kept by him for a long time: 'If the war had not given the printing presses a holiday,' writes Calvin to M. de Falais in November of the same year, 'I would have sent Wendelin my Galatians; but Corinthians lies quiet in his desk and there is no need for me to hurry.'[12] It was more convenient for Calvin to use one of the Geneva printers and it was of course a disadvantage for him that
180

Rihel possessed no Hebrew type[13] (this, no doubt, is the reason why Calvin uses no Hebrew words in the first edition of Romans). When, therefore, the partnership lapsed, all his commentaries were printed in Geneva.

That Calvin early determined to write commentaries on the whole Pauline Corpus (including Hebrews, whose Pauline authorship he denied as a scholar but accepted as a churchman) is confirmed both by the speed with which he brought them out and by some internal evidence. The gap of six years between Romans and I Corinthians may be explained partly by his renewed distractions in Geneva, partly by Rihel's slowness in publishing it. It is clear from the passages in the letters to M. de Falais and Farel that by November 1546 both epistles to the Corinthians were off his hands and he was already working on Galatians (or the Galatians group), which, indeed, he could have finished had there been need. It is reasonable to assume, therefore, that the Corinthians commentaries were written in 1545 or earlier. He had finished the Galatians group before February 1548 and it was published that year, as also were the commentaries on I and II Timothy. In 1549 followed Hebrews and Titus, and when the Corpus had been completed with I and II Thessalonians in 1551 (though written before February 1550), the collected edition, revised only slightly for the later epistles but considerably for Romans, was published in 1551. The first part of the task he had set himself was now completed and he had already started on other parts of the Bible.

The internal evidence is more scanty but no less conclusive. Calvin often refers back to earlier commentaries, advising the reader to look up what he has written in Romans or Galatians or elsewhere. This he does, of course, to avoid prolixity and repetition, though it also has the effect of unifying the commentaries. What is more remarkable is that he very occasionally refers forward to commentaries not yet written. Thus, writing at the very latest in 1546 but, as we have seen, probably some time before, he promises in I Corinthians to deal with the word *testamentum* when he comes to write on Hebrews, which still lay at least three years ahead: 'On the word *testamentum* we shall speak, if the Lord allows us time, in the Epistle to the Hebrews.'[14] Similarly, earlier in I Corinthians he defers the treatment of the proverb about leaven until he writes Galatians: 'I said, "In this

G

passage", because Paul uses it elsewhere in a different sense, as we shall see.'[15]

Theologian and commentator

ENOUGH has now been said to establish the truth behind Hooker's statement. Calvin is not just a dogmatic theologian who also wrote commentaries; his genuine life's work consisted of these two equal activities, dogmatic theology and exposition of Scripture. But it would be more true to say that they are not two separate activities but are related and connected as the two parts of one activity. On the one hand, his biblical work exercised a great influence on the *Institutio*. As fresh editions appeared, it is possible to see how in the meantime his thought has been moulded by the closer study of this or that book of the Bible. It would probably also appear from a comparison of the commentaries how they in their turn had been enriched by the deeper meditation demanded by revisions of the *Institutio*. But all this still considers the *Institutio* and the commentaries as two separate activities. Such a view is contrary to Calvin's declared intention in his preface to the *Institutio*, written first in 1539. Here he not only says that he writes so as to open up the understanding of Scripture, but expressly connects the *Institutio* with his commentaries and in particular with that on Romans, to be published the following year. Warned by the fearful lengthiness of Bucer, which was partly caused by his introducing full-scale dogmatic discussions into the body of his work, Calvin saw that these *loci communes* could stand on their own in a book which would be a companion to the commentaries while they also would be a companion to it.

It has been my purpose in this labour so to prepare and train aspirants[16] after sacred theology for the reading of the divine Word that they may have an easy entrance into it and then go on in it without stumbling. For I think I have so embraced the sum of religion in all its parts and arranged it in order, that if anyone rightly grasps it, he will have no difficulty in determining both what he ought especially to seek in Scripture and to what aim he should refer everything in it. And so I have, as it were, paved the way, and if I shall hereafter publish any commentaries on Scripture I shall always condense them, for I shall have no need to undertake lengthy discussions on doctrines and digress with *loci communes*. In this way the reader will be spared great trouble and boredom, provided he approaches them[17] fore-armed with a knowledge of the present work, as a necessary tool. But because the commentary on the Epistle to the Romans will furnish an example of this intention,[18] I prefer to let the thing itself show rather than forecast it with words.[19]

It only remains to trace the course of his later work on the Bible. The collected edition of the Pauline epistles and Hebrews came out, as we saw earlier, in 1551. This had been preceded by the first edition of Isaiah in 1549 and the Catholic epistles in 1551. The rest of his life was given up to finishing the New Testament and making inroads on the Old. It will be more convenient to treat them separately. Acts was published in two parts, 1552 and 1554. In the intervening year came St. John's Gospel; and the New Testament commentaries were concluded with the Harmony of the Synoptic Gospels in 1555. But 1556 and 1557 saw two revisions of the complete epistles, in 1560 he revised Acts and undertook a certain revision of them all in 1562. No commentaries exist on II and III John or Revelation. There have been suggestions that Calvin did in fact write on Revelation and that it has been completely lost. Indeed, John Bale, the English Reformer expressly ascribes a commentary to him. He gives a long list of past and present commentators and for his contemporaries, names Luther, Sebastian Meyer, Georgius Aemilius, Francis Lambert, Zwingli, Brenz, Calvin, and Melchior Hofman.[20] Against this it must be said that Bale identifies some of these works in the customary way of quoting the first words, and, he says, 'I have seen almost so many as have their beginnings here registered'.[21] Calvin is not so signalised. We assume, therefore, that he was writing merely from hearsay. There is, in the *Bibliothèque publique et universitaire* at Geneva an anonymous commentary which the catalogue ascribed to Calvin: *Familiere et briefve exposition sur l'Apocalypse de Sainct Jehan l'apostre*. Geneva. Jehan Gerard. 1539. 8⁰. It is most improbable that Calvin is the author; indeed, only the accident that it is bound in one volume with his *Exposition sur l'epistre de Sainct Judas* (1542) connects him with it.

The first Old Testament commentary, Isaiah, appeared in 1551, before he had completed his New Testament work. Three years passed before Genesis, the next in order, was published. In 1557 came Psalms and then Hosea the same year, a mere transcript of his lectures and apparently unrevised. The second and revised edition of Isaiah followed in 1559 and thereafter, all the Minor Prophets (1559), Daniel (1560), Jeremiah and Lamentations (1563), Genesis and the Harmony of the rest of the Pentateuch (1563), and, posthumously, Joshua (1564) and Ezekiel 1-20 (1565). That his colleagues believed he intended to comment on the whole Bible, Beza shows us in his dedication of Ezekiel to Coligny: 'Had God granted us the enjoyment of such a great light for another year or two, I do not see what could be wanting to the perfect understanding of the books of both covenants.'[22]

Calvin's secretaries

CALVIN continued in his prefaces or dedications to lament the lack of time: 'What may be expected of a man of leisure cannot be expected from me, who, in addition to the ordinary office of a pastor, have other duties which allow me hardly the least relaxation. Yet I shall not consider my spare time better spent in any other way.'[23] But his work had been facilitated from 1549 by the assistance of three secretaries. We have explained elsewhere[24] how Denis Raguenier, the stenographer, preserved Calvin's sermons from that year. He and Jean Budé, the son of the mighty Guillaume Budé, and Charles de Jonviller also undertook to write down and transcribe his lectures at the school and at the 'Congrégations'. Thanks to the prefaces, we can see a little more clearly Calvin at work as a lecturer and commentator. In the first place, Budé confirms the fearful pressure of work that forced him 'to leave home after having had usually hardly half an hour to meditate on these lectures'.[25] Then we are told that he lectured extemporarily, not like those 'who repeat to their hearers from a written paper what had been previously prepared at home'.[26] This is confirmed by Jean Crespin, the printer: 'He occupied a whole hour in speaking and used not to write in his book a single word to assist his memory.'[27] The book mentioned was apparently his Hebrew Bible, for the Printer's Preface to Daniel says that 'Calvin is accustomed first to read each verse in Hebrew and then translate it into Latin'.[28] Crespin
184

CALVIN THE BIBLICAL EXPOSITOR

also shows, in the Minor Prophets' Preface, the secretaries at work:

> In copying, they followed this plan. Each had his paper ready in the most convenient form, and each separately wrote down with the greatest speed. If a word escaped one (which sometimes happened, especially on points of dispute and in those parts that were delivered with some warmth), it was taken down by another. . . . Immediately after the lecture ended, de Jonviller took the papers of the other two, placed them before him, consulted his own, and collating them all dictated to someone else so as to copy down what they had hastily taken down. At last he read it all through in order to be able to read it back to M. Calvin at home the following day. When any little word was missing, it was added; or if anything seemed not explained sufficiently, it was easily made plainer.[29]

It would seem that at first, from 1549 to 1552 or so, the secretaries gave their transcriptions to Calvin who himself revised them thoroughly and made an independent commentary out of them. But as time went on, he was no doubt only too glad to make use of the zeal of his admirers and to be content with the scanty revision that Crespin notes. No doubt these later commentaries would have been the better had they received the great care that he gave to the epistles; but, since that was impossible, it is still sufficient to say that they are worthy of Calvin the commentator—'Two things there are of principal moment which have deservedly procured him honour throughout the world: the one his exceeding pains in composing the Institutions of Christian religion; the other his no less industrious travails for exposition of holy Scripture according unto the same Institutions.'

1. *Saint Augustin dans l'Oeuvre de Jean Calvin*, I, p. 1.
2. See W. Niesel: *Calvin-Bibliographie 1901–1959*, pp. 75–78.
3. CO XIV. 37. CTS p. xx.
4. OS III. 6.
5. OS III. 8.
6. There were very few biblical scholars, either Roman Catholic or Protestant, with whom Calvin was not closely connected.
7. *Revue de Théologie*, vol. III, pp. 217 ff., vol. IV, pp. 1 ff., 281 ff. and 388 ff. 1865–66.

JOHN CALVIN

8. CO X. 51–52. ET pp. 18 f.

9. CO X.402. CTS xxiii.

10. CO X.404. CTS xxvi.

11. CO XII.391. ET II. 58–59.

12. CO XII.423. ET II. 70.

13. See F. Ritter: *Histoire de l'Imprimerie Alsacienne aux XVe et XVIe* Siècles, Strasbourg and Paris, 1955, p. 266.

14. CO XLIX. 489. CTS 383.

15. CO XLIX. 382. CTS 187.

16. *Candidatos* does not refer especially to what we should call 'theological candidates', but to anyone who wishes to study theology. This appears from Calvin's French translation which is, literally, 'those who wish to devote themselves to the study of theology'.

17. The translator of the *Library of Christian Classics* edition of the *Institutio* is surely mistaken in supplying 'Scripture' as the object of 'approaches'. The context very clearly shows that Calvin is speaking of his commentaries. Will Scripture be troublesome and boring to us unless we approach it armed with the *Institutio*?

18. Not 'instruction', as LCC, which is a translation of *institutionis*, not of *instituti*.

19. OS III.6.

20. *Select Works* (Parker Society), p. 258.

21. *ibid*., p. 255.

22. CO XL. 9–10. CTS xl.

23. Dedicatory Epistle of Minor Prophets. CO XLII. 183–184. CTS I. xix.

24. *The Oracles of God*, pp. 39 f.

25. Preface to the Minor Prophets. CO XLII. 185–186. CTS I.xxvi.

26. *ibid*., CO XLII. 185–186. CTS xxvii.

27. To the Reader, Minor Prophets. CO XLII. 189–190. CTS I.xxx.

28. CO XL. 523–524. CTS I.lxii.

29. CO XLII. 189–190. CTS I.xxxi.

APPENDIX 1

Chronological List of the Commentaries

(L.=Latin. F.=French translation. Cong.=lectures in *Congréga-tion*. Lect.=*Leçons* at School. Pr.=preached. The dates of lecturing or preaching are given only where there is reason to believe that the lectures or sermons formed the basis of the commentary.)

1540 Romans, L. 1550, F.
1542 Jude, F.
1545 I and II Peter and Jude, F.
1546 I Corinthians,L. 1547, F.
1547 II Corinthians, F. 1548, L.
1548 Galatians, etc., L. 1548, F.
     I and II Timothy, L. 1548, F.
1549 Titus, F. 1550, L.
     Hebrews, L. 1549, F. Cong. up to 1549. Pr. up to 1549.
1550 I and II Thessalonians, L.
1551 Isaiah (1st edn.), L. 1552, F. Lect. up to 1549. Pr. before 1549.
     Collected edition of Pauline letters and Hebrews, L.
     Catholic epistles, L. 1556, F. Cong. 1549-50.
     I John, F. James, F. Jude, F.
1552 Acts (a), L. 1552, F. Pr. 1549–54.
1553 John, L. 1553, F. Cong. 1550 ff.
1554 Genesis, L. 1554, F. Lect. 1550 ff.
     Acts (b), L. 1554, F. Pr. 1549–54.
1556 Collected edition of all epistles, L. Revision.
1557 Psalms, L. 1558, F. Lect. 1552 ff. Cong. 1555 ff.
     Preached variously.
     Hosea, L. 1557, F. Lect. pre-1557. Pr. 1551.
     Collected edition of Pauline letters and Hebrews, L. Revision.
1559 Isaiah (2nd edn.), L. 1572, F. (not by Calvin). Pr. 1556–59.
     Minor Prophets, L. 1560, F. Lect. 1557 ff. Pr. 1550-52.
1561 Daniel, L. 1562, F. Lect. 1559–60. Pr. 1552.

JOHN CALVIN

1563   Jeremiah and Lamentations, L.   1565, F. (not by Calvin).
       Lect. 1560–62.   Pr. 1549–50.
       Pentateuch, L.   1564, F.   Cong. 1559 ff.   Pr. (Deutero-
       nomy), 1555–60.
1564   Joshua, F. 1564, L.   Cong. 1563 f.
1565   Ezekiel 1-20, L.   1565, F.   Lect. 1564–64.   Pr. 1552–54.

APPENDIX 2

Chronological Chart of Leçons and Congrégations

(The date following the book refers to date of publication. For the sake of simplicity I have not given reference, but each date is to be found in CO XXI. 71–96.)

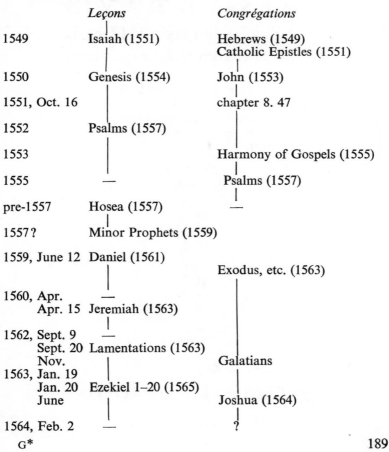

	Leçons	*Congrégations*
1549	Isaiah (1551)	Hebrews (1549)
		Catholic Epistles (1551)
1550	Genesis (1554)	John (1553)
1551, Oct. 16		chapter 8. 47
1552	Psalms (1557)	
1553		Harmony of Gospels (1555)
1555	—	Psalms (1557)
pre-1557	Hosea (1557)	—
1557?	Minor Prophets (1559)	
1559, June 12	Daniel (1561)	
		Exodus, etc. (1563)
1560, Apr.	—	
Apr. 15	Jeremiah (1563)	
1562, Sept. 9	—	
Sept. 20	Lamentations (1563)	
Nov.		Galatians
1563, Jan. 19		
Jan. 20	Ezekiel 1–20 (1565)	
June		Joshua (1564)
1564, Feb. 2	—	?

10 Calvin and Louis Budé's Translation of the Psalms

R. Peter

LES PSEAV-
MES DE DAVID
traduicts selon la verité Hebraique, auec annotations tresvtiles.

PAR LOYS BVDE'.

Preface de Iehan Caluin, touchant
l'vtilité des Pseaumes, & de la tranſla-
tion preſente.

A CENEVE,
De l'Imprimerie de Iehan Creſpin.
M. D. L I.

THIS ESSAY is concerned with Calvin's preface to a translation of the Psalms by Louis Budé, a work which escaped the notice of the *Opera Calvini* editors. The full title of the work is *Les Pseaumes de David traduicts selon la verité hebraique*, Geneva, 1551, 8⁰. The book measures 117 by 68 mm., and contains 367 pages of 28 lines each plus 8 unmarked sheets. The print covers the whole of the page for Calvin's preface, but is divided into two columns for the work itself. The column on the left takes up two thirds of the page giving the translation of the Psalms. That on the right consists of notes in the form of glosses, or references to the original Hebrew. Roman lettering is used for the preface and translation, italics for the notes. There are announcements and a decorated letter at the beginning of the preface.

Certain copies designed for distribution in France omit the place of printing from the title page, and Calvin's name does not appear either in the title or at the end of the preface. About a dozen copies of the work exist; among them are those in Paris (Bibliothèque de l'Arsenal, 8⁰ T 301), in Basle (Universitätsbibliothek, F. NP. IX. 58), and in Geneva (Bibliothèque Publique et Universitaire, Bb 582 Rés. and for the variant S 91 Rés.).

The author of the work

LOUIS Budé, sieur de La Motte, sixth son of the humanist Guillaume Budé and of Roberte Le Lieur,[1] was born in Paris early in 1520.[2] While his father and some of his brothers and sisters remained in France and adhered to the Roman faith,[3] Louis and the other members of the family embraced the Reformed faith and sought asylum in Geneva. Their departure was not sudden. Hesitations remained to be overcome. In 1546, Calvin wrote to Mme. Budé, a widow since 1540, and advised her to withdraw to another country.[4] Louis and his brothers, Matthew and John, more determined than their mother,[5] sought help from Geneva, and developed a friendship with Calvin.[6] However, when Madame had accepted the idea of exile, another son, François, who had equally gone over to the Evangelical cause, seems to have had second thoughts about leaving. Not that he put a stop to the family's exodus, but he himself could not make up his mind. So he held up the enterprise.[7] And further, Matthew, the most resolute of all, died at the end of 1547.[8]

Finally, in the first half of 1549, 'the company moved house'.[9] By the beginning of June the Budés were in Geneva,[10] that is to say, Madame, her two sons, John and Louis, and her daughter Marguerite.[11] On 27 June they made a request to the Council for housing[12] and set up home in the rue des Chanoines.[13] Accustomed to humanist studies, the two sons were not slow to find work.[14] Louis was a hebraist[15] and had spent a long period in Italy to perfect his knowledge.[16] The Hebrew scholars of the Reformed faith were still very few, at least on French soil. It is not surprising that interest was shown in Louis Budé even before he had arrived. The Hebrew Professor at the Lausanne School had died in 1548,[17] and Viret was looking for a replacement. Quickly he asked Calvin, who had put forward Budé's name, if this expectation was likely to materialise. He showed himself enthusiastic at the arrival of Budé in Geneva, for the smooth running of the School no longer permitted further delay.[18] Calvin meanwhile would only send a refusal on Budé's behalf.[19] Budé was in fact to expound the Old Testament at the Collège de Rive in Geneva right up to his death, which followed scarcely two years later. Actually he died 25 May 1551[20] at the age of thirty-one. Contemporary documents reveal not only his learning,[21] but also his godliness[22] and his generosity.[23]

The translation of the Psalms

BY his labours Louis Budé contributed to a better understanding of the Old Testament text. He collaborated on the second revision of Olivétan's Bible,[24] concentrating especially on the Psalter, for which he put forward a new translation. It appeared posthumously in 1551, and was published both as a separate book and as an integral part of Genevan Bibles. It was John Crespin the printer who first published it with the approval of Calvin. He put out a separate edition of it (described below), with a preface by the Reformer which we reproduce in an appendix.[25] At the same time he published it in the Bible which he brought out in 1551.[26] From the point of view of textual revision

192

the importance of this Bible has yet to be recognised.[27] Nevertheless, Calvin here again speaks and explains himself in the introduction. Certainly, this piece, which serves as the preface in the majority of the old Genevan Bibles after 1546,[28] was reproduced by the editors of the *Opera Calvini*.[29] But they reprinted the current version, the one which appeared in 1546 and again in 1555,[30] without giving the variants of the 1551 Crespin edition. We have reproduced in an appendix the end of this preface which gives the variants accurately.

The value and importance of the translation

TO give an idea of the translation Budé made, we have taken as an example the first fourteen verses of Psalm 49. The 1535 Olivétan Bible version[31] and Budé's 1551 Psalter are in parallel. The notes in the left-hand column give certain improvements made by Calvin at the time of the first revision and incorporated into the 1546 Bible.

Those on the right are Budé's own corrections from the original Hebrew. To facilitate comparison verse divisions are added. Such divisions first appeared in the 1551 New Testament of Robert Estienne.

Olivétan Version 1535

(2) Vous tous peuples ouyez ceste chose,[a] vous tous qui habitez au monde,[b] escoutez.
(3) Vous aussi filz d'Adam et vous filz de l'homme,[c] ensemble le riche et le paovre.
(4) Ma bouche parlera[d] sapience et la meditation de mon coeur, prudence.
(5) Ie presteray l'aureille au proverbe, i'exposeray mon dicton obscur à tout la[e] harpe.
(6) Pourquoy auray-ie crainte au temps d'adversité, et quand la malice de celuy qui est à mes talons m'environne?[f]

Budé Version 1551

(2) Vous tous peuples oyez cecy, vous tous qui demourez en ce monde,[a] prestez l'aureille,
(3) tant ceux de bas estat comme nobles, et tant le riche comme le povre.
(4) Ma bouche dira propos de sapience et mon cueur a conceu choses d'entendement.[b]
(5) I'enclineray l'aureille à mon proverbe, i'exposeray mon dire obscur sur la harpe.
(6) Pourquoy craindray-ie au mauvais temps,[c] lors que l'iniquité de mes talons m'environnera?

193

JOHN CALVIN

Olivétan Version 1535	Budé Version 1551

(7) Ilz se fient en leur vertu et se vantent en l'abondance de leurs richesses.

(8) Toutesfoys l'homme ne rachetera point son frere et ne donnera point à Dieu la ranceon d'iceluy.

(9) Car la ranceon de leur ame est precieuse, et l'eage de perpetuité.[g]

(10) Et qu'il vive à tousioursmais, ne voyant point la fosse?[h]

(11) Car il voit les sages qui meurent, ensemble le fol et le niayz qui perissent et qui laissent leur substance aux autres.

(12) Toutesfois leur desir[i] est que leur maison soit eternellement et que leurs habitations soient en tout eage, et se sont donné bruit par leurs noms[j] sus la terre.

(13) Mais l'homme ne demourera point en sa magnificence, il sera semblable aux bestes, lesquelles perissent.

(14) Telle voye d'iceulx est follie à eulx-mesmes,[k] et leurs successeurs ensuyvent voluntiers leurs commandemens.

(a) ouyez cecy, (b) vous tous les habitans du monde, (c) et vous filz du puissant, (d) proferera (e) obscur avec la (f) quand la malice de mes talons m'environne? (g) et renouvellement à perpetuité. (h) sans veoir le sepulcre. (i) leur meditation (j) et se ont donné bruit à leur nom (k) d'iceux leur tourne follie.

---

(7) De ceux qui se fient en leurs biens et se glorifient en l'abondance de leurs richesses?

(8) Personne ne pourra nullement racheter son frere, ne donner à Dieu sa rançon.

(9) Car le rachat de leur ame est par trop cher et ne se fera iamais.[d]

(10) Et qu'il vive à tousioursmais[e] et ne veoye point la fosse?

(11) Car il peut veoir[f] que les sages meurent, et qu'ensemble le fol et l'homme abbruti perissent et laissent leur sustance à d'autres.

(12) Toute leur affection[g] est que leurs maisons durent perpetuellement et que leurs manoirs demeurent en tous eages;[h] et pourtant ils imposent leurs noms aux terres.[i]

(13) Mais l'homme ne demourera point en honneur, ains sera semblable aux bestes[j] brutes qui perissent du tout.

(14) Telle voye d'iceux leur tourne à folie, toutesfois leurs successeurs ensuyvent volontiers leurs enseignemens.[k]

(a) le mot Hebrieu signifie la vie presente et le temps d'icelle.

(b) en Hebr. ma bouche dira sapiences et la meditation de mon cueur intelligences.

(c) en Hebr. aux iours de mal.

(d) en Hebr. Et sera cher (ou : precieus) le rachat de leur ame et cessera à iamais (aucuns : et qu'il vive en ce monde à iamais).

(e) en Hebr. Et vivra encores à iamais.

(f) en Hebr. Car il verra.

(g) en Hebr. leur dedans.
(h) en Hebr. en generation et generation.
(i) en Hebr. ils ont appellé leurs noms sur les terres.
(j) en Hebr. il a esté faict semblable comme les bestes.
(k) en Hebr. Ceste leur voye, folie à eux, et après eux en leur bouche les enfans aimeront.

In comparing the two translations it is indisputable that definite progress has been made from one to the other. And Budé's version is known to have been adopted for the Genevan Bibles after 1551.[32] There remains one point on which Budé's version throws indirect light, and the point is not unimportant. It concerns the problem of the version Calvin used in his tracts, commentaries and preaching. Quite recently an historian stated with good reason: 'Up till now, the problem of Calvin's Bible remains open and the attempts which have been made to establish the text cannot be regarded as conclusive.'[33]

We know that Calvin often cited the Bible from memory, *ad sensum*, rather than *verbatim*. And if proof were needed, what better than that of Augustin Marlorat[34] who knew and frequently used to visit the Reformer? A little before he was martyred, as minister of Rouen, he put together an excellent index for Calvin's *Institutio*.[35] In the introduction to these tables, dated 1 May 1562, he defines his own method by comparison with Calvin's: 'As to the version which I have followed [i.e. for making the biblical index], I hope readers will not find it strange if I refer to the text itself, as it appears in the Bible [a little lower down he adds: "in the latest version of the Bible"] in preference to what Master John Calvin has within his *Institutio*. For he is an excellent and widely-read man, and all his works bear sufficient witness that holy scripture is familiar to him, but he does not always have the Books open when he writes (since he has no need) to put word for word what he reads both in the Old and the New Testament. It is enough if the sense is there truly preserved and the meaning of the words very carefully noted, so that there is nothing there to attack and refute.'[36]

But it is nonetheless true that Calvin generally follows in his commentaries, and sometimes even in the middle of his preaching,[37] a text which is as close as possible to the original Hebrew

195

or Greek. Take the Reformer's *Commentary on the Psalms*. It appeared in 1557 in Latin, and in 1558 in French.[38] The biblical texts which the two editions use[39] show serious variations by comparison with Budé's officially accepted version. But on closer inspection one sees that the main changes introduced by Calvin stem from the incorporation into the text of notes made by Budé on the original Hebrew. Here then is the beginning of Psalm 49 in the 1558 *Commentary*:

(2) Vous tous peuples oyez ceci, vous tous qui demeurez en ce monde, prestez l'aureille,

(3) tant les fils d'Adam que les fils de l'homme, le riche et le povre ensemble.

(4) Ma bouche dira sapience et la meditation de mon coeur est intelligences.

(5) I'enclineray l'aureille à mon proverbe, i'exposeray mon enigme sur la harpe.

(6) Pourquoy craindray-ie aux iours du mal? l'iniquité de mon talon m'environnera.

(7) Ils se confient en leurs biens et se glorifient en l'abondance de leurs richesses.

(8) Le frere ne pourra nullement racheter, l'homme ne donnera à Dieu pris de sa rançon.

(9) Et sera precieux le rachat de leur ame, et leur durée à iamais.

(10) Afin qu'il vive encore à iamais et ne voye point le sepulchre.

(11) Car il verra que les sages meurent, ensemble le fol et l' homme brutal perissent et laisseront leurs richesses à des estrangers.

(12) Le dedans d'iceux leurs maisons à iamais, leurs manoirs de generation en generation; ils ont appelé leurs noms sur les terres.

(13) Mais l'homme ne demeurera point en honneur, il est fait semblable aux bestes brutes, ils perissent du tout.

(14) Telle voye d'iceux leur est folie, et leurs successeurs accorderont à la bouche d'iceux.[40]

In conclusion, to recognise the Bible Calvin used, it is necessary to look at the Genevan Bibles of the time which, in the folio editions, are surrounded by glosses, references to the original texts, summaries, prefaces, introductions, maps, figures, an index, and appendixes of all sorts. The margins of the Bible which came from François Jaquy's Geneva press in 1562, 2°, are crammed with notes which often spill over even into the space for the text. But, it is with the help of these notes, already

196

numerous in Budé's Psalter[41] and improved[42] in the great Genevan
Bibles from edition to edition, that one can, in conjunction
with the version he puts forward, reconstruct the Bible of Calvin.[43]

NOTES

1. Eleven children, seven boys and four girls, from this marriage, con-
tracted in 1506. On Budé's family and genealogy see: Doumergue III.
606 f. E. and E. Haag, *La France Protestante*, 2nd edit., Paris, 1877–1888,
III. 372 f.

2. In a letter dated 6 March 1520 Guillaume Budé chose his correspon-
dent Louis Ruzé as godfather for little Louis (*infantuli mei Ludovici*). Cf.
Louis Delaruelle, *Répertoire analytique et chronologique de la correspondance de Guillaume Budé*, Paris, 1907, pp. 106 f. In naming his son Louis,
Guillaume Budé preserved the memory of his brother Louis, whose death
in November 1517 had caused him great distress. See G. Budé's letter to
Erasmus, 21 December 1517 in Allen, *Erasmi Epistolae*, Oxford, 1913, III.
174. On Guillaume Budé's brother Louis, see M. Duhem, 'Deux frères de
Guillaume Budé, Chanoines de Troyes, Etienne et Louis Budé in *Mémoires
de la Société Académique de l'Aube*, Troyes, 1933, pp. 7 f.

3. On Guillaume Budé's alleged protestantism see A-L. Herminjard,
Correspondance des Réformateurs dans les pays de langue française,
Geneva, 1866–1897, III. 239, note 3; Haag, *op. cit.*, vol. III. 373; and Jean
Plattard, *Guillaume Budé et les origines de l'humanisme français*, Paris, 1923,
pp. 33 ff.

4. CO XII. 452 f. That Mme. Budé was in effect the destination of this
anonymous letter seems beyond doubt. The address 'Mademoiselle' does
not rule this out. In the sixteenth century this title indicated social rank
and could be used of a married woman.

5. '. . . Our Lord has given you this advantage', wrote Calvin to Mme.
Budé, 'that you have children who not only present themselves to take
you out of captivity, but even urge you to this.' *ibid.* 454. The two refugee
sons were studying in Strasbourg in 1545.

6. Matthew Budé went to Geneva in 1545 with Crespon and Diaz 'to see
the state of the church in that city and its good order'. J. Crespin, *Histoire
des Martyrs*, Toulouse, 1885–1889, I. 468. Matthew Budé rejoices in a
letter to Calvin, 26 April 1546, that their friendship which began in a
personal encounter is confirmed in their letters. CO XII. 340. In another
letter to Calvin, 23 March 1547 from Paris, Matthew commends his brother
Jean, and asks Calvin to receive him with the same kindness he showed his
brother Louis and himself. CO XII. 501 f. Calvin, for his part, took to Jean
and recommended him in glowing terms to M. de Falais, through whose
house he had to pass before returning to Paris. Letter, 4 June 1547. CO
XII. 535.

JOHN CALVIN

7. Calvin to [François] Budé, 19 June 1547. CO XII, 541 ff. The opening words can only apply to François. 'Sir, though your face is still unknown to me. . . . ' François settled in Geneva only in 1554. CO XV. 298.

8. Calvin to Jean and Louis Budé, 1547. CO XII. 644–648, esp. 644 note 1.

9. Calvin's expression. CO XII. 541. It is true that at this point Calvin only mentions the preparations.

10. Viret to Calvin, 12 June 1549, 'I rejoice that the Budés have come with their mother'. CO XIII. 298.

11. Melanchthon also records the move, but writes of 'daughters'. To Camerarius, 11 September 1549 and to an unknown person, 16 September 1549. *Corpus Reformatorum*, Halle, 1840, VII. 461, 464. Nevertheless Marguerite appears to be the only one. In 1550 she married Guillaume de Trie, seigneur of Varennes, and friend of Calvin. Doumergue, III. 630 ff.

12. Council Register for 27 June (not 27 January as Galiffe). 'Me. Budé, of Paris, requests in the name of himself, his brothers and their mother to live in Geneva. Granted.' cf. CO XXI, 453.

13. Doumergue, III. 609.

14. For Jean Budé in Geneva, see Doumergue III. 606-10.

15. Doumergue writes of Louis Budé as if he had studied law in Padua in 1550, but this is based on a false interpretation of a letter from de Jonviller to Calvin, 24 March 1550. CO XIII. 552.

16. At least from 1546 to 1547 and perhaps longer. CO XII. 340, 502, and XX. 391 '. . . Rabbinos evolvet . . . '

17. One Imbert Pacolet. See H. Vuilleumier, *Histoire de l'Eglise réformée du pays de Vaud sous le régime bernois*, Lausanne, 1927–1933, I. 416. Herminjard, IV. 459 note 8.

18. Viret to Calvin, 8 May, 7 June, and 12 June 1549. CO XIII. 269, 293, 298.

19. Calvin to Viret, 6 July 1549. CO XIII. 318. It is not impossible that Calvin influenced Budé to stay in Geneva. Such a specialist would be precious. At Lausanne the appointment went to the deacon Jean-Reymond Merlin, from Dauphiny, a protégé of Calvin and Viret.

20. CO XX. 391, not 1552 as Haag. Nevertheless Haag, p. 375 says, 'Louis Budé died leaving his wife Barbe Le Bouch childless after their marriage 9 August 1550. She was the daughter of Jean Le Bouch, sieur de la Bourdonnière, in Berry, and of Jeanne de Prégremau. Later she married again, to Guy de Sérignac, sieur de Tillac . . ' Calvin also mentions the young professor's death: '. . .feeling great pain from the disease, which had seized the youth and strong complexion of the man. He had only been in bed six days, but he was quite subdued and gentle as a lamb ready for the slaughter,' cf. the end of Calvin's Preface to Budé's Psalms. Viret to Farel, June 1551, mentions the nature of the disease, 'colico morbo exstinctus'. CO XIV. 131.

21. According to Calvin '. . he was well read in the language [Hebrew], and was so learned in humanist studies that nothing passed him. Such was his diligence that he spared neither time nor effort to examine the things critically up to the end. . . . 'See Calvin's Preface to Budé's Psalms. Farel to

Calvin, 29 June 1551, says '... transitu doctissimi L. Budei ...' CO XIV. 143.

22. Calvin says in the Preface to Budé's Psalms 'I have not seen such profound [exquis] learning as was in him, and I have not found greater godliness and fear of God than here'. Farel says, '... de quo merito quererer, nisi certo scirem pietatis fructum iam copiosum metere. ...'

23. 'Budé ... gave a great sum to the fund for impoverished foreigners.'

24. The first revision, done by Calvin, took place in 1545. On the second, Calvin to Farel, 10 November 1550, CO XIII. 656. 'The correction of the NT has occupied me the last four months. Now, despite myself, I am forced to go over a large part of the OT. I have meanwhile invited the printers to choose capable men, and others beside myself to look to this task. They have taken no notice and I bear the burden of their idleness. I have got hold of Louis Budé to look over David, Solomon and Job. His help relieves me from carrying the whole burden. I have also given Beza the Apocrypha. What am I to do? A vast number of Bibles are sought after and there are no more copies. As no one will take the load, the ox has to be harnessed.'

25. Budé's translation of the Psalms appeared separately on other occasions (wihout Calvin's preface). Eg., from the Lyons press of Guillaume Rouille in 1558 (16° with 343 two columned pages). But already in 1556 and then in 1561, together with versified Psalms by Beza and Marot.

26. *La Bible*, Geneva, 1551, J. Crespin, 4°, described in W-J Van Eys, *Bibliographie des Bibles et des Nouveaux Testaments en langue française des XV et XVI siècles*, Geneva, 1900–1901, vol. I, number 65. A variant existed for distribution in France. The title page gives no place of origin, and the word 'Preface' is substituted for 'Iehan Calvin au Lecteur'. A copy is to be seen in the Musée Calvet at Avignon. No. 69 in Van Eys is the same except for a date change, which Crespin made simply to encourage sales, in the following year.

27. CO LVI. iii–x does not mention it. O. Douen in a bird's-eye view of the history of Olivétan's Bible 1535–1560 in the *Revue de Théologie et de Philosophie*, Lausanne, 1889 speaks of it, but has not seen it.

28. CO IX. lxiv. Van Eys, nos. 54–55.

29. CO IX. 823–826.

30. Van Eys, no. 82. *La Bible*, Geneva, 1555, P. Sorel, 4°.

31. Van Eys, no. 35. *La Bible*, Neuchâtel, 1535, Pierre de Wingle, 2°.

32. We have looked at Crespin's 1551 4° Bible and Jaquy's 1562 2° Bible. Both give Budé's version of the Psalms with these very small changes: v. 4. 1551—et (this particle was restored in 1562). v. 11. 1551 & 1562—l' homme brutal (in place of l'homme abbruti). v. 14. 1551 & 1562—toutesfois. From 1551, at Calvin's instigation, Beza continued the versification of the Psalms, begun by Clement Marot (P. Pidoux, *Le Psautier huguenot*, Basle, 1962, II, 49). Beza relied very closely on Bude's version, which had become the official version of the Psalms. For example Ps. 49. 3:

Car le rachet de leur ame est trop cher
Pour en finer, quoi qu'on veuille tascher

JOHN CALVIN

De vivre ici perpetuellement,
Sans iamais voir fosse ne monument.

Thus Budé's version was perpetuated not only in the Genevan Bible but also in the Psalter. See also the 1556 Psalter (edition D) with its preface in Pidoux, *op. cit.*, II. 95 and 97 f.

33. *Supplementa Calviniana. Sermons inédits.* Vol. II. *Sermons sur le livre d'Esaie*, published by G. A. Barrois, Neukirchen, 1961, p. xi. For the attempts to which Barrois alludes see CO LVI, LVII.

34. On Augustin Marlorat (1506–1562), see Haag, 1st ed. VII. 256 f.

35. An appendix is first found in most copies of the *Institutio*, edition of J. Bourgeois, 1562, 4°. Subsequent editions copied this.

36. *ibid.*, appendix a.i. verso.

37. We refer to the biblical text placed *at the top* of the unpublished or unprinted sermons, for the secretaries or the printers simply reproduce the official version.

38. 1557, R. Estienne, Geneva, 2°, Latin; 1558, C. Badius, Geneva, 2°, French.

39. Latin CO XXXI, XXXII; French CO LVI, 365 f.

40. Note besides that Calvin saw the need of restoring to the margin of his commentary two readings from the Budé version. At the beginning of v.3: we read in the margin: or '[tant] ceux de bas estat [que] les nobles'. And v.5 for 'enigme': or 'dire obscur'.

41. Olivétan had started the practice in his 1535 Bible. In some difficult passages he puts the original Greek or Hebrew in the margin.

42. The notes are not due to Calvin only but also to his fellow workers, Louis Budé, Theodore Beza, Nicolas des Gallars, and Robert Estienne. Calvin gave them all his attention and revised them. CO XXI. 97.

43. We might ask why Calvin did not put into the Genevan Bibles such and such a reading which was close to his heart, readings which are found in his commentaries and which appear again in the official version simply as notes? Is this out of respect for the work of such and such a translator? Rather it seems that the elegance of the original style appeared to him more valuable for continuous reading than a word for word translation, which he kept for the commentaries.

Calvin's Preface at the Head of Louis Budé's Work

---

*.ii.ʳ PREFACE DE IEHAN CALVIN AUX LECTEURS FIDELES,
TOUCHANT L'UTILITÉ DES PSEAUMES[1]
ET DE LA TRANSLATION PRESENTE

Combien que la corruption de nostre nature se monstre en tout et par tout,[2] si est-ce qu'entre les autres vices, cestuy-cy est notable et par trop enorme: qu'estans pressés de tant de maux, nous n'avons pas le sens ou courage de nous retirer à Dieu pour luy demander secours; et en tant de biens qu'il ne cesse de nous elargir,[a] nous ne pensons point de luy faire aucune recognoissance; et toutesfois voilà le principal où il nous falloit appliquer et exercer. Parquoy
*.ii.ᵛ d'autant plus devons-nous estre soin-// gneux de cercher[b] remede à un si grand mal. C'est qu'estans advertiz de noz miseres et de tant de necessités, nous soyons solicités d'invoquer Dieu; que nous cognoissions en second lieu la forme de le bien prier et les requestes que nous avons à luy faire; tiercement que nous cognoissions sa bonté par laquelle il nous convie tant doucement que rien plus[c] de venir à luy; et que cela nous y pousse tant plus vivement, quand nous sommes asseurés de n'y point venir à l'aventure. D'autre part, que nous meditions mieux ses graces et benefices, pour luy en rendre la louange qui luy en est deue; non pas qu'il en ait besoin, mais pour nostre salut, à fin que ce qu'il nous donne en ce monde pour nous faire gouster son amour inestimable ne nous

201

*.iii.^r soit point// tourné en condamnation par nostre ingratitude.

    Or combien que ceste doctrine et telles admonitions se trouvent par toute l'Escriture saincte, il n'y a livre qui en soit si plein que le Psautier. Car il semble que Dieu nous ait voulu donner en la personne de David, qui en a composé la plus grand' part,[3] comme un miroir où nous peussions contempler tout ce qui nous doit induire à le bien prier, et le louer quand il nous a exaucés. Mesmes à parler plus proprement, les Pseaumes contien[n]ent comme une anatomie de toutes les affections de l'ame,[4] qui se doyvent desployer devant Dieu soit en tristesse ou en fascherie, soit en ioye. Car il est impossible de sentir nulle tentation en nous, dont nous n'ayons icy exemple, et à laquelle le remede

*.iii.^v n'y soit quand// et quand[d] appresté. Mesmes il n'y a pas seulement de quoy nous soulager aux afflictions qui nous pressent; mais beaucoup de vices qui nous seroyent autrement cachés sont descouverts, comme il est certain que d'un si profond abysme de maladies spirituelles dont nous sommes entachés, nous n'en cognoissons pas la centieme partie. Or les Pseaumes bien medités nous contraignent d'entrer en examen de ce que nous tenons comme ensevely. En sorte que quiconque aura profité en ce livre comme il doit, aura comme tous ses sens et esprits ouverts pour s'addresser privément à Dieu et communiquer avec luy, pour trouver allegement et repos de tous les troubles et passions dont il sera agité. C'est l'article que nous avons cy-dessus mis// le premier entre trois, asçavoir de bien sentir les necessités que nous

*.iiii.^r avons d'invoquer Dieu pour estre secouruz de luy. Car combien qu'elles soyent quasi infinies et dedans et dehors, toutesfois les tentations interieures qui procedent ou de nostre incredulité, ou d'impatience, ou d'autres infirmités de nostre ame, doyvent tousiours estre mises au premier rang. Quant aux ennemis qui nous environnent et nous molestent de toutes parts, nous les sentons bien, mais nous ne sommes pas si bien advisés de cognoistre que c'est à Dieu de nons donner la vertu d'y resister. Il y a encores une autre faute aussi grande et plus, qu'en nous attachant aux hommes qui nous persecutent, ou aux afflictions qui nous faschent et tormentent, nous laissons le prin-// cipal ennemi duquel il nous falloit garder sur tout, asçavoir Sathan. Outre plus, iamais nous ne venons à la source de toutes les adversités que nous endurons: c'est de considerer que Dieu nous punit iustement, d'autant que nous l'avons irrité pas noz pechés. Ces choses, comme i'ay dict, nous sont si bien descouvertes aux Pseaumes, que les plus endormiz et stupides en porroyent estre resveillés.

Il y a encore plus,[5] c'est que nous y sommes incités d'estre touchés et avoir compassion des miseres de noz prochains pour y cercher allegement comme aux nostres. Car en priant Dieu, ce n'est pas raison que chacun pense seulement pour soy, mais nous faut ietter les yeux sur tout le corps de l'Eglise et sur les membres d'icelle. Or pource que nous// sommes si froids et tardifs en cest endroit, mesmes quasi eslourdiz[e] du tout, nous avons mestier[f] d'estre picqués. Et il y a plusieurs Pseaumes qui nous peuvent servir comme d'esperons: singulierement ceux qui ont esté composés par les saincts Prophetes qui ont vescu du temps que Dieu affligeoit son peuple par diverses calamités. Car là il nous est monstré comment noz cueurs doyvent estre dechirés[g] quand nous voyons l'Eglise en dissipation, comment nous devons gemir, plorer[h] et estre en angoisse continuelle la voyans opprimée par ses ennemis.

Mesmes il n'est pas icy question que nous soyons esmeuz seulement de pitié envers les hommes, mais que le zele de la maison de Dieu nous ronge et brusle le cueur: comme de faict sa gloire, la// saincteté de son nom et tout ce qui appartient à son royaume, doit bien surmonter l'amour et le regard que nous avons aux creatures. Sur cela, les requestes nous sont formées et mises en la bouche, à fin que nous sachions que[i] nous avons à demander à Dieu, comment nous avons à desployer noz cueurs devant luy, car autrement nous

[*.vi.]ʳ ne sçaurions que faire, sinon ronger nostre frein, d'autant que nous avons les cueurs serrés, et noz langues sont comme muettes. Et d'autant que telle ouverture ne se peut faire sinon quand nous apprehendons la misericorde de Dieu, laquelle seule nous donne hardiesse de venir à luy, le sainct Esprit quasi par tous les Pseaumes nous met en avant comment il nous faut mediter, au milieu de noz troubles// et perplexités, la douceur, humanité, et l'amour inestimable que Dieu nous porte: à fin d'appliquer le tout à nostre usage en priant, et que nostre lascheté soit corrigée tellement que nous allions d'un franc courage et pleine fianceʲ à celuy qui est si prest et enclin à nous recevoir.

Il reste quand nous avons prié Dieu, qu'aussi nous luy rendions action de graces pour ses benefices. Dequoy les enseignemens sont si amples en tout le Psautier, qu'on ne sçauroit point exprimer ce qui y est en peu de parolles. Et d'autant que nous sommes si mescognoissans, l'Esprit de Dieu qui cognoist noz maladies insiste tant plus fort à nous remonstrer combien nous sommes tenuz de magnifier son nom, et de quel ardeur il nous y faut efforcer; mesmes ne [*.vi.]ᵛ se// contentant point que chacun y employe toutes ses forces, il nous solicite d'appeller et attirer entant qu'en nous est toutes creatures pour nous tenir compagnie à ce faire.

Telles et si grandes utilités nous monstrent assez en quelle recommandation nous devons avoir le Psautier, si nous desirons de profiter en l'eschole de Dieu. Et combien que ie les ay touchés en brief, si est-ce que ce petit goust que i'en ay donné suffira aux enfans de Dieu pour les mener à l'experience, laquelle les instruira plus a à plein.

Il y a l'aide que trouveront icy ceux de la langue Françoise. Car pource que le style des Pseaumes est [*.vii.]ʳ difficile, il est bien requis que ceux, qui ne sont gueres exercés en l'Escriture et n'entendent point la langue Hebraique, soyent conduicts// et addressésᵏ pour comprendre le vray sens naturel.⁶ Or (comme i'ay

204

dict) telle addresse est icy donnée. Car nostre bon frere, maistre Loys Budé, y a travaillé aussi fidelement qu'il estoit possible et qu'on sçauroit requerir. Car outre ce qu'il estoit bien entendu en la langue, et qu'il avoit esté si bien enseigné aux lettres humaines que rien ne luy defailloit, il y avoit une telle diligence en luy, qu'il n'espargnoit ne temps ne labeur pour esplucher les choses iusques au bout devant que se resoudre. Mesmes la singuliere reverence qu'il portoit à la parolle de Dieu, le rendoit beaucoup plus attentif à cest ouvrage, pour la crainte qu'il avoit de polluer les choses sacrées. Et de faict, ie ne prise pas tellement le sçavoir [*.vii.]ᵛ exquis qui estoit en luy, que ie// ne prefere la pieté et droite crainte de Dieu que i'y ay cognue.

Ce que ie ne dy pas tant pour la louange de l'homme que Dieu a retiré d'avec nous, que pour l'instruction des vivans, et sur tout pour admonester un tas d'esprits glorieux[1] et enflés de vent de fole monstre,ᵐ qu'ils appren[n]ent au lieu de bastir en l'air de cercher le fondement de vraye sagesse et science, sans lequel il n'y a nulle fermeté en tout ce que les hommes pourront sçavoir. Au lieu doncques que beaucoup de fols eventés et volages ne cuidentⁿ point estre sçavans et gens d'esprit, s'ils ne sont profanes et mocqueurs de Dieu,[7] le bon Loys Budé, estant pour le moins aussi excellent qu'eux aux lettres humaines, n'a pas laissé de cheminer en simplicité Chrestienne tant en la vie// [*.viii.]ʳ qu'en la mort, ie dy depuis que Dieu l'avoit rengé à l'obeissance de l'Evangile.

Ausurplus ie ne doute point que Dieu par sa grace ne luy ait adressé cest oeuvre en mains pour le conduire à une mort si paisible et heureuse comme a esté la siene. Car alors il monstroit bien qu'il n'avoit pas tellement vacqué aux Pseaumes pour le profit des autres, qu'il ne s'en fust approprié la vertu. Outre la confession qu'il feit de sa foy, autant entiere et pure que lon sçauroit desirer d'un Chrestien, outre le soin et zele ardant qu'il avoit à invoquer Dieu, on po[u]voit bien iuger que les meditations qui y sont contenues, luy estoyent bien imprimées au cueur, en ce que sentant

205

JOHN CALVIN

[*.viii.]ᵛ grandes violences de sa maladie, attendu la ieunesse
et forte complexion° de l'homme, et// qu'il n'avoit esté
que six iours au lict, neantmoins il estoit là tout
dompté et aussi debonnaire qu'un agneau appresté
au sacrifice.

Maintenant vous Chrestiens qui cerchez Dieu,
iouyssez du labeur de ce bon personnage, iusques à ce
que vous soyez recueilliz avec luy au royaume de
Dieu.

(*a*) elargir, *distribuer*. (*b*) cercher, *chercher*. (*c*) tant doucement que rien
plus, *on ne peut plus doucement*. (*d*) quand et quand, *chaque fois*. (*e*)
eslourdir, *rendre lourd, hébété, stupide*. (*f*) avoir mestier de, *avoir besoin
de*. (*g*) dechirer, *abattre*. (*h*) plorer, *pleurer*. (*i*) que, *ce que*. (*j*) fiance, *con-
fiance*. (*k*) addresser ou adresser, *diriger*. (*l*) glorieux, *vaniteux*. (*m*) monstre, *apparence*. (*n*) cuider, *croire, penser*. (*o*) complexion, *constitution*.

1. On the importance of the Psalms for Calvin, see E. Mülhaupt, *Der
Psalter auf der Kanzel Calvins*, Neukirchen, 1959, pp. 8–12. And R. Martin-
Achard, *Calvin et les Psaumes*, in *Les Cahiers Protestants*, Lausanne, 1960,
pp. 102–112.

2. *Inst*. II. iii.

3. On Calvin's view of inspiration such a passage counterbalances others
like: '... we cannot find better songs than David's Psalms: which the Holy
Spirit has spoken and created.' *Epistle to the Reader*, at the head of the
Psalter, 10 June 1543. CO VI. 171.

4. An allusion to the preface to his commentary on the Psalms: 'I am
accustomed to call this book an anatomy of all parts of the soul, because
there is no state of mind in man which is not seen here as in a mirror.'
CO XXXI, 16. The two texts deserve comparison. That of 1551 is more
objective, that of 1557 more personal.

5. The two following paragraphs develop ideas not found in the 1557
preface.

6. Calvin recommends the literal sense of Scripture. See the other preface.

7. Calvin's *De Scandalis*. CO VIII. 44 f. 'Others mock the Gospel ... they
even make themselves believe it is semi-divine, when they dare to defy
the heaven and all divinity. ... Everyone knows that Agrippa, Villeneuve,
Dolet, and their likes are always violently contemptuous of the Gospel....
Rabelais, Degovea, Desperiers and many others, having had a taste of the
Gospel, have been broken by their own blindness.' On these humanists
'profane mockers of God' see J. Bohatec, *Budé und Calvin*, Graz, 1950,
passim.

206

Calvin's Preface at the Head of the Bible Printed by J. Crespin in Geneva, 1551

---

*ii.ʳ   IEHAN CALVIN AU LECTEUR

    Si ie voulois icy user de longue preface, i'auroye
trois poincts à desduire. . . .

*ii.ᵛ   Le troisieme poinct ne requiert pas si long propos.
C'est touchant la translation de la saincte Bible: ie dy
en la langue Françoise. Entre ceux qui ont travaillé
après, feu maistre Pierre Robert,[1] en son vivant fidele
serviteur de l'Eglise Chrestienne et maintenant après
son trespas de bonne et heureuse memoire, s'y est
porté en sorte que son labeur est digne de grand'
louange. Et de faict, il n'y a homme de sain iugement

*iii.ʳ   qui ne luy donne ce// los. Toutesfois il ne se faut pas
esbahir s'il luy estoit eschappé beaucoup de fautes en
un tel ouvrage, i'enten si long et si difficile. *Pourᵃ*
amender ce qui defailloit là, il y a environ six ans[2]
qu'on avoit fidelement travaillé tant à polir et adoucir la
rudesse du langage qu'à redresser le tout au vray sens
et naturel. Et i'espere que la peine qui a esté prinse,
comme elle n'a pas esté inutile, aura esté bien receue
de toutes gens craignans Dieu et desirans de profiter
en la pure intelligence de sa parolle. Maintenant celuy
qui desia y avoit mis la main s'y est encor appliqué
plus songneusement, tant pour accommoder tousiours
mieux le langage à la façon de parler commune et receue
et telle facilité qu'il puisse estre entendu de chacun, que
pour restituer en son entier ce qui avoit esté mal prins,

ou corrompu, ou trop obscurement translaté. Combien qu'il a esté deschargé par d'autres de quelque partie du labeur, comme de la translation du Psautier par feu maistre Loys Budé, nostre bon frere, et de celle des livres Apocryphes par nostre frere, maistre Theodore de Besze, lequel, selon le savoir qu'il a en la langue Grecque, la dexterité d'esprit et le iugement que Dieu luy a donné, et le zele de servir à l'Eglise, y a tellement vacqué, que ceux qui iouyront de sa peine auront de quoy louer Dieu. Mesme aux petis Prophetes (qu'on appelle) il s'est aidé de quelques corrections qui avoyent esté notées par un troisieme.[3] *Mais pource que selon la liberté que cestuy-là luy permettoit, il a suyvy ce que bon luy a semblé, il n'en fait point plus ample mention. Or quelque travail qu'on y ait prins, tant s'en faut que ie recommande l'ouvrage comme parfaict, que celuy qui en a soustenu le principal faiz ne se contente pas encor de ce qu'il y a peu faire. Qui plus est, selon qu'il l'a protesté cy-devant, son desir*[b] seroit que quelcun, ayant bon loisir et estant garny de tout ce qui est requis à un tel œuvre, y vousist employer une demi-douzaine d'ans et puis communiquer ce qu'il auroit faict à gens entendus et experts, tellement qu'il fust bien reveu de plusieurs yeux. *Voire s'il estoit possible, il seroit bien à souhaiter que tout un monde s'y employast, et le pris et dignité de l'ouvrage le merite bien. Et de faict, ce qu'il entreprint il y a six ans de faire ceste correction ne fut pas pour s'avancer en preoccupant le lieu; et maintenant ce qu'il a redoublé, taschant de tou-siours plus avancer, ne doit estre que bien pris; et ne luy doit-on imputer à trop grande hastiveté, si, estant requis*[c] et importuné de ceux qui desirent la gloire de Dieu et l'edification de l'Eglise Chrestienne, acquies-çant à leurs prieres, il a par faute d'autre mis *derechef*[d] en avant ce que Dieu luy avoit donné. Tant y a, qu'il estime bien sans arrogance et ose promettre qu'on trouvera qu'il a *icy*[e] beaucoup amendé les translations precedentes, voire plus que ie ne dy. Quoy qu'il en soit, il desdie (*comme il a faict par cy-devant*)[f] en bonne conscience son labeur tel qu'il est à Dieu, en signe de recognoissance qu'il a receu de luy tout ce qu'il communique à ses prochains, le priant d'avoir ce sacrifice agreable; il le desdie pareillement à l'usage de l'Eglise de Dieu, esperant qu'il ne sera pas inutile, qu'il ne fructifie à l'honneur de celuy auquel appartient tout honneur.

(a) We print the variants in italics. The notes reproduce the current text in CO IX. 826. (b)... et si difficile. Premierement donc, pource qu'en sa translation le langage estoit rude et aucunement eslongné de la façon commune et receue, il s'est trouvé homme qui a mis peine de l'adoucir, non seulement en le polissant, mais aussi l'accommodant à une plus grande facilité, pour estre mieux entendu de tous. Secondement, quant au sens, selon la faculté que Dieu luy a donnée, et le iugement qu'il a peu acquerir par le long et continuel exercice qu'il a en l'Escriture, il s'est diligemment employé à restituer en son entier ce qui avoit esté mal prins, ou corrompu, ou trop obscurement translaté. Comment il en est venu à bout, et combien son labeur a esté profitable, on en pourra iuger en le lisant. Vray est que desia il declaire et proteste qu'il ne se contente pas encor de ce qu'il y a faict. Qui plus est, son desir... (c)... de plusieurs yeux. Et de faict, ce qu'il a entreprins de faire ceste correction n'a pas esté pour s'advancer en preoccupant le lieu. Mais comme on luy eust peu imputer à temerité, s'il se fust ingeré pour se ietter hastivement aux champs, aussi ne merite il aucune reprehension de ce qu'estant instamment requis... (d) —derechef. (e)—icy. (f) —(comme... devant).

1. i.e., Olivetanus.
2. This figure is repeated a little later. Calvin then revised the Olivétan Bible for the first time in 1545. The result was Jean Gérard's 1546 Genevan Bible, 4°, described by Van Eys, no. 54 f. Our preface appears for the first time in this Bible but in the current version.
3. The third fellow labourer is not known.

11 Calvin's View of Ecclesiastical Discipline

R. N. Caswell

The necessity of discipline

IT WOULD SOUND strange to many ears if a minister refused to consider a call to a congregation unless granted these two things, that he might use a catechism and institute ecclesiastical discipline. Yet when Calvin returned to Geneva in 1541 from exile in Strasbourg, to be one of the city ministers, these were precisely his demands of the city authorities. He wrote to Farel in that year: 'Immediately after I had offered my services to the Senate, I declared that a church could not hold together unless a settled government should be agreed on, such as is prescribed to us in the Word of God, and such as was in use in the ancient church' (*Letters*, 1855, ET I. 260). From his earliest days it was his view that discipline is one of the essential activities of the church. In the 1539 edition of the *Institutio* he wrote: 'Those who think that the church can stand for long without this bond of discipline, are mistaken; unless by chance we can afford to omit that support which the Lord foresaw would be necessary for us' (CO I. 550). In the 1537 *Ordonnances* he argues that the church cannot fulfil its true function without the use of discipline, and he fears that God will take vengeance on their neglect of it (CO X. 5n, 10). The refusal of the city authorities at that time to grant his request for discipline was one of the causes of his leaving in 1538, and although in his second period of labour in Geneva, the right to excommunicate was gradually accorded to the church, it was only after years of patient teaching from the pulpit and in the teeth of bitter opposition from the freedom-loving party, generally styled 'the *Libertins*'.

To Calvin discipline was essential because it was taught in the Word of God. This is the secret of all Reformed ecclesiology. Discipline was desirable, not because men thought the church should be so organised in view of its task, but because these same men declared that the Word of God was explicit regarding this institution. 'The church, in its visible form, is not an institution which can be organised just as we like; but already in this matter, the Lord indicates that the Church is His, by laying out the way in which it must be arranged' (J. Courvoisier, *Le Sens de la discipline ecclésiastique dans la Genève de Calvin*, 1946, p. 22). The Reformation itself was brought about by the Word, not by the Reformers' insight, and in this Word discipline was ordained as part of the power of the keys (*Inst.* IV. xi. 1). For these men that was enough.

Calvin, in one place, states quite bluntly that whoever opposes the establishment of ecclesiastical discipline is an enemy of the Christian faith. Discipline was not invented by men, but was given as an inviolable rule by the Lord to His followers. We may not dispense with it, for by instituting it in His church the Lord declares that He wishes it to remain to the end of the world (CO LIII. 123). The abolition of discipline would mean the entire dissolution of the church. It is as necessary for the church as ligaments for the body (*Inst.* IV. xii. 1). It is easy to understand why Calvin was so dogmatic as to its necessity, when we consider how closely he linked it with the care of souls and the preaching of the Word. This care and this preaching are not two separate things, but two parts of one activity, the effective application of the Word, and discipline is a necessary appendage (*Harmony of the Gospels*, CTS II. 358). 'The preaching of the doctrine is to be accompanied by private admonitions, reproofs, and other means to enforce the doctrine, and prevent it from being altogether ineffectual' (*Inst.*, *ibid.*). This close link with the Word, discipline being that activity that mediates between the *Ecclesia docens* and the *Ecclesia discens*, explains why Calvin did not need to posit discipline as a mark of the church, as did Bucer and Knox.

Men had been called by the Gospel to the forgiveness of sins and to holiness of character. Reformed life must become a product of the Reformed Church, and doctrine had to be applied to the believer with that end in view. When in 1537 Calvin proposed

211

that the citizens of Geneva should subscribe a Confession of Faith, it was not just a matter of establishing them as Protestants. The church, made up of the adherents of the new Confession had something else to do, as Calvin saw it, than merely to assure the preaching of the Word and the administration of the sacraments, although these were the marks by which the true church could be recognised.The church must be a living fellowship, a kingdom of Christ on earth. So it must approach as near as possible the ideal of holiness implied in that conception, though without becoming a perfectionist *élite*. Positively its mission was to contribute, by all the means at its disposal, to the growth in grace of members.

This sanctification is brought about by the Word, but the ministry of the Word is not discharged by preaching a couple of sermons on Sunday. The Word has to be applied by personal advice and admonition from house to house, with reproof where necessary. Harsher measures will follow when unavoidable. The primary aim of discipline, Calvin declares, is the prevention of offences, only secondarily the abolition of any scandal that may have arisen (*Inst*. IV. xi. 5). Discipline is, then, the ordering of the life of the church in its learning obedience to Christ and in its response to the teaching of Scripture.

Preaching without this ordering is useless—'throwing the Word into the air'—and for a preacher to be silent when he is out of the pulpit shows a fundamental misunderstanding of Christianity and of God's order. 'When the one who proclaims the Word of God has taught the people, he must then think of particular persons who need to be admonished, as we see in Ezekiel, where it is not only mentioned that the pastor is commissioned by God to lead the flock to pasture, but also that his office is to assist the weak, to restore the diseased and to remedy all their infirmities' (CO LIII. 442). 'The business of teaching is not confined to public discourses, but extends also to private admonitions' (*Inst*. IV. iii. 6). These are the foundations of discipline.

Further, it is the right and duty of every member to admonish his fellow members and provoke them to good works, and thus prevent the preaching from becoming 'frigid'. Doctrine only obtains its full authority when supported by personal admonition, a 'spur to stimulate the inactive' (*Inst*. IV. xii. 1, 2). Children need a teacher's help: this pedagogic aspect of discipline is vital, for the pastoral authority of the church to which it is linked, was given not for casting down but for building up. It is unfortunate that many think of discipline as purely or primarily repressive.

Calvin himself, as has been pointed out by Jean-Daniel Benoît,[1] was above all a pastor. He was only a theologian in order to be a better pastor, theology being for him the servant of piety, and his own reforming work simply an extension of his pastoral activity. Much of his thought on pastoral discipline, as it might be called, can be traced to the first great work on pastoral theology in the Reformed Churches, Bucer's *De Vera Animarum Cura*. In this work the exercise of discipline is linked with the office of the pastor and with the elders' task of caring for souls.

The abolition of offences

WHEN offences are not prevented by the constant application of the Word, then the other parts of discipline must be applied. In writing of the *Necessity of Reforming the Church* Calvin gives an analysis of discipline thus: 'Where their admonitions? Where their censures? To omit other things, what use is made of excommunication, that best nerve of discipline . . . the most salutary remedy for chastening the guilty?' (Tracts, CTS I. 205).

It is to be borne in mind, before expanding disciplinary procedure, that in the case of notorious public sins the successive steps laid down by Christ are not necessary. Solemn and public correction by the church is to be used immediately. Calvin refers to Paul's directive in I Timothy 5.20 and example in Galatians 2.11, 14. (*Inst.* IV. xii. 3.) Still more serious crimes will merit prompt excommunication. 'For the correction of atrocious crimes it is not sufficient to employ admonition or reproof; recourse must be had to a severer remedy; as Paul shows, when he does not content himself with censuring the incestuous Corinthian, but pronounces the sentence of excommunication immediately upon being certified of his crime' (*ibid*). Secret sins, of course, and the sins of hypocrites which are unknown to men, force us to acknowledge that discipline, no matter how carefully applied, will never result in an entirely pure church. Tares

H   213 will always be mixed among the wheat. Calvin does speak, however, of a certain spirit of discernment imparted to the church, so that 'we may not always be deceived by hypocrites, and that the church may not be too much exposed to their wicked impostures' (*Comment. on Jn.* 2.24, 25). But even so, it seems inevitable that 'many hypocrites, who have nothing of Christ, but the name and appearance' will be found among the true children of God.

The steps of disciplinary procedure are three. 'The first is to give a private advice to the person who has offended. The second is, if he shall give any sign of obstinacy, to advise him again in the presence of witnesses. The third is, if no advantage shall be obtained in this way, to deliver him up to the public decision of the church.' The thought of the duty of mutual reproof is implicit here. 'It would be outrageous cruelty to betray, by our silence and concealment, the salvation of those whom we might, by mild reproof rescue from perdition.' We may not be successful, but we should try; the course has been laid down for us by the Lord and follow it we must. Two common extremes are to be avoided; one is, to praise and flatter those whom we ought to reprove; the other, to be excessively bitter against those whom by love, we should attempt to cure (*Harmony*, CTS II. 352 ff.).

The third step is not to be entrusted to an individual. 'Even Paul', Calvin stresses, 'though an apostle, does not himself as an individual excommunicate according to his own pleasure, but consults with the church, that the matter may be transacted by common authority" (*Comment. on I Cor.* 5. 4). A legitimate assembly is necessary for the proper use of this power (*Inst.* IV. xi. 5). What, then, is this legitimate assembly? Our Lord, in Matthew 18, uses the phrase 'Tell it to the Church', though there was then no church in existence, 'He looked', comments Calvin, 'at the form of discipline which was observed among the Jews . . . the power of excommunication belonged to the elders' (*Comment. ad loc.*). In the early church there was 'a Presbytery, that is, an assembly of elders, who by the consent of all, had the power of first judging in the case. From them, the matter was brought before the people, but it was as a thing already judged of.' When the church gathers, it should act in accordance with the Word of God, and with the hearty prayer that they should be

CALVIN AND CHURCH DISCIPLINE

directed by his Spirit . . . 'Whatever is done in such an assembly is the work of Christ' (*Comment. on I Cor.* 5). Discipline then is *ecclesiastical* discipline; it was one of the faults of the papacy that it took the power of discipline out of the hands of the people. It was Calvin's aim, in conformity with the New Testament, to restore this power to the lawfully elected representatives of the laity. (*Ordonnances.* CO X.10.)

It is important that the spirit behind discipline should be one of real sorrow and mourning. The ultimate aim with offenders is not to exclude them, but in tenderness to seek them and regain them for the fellowship. Even when punishment is used, it is used as a 'medicine to bring sinners back to our Lord' (CO X.30). The most rigorous treatment of all, namely that of handing over the offender to Satan, was inflicted by Paul so that the spirit might be saved in the day of the Lord Jesus.

The power of the keys

THE power to 'bind' sinners and to 'loose' them, when repentant, belongs to the power of the keys. Here Calvin distinguishes two shades of meaning. The first (Matthew 16.19; John 20.22 f.) has to do with the preaching of the Gospel, by which the repentant are loosed and the unrepentant bound. This power, he adds, is more ministerial than authoritative, 'for, strictly speaking, Christ has not given this power to men, but to His Word, of which He has appointed men to be His ministers' (*Inst.* IV. xi. 1).

The second shade of meaning refers to the use of ecclesiastical discipline (Matthew 18.17–18). When a man is 'bound' by the church, it is another way of saying that he is excommunicated; when he is received again into the fellowship he is 'loosed'. The church's authority is God's authority: 'Whoever, after committing a crime, humbly confesses his fault, and entreats the church to forgive him, is absolved not only by men but by God himself; and on the other hand, whoever treats with ridicule the reproofs and threatenings of the church, if he is condemned by it, the decision which men have given will be ratified in heaven.' (*Inst.* IV. xi.2; cf. *Harmony* II. 358.) This does not, of course, give the rein to ecclesiastical tyranny, for these proceedings are

215

JOHN CALVIN

to be carried out with hearty prayers to God for the guidance of
the Spirit, asking that discernment may be given in dealing with
offenders. God is not, therefore, a sort of 'petty judge, who con-
curs in the sentence of mortal men' (*ibid.*). He only ratifies a
decision over which He by His Spirit has presided.

The aims of discipline

THE prime aim is the glory of God, that the honour of the head
should not be diminished by anything unworthy in the body.
Niesel speaks of Calvin paying 'vigilant attention to the life of
the church and of every single one of its members; not with a
view to achieving some sort of moral standard but for the sake
of Christ and His honour'.[2] It is scarcely possible to imagine
any other, lesser, motivation driving the Reformer to such
heroic endeavours to establish discipline in Geneva.

The second aim springs from the apostle's words 'A little
leaven leaveneth the whole lump'. In the intimate fellowship
that would exist in the church, association with the wicked would
soon corrupt the good, especially bearing in mind the propensity
of the heart of men to evil. Calvin refers to the fact that the
apostle forbad even normal fellowship with the wicked (I Corinthians 5. 11).

The third aim concerns the well-being of the offender himself.
Rebuke and exclusion may bring him to himself and be the
means of his repentance. 'Thus it is even conducive to their own
benefit for their iniquity to be punished, that the stroke of the
rod may arouse to a confession of their guilt, those who would
only be rendered more obstinate by indulgence' (*Inst.* IV. xii. 5).

Discipline and the sacraments: the Lord's Supper

IT is not only necessary to exclude offending believers from the
Table, but it is also the duty of the church to ensure that those
who present themselves for admission are worthy of this holy
mystery. Not to do this is to 'prostitute' the sacrament (CO
X.207). 'To admit all and sundry without discrimination is a
contempt which the Lord cannot tolerate. The Lord himself
216

distributed the Supper only to the disciples. So whoever is not established in the doctrine of the Gospel should not come to the institution of the Lord. . . . This also is to be fixed in the whole constitution and order of discipline—which ought to thrive in the church—not to admit those who are adjudged unworthy, (from a circular letter, CO X.258). One of the main activities of discipline, then, is this examination of intending communicants regarding their faith and life. Calvin expected that this care for the purity of the church would be the foremost task of the newly formed Consistory (CO X.8). Those who show by their sinful lives that they do not belong to Jesus should be forbidden to approach the Table. Our negligence in this matter may, thought Calvin, call down that vengeance which Paul speaks of as falling upon those who partake unworthily. And the one who is responsible for administering the sacrament is bound to take action. 'If he knowingly and intentionally admit an unworthy person, whom he might justly reject, he is as guilty of sacrilege as if he were to give the Lord's body to dogs' (*Inst.* IV. xii.5). He quotes Chrysostom's remark 'Blood shall be required at your hands', when speaking of the minister who fears to exclude the unworthy because of social status or wealth.

In Strasbourg, and later in Geneva, Calvin interviewed all who wished to partake of the sacrament. That it savoured of the Roman Confessional did not deter him. 'It is', he explains, 'like the examination which Paul speaks of in I Corinthians 11. To approach the holy Table without due consideration would be a blasphemous defilement of it'. Hence the need for such a 'double examination'. People are so confused, he laments. They think they are saved by doing good. They are as bad as the Turks or the pagans. Others are so careless they hardly know whether they have a conscience at all. They despise the preaching, live scandalously, blaspheme, stagger drunkenly, not caring whether they have offended God, yet they come religiously to the Lord's Table! (From a sermon on I Cor. 11.26 ff. CO XLIX. 808 ff.)

He explained his plan in a letter to Farel: 'In this place [Strasbourg] hitherto many individuals were in the habit of making a rash approach to the sacrament of the Supper. On Easter-day, when I gave out the intimation that we were to celebrate the Supper on next Lord's Day, I announced, at the same time, that no one would be admitted to the Table of the Lord by me, who had not beforehand presented himself for examination' (*Letters*, Bonnet, I.152). There was so much hesitation, however, on the part of his friends, that two months later he found it necessary to explain to Farel again. 'I have often declared to you that it did not appear to me to be expedient that confession should be abolished in the churches, unless that which I have lately taught be substituted in the place of it. In order that I may better explain to you my method, let me first of all state the real nature of the case. When the day of the sacrament of the Supper draws nigh, I give notice from the pulpit that those who are desirous to communicate must first of all let me know; at the same time, I add for what purpose, that it is in order that those who are as yet uninstructed and inexperienced in religion may be better trained; besides, that those who need special admonition may hear it; and lastly, that if there are any persons who may be suffering under trouble of mind they may receive consolation. . . . What shameless effrontery would it be for any one not even to condescend to avouch his faith in the face of the church with whom he sought communion, and how wretched would be the state and condition of the church if it could be compelled to receive to the partaking in so great a mystery those of whom it is altogether ignorant, or perhaps regards with suspicion! And to say nothing about the church, how shall the minister himself to whom the dispensation of this grace is committed on condition that he may not cast it before dogs and swine, that he must not pour it out to the worthy and the unworthy without distinction, discharge this onerous duty, unless he proceeds upon some fixed and certain method for separating the worthy from the unworthy communicants' (*Letters*, I. 160 f.).

Perhaps his examination would follow the lines laid down in his treatise on the Lord's Supper, 'whether we have a true repentance in ourselves and a true faith in our Lord Jesus Christ' —yet not such a strict examination as would bring the conscience into perilous perplexity—'We must hold in firm and hearty confidence the Lord Jesus Christ as our sole righteousness, life and salvation, receiving and accepting the promises which are given us by Him as certain and assured; renouncing on the other hand all other confidence, in order that, distrusting ourselves and all other creatures, we may rest fully in Him and content ourselves with His grace alone'. We cannot partake if we walk in darkness, 'for it is absurd to pretend to be of the body of Christ while we abandon ourselves to all licence and lead a dissolute life'. Above all there must be no bitterness toward any, for this sacrament exemplifies and recommends love most of all. We will also testify openly to our debt to Christ that others may be edified by our example. Yet no one with trembling faith should absent themselves; all we need is that 'we feel in our heart that, without hypocrisy and deceit, we hope for salvation in Christ, and desire to live according to the rule of the gospel. . . . Let us not come without faith and repentance' (*Treatises*, ed. J.K.S. Reid, p. 150 ff.).

Discipline and the sacraments: baptism

BY definition, 'Baptism is a sign of initiation, by which we are admitted into the society of the church, in order that, being incorporated into Christ, we may be numbered among the children of God'. It was given for two purposes: 'first, to promote our faith toward Him; secondly, to testify our confession before men'. It is a sign accompanying the Word, by which the remission of sins and the mortification of the body of sin are brought about. And 'from this sacrament, as from all others, we obtain nothing except what we receive by faith'. By it we testify 'that our confidence is in the mercy of God, and our purity in the remission of sins, which is obtained by Jesus Christ; and that we enter into the church of God in order to live in the same harmony of faith and charity, of one mind with all the faithful'.[3]

In a lengthy chapter Calvin argues the case for paedobaptism, basing it on the similarity of the old and new covenants. Discipline applied to this sacrament means in the case of adults that they will only be admitted to it when the minister is satisfied that their profession of faith is credible. In the case of infants, Calvin envisaged some of them too remaining unbaptised, for baptism belongs only to Christians and to their children. 'He who is an unbeliever, descended of impious parents, is accounted an alien from the communion of the covenant till he

219

be united to God by faith. It is no wonder, therefore, if he be not a partaker of the sign, the signification of which in him would be delusive and vain' (*Inst.* IV. xvi.24). In a letter to John Knox, however, he adopts a much broader view and allows the use of sponsors (*Knox's Works*, ed. Laing, VI. 94 f.). 'The interruption of true religion, which has prevailed under Popery, has not abstracted the virtue and efficacy of baptism. The progeny of holy and pious ancestors, although their grandfathers and parents may have been apostates, belong notwithstanding to the body of the church. . . . Whatever infant is presented on the ground of a legitimate sponsorship, we see not why he should be rejected.'

Discipline and marriage

IN 1537 Calvin requested the Council to set up a commission to regulate marriage matters, this commission to work in conjunction with the ministers of the Word. The request was ignored.

The 1541 Ordonnances have only two articles on marriage. The civil power still retained jurisdiction in a realm where Calvin desired to see the ministers of the Word supreme. True, in his own conduct of the marriage service, he did issue a general challenge to the couple with regard to impediments, and it was his view that people married otherwise than God's word allows, were not lawfully married.[4] Some progress does seem to have been made in the 1545 *Projet d'Ordonnances sur les mariages* (the corrections appear to be in Calvin's hand), but only in 1561 is there a full chapter on marriage in the Ordinances. (CO X. 105 ff.)

Marriage may be celebrated on weekdays and Sundays, though not on Communion Sundays. The Consistory was to make the preliminary hearing in matrimonial cases and report to the Council. Some persons need permission to marry; the minimum age without permission for boys is 20, for girls 18. Widows and widowers may marry without permission. A promise of marriage is not to be made lightly, and may only be retracted if, for instance, one of the parties proves to have an incurable illness. Marriage is not to be delayed more than six or seven months after the engagement. 'Banns' are to be read on three successive Sundays. The ceremony itself is to be grave and modest—without tambourines or minstrels! The degrees of consanguinity are noted. A marriage may be declared null due to physical malformation of one of the partners, and may be revoked because of adultery in either partner (the innocent party being free to remarry), long absence deemed equivalent to reasonable assumption of death, or wilful desertion.

Discipline of pastors

PASTORS had, in addition to the general discipline, a discipline of their own. They were constantly examined as to their doctrine and conduct. Differences could be referred from the weekly conference of ministers to the elders or even to the magistrates. Any tendency to schism or rebelling against the order in the church was noted. Simony, intrigues for better paid posts, absence from the parish without good reason, were dealt with, together with a list of crimes ranging from lies to lewdness, from dancing to drunkenness. But there were offences peculiar to the ministry, strange methods of expounding Scripture, negligence in study, scolding the congregation, clothes not befitting the position, all of which merited reproof.

The use of elders in discipline

IN the 1537 Ordonnances the request is made for certain persons to be chosen to assist in discipline. 'We have deliberately required of you to be pleased to ordain and elect certain persons of good life and witness from the faithful, persevering and not easily corrupted, who should be dispersed and distributed in all the quarters of the city, having oversight of the life and government of each of them; and if they see any vice worthy of note to find fault with in any person, that they communicate about it with some of the ministers, to admonish whoever it is that is at fault, and to exhort him in brotherly fashion to amendment' (*Treatises*, Reid, p. 52).

These elders were chosen to rule, not to preach. They were lay-helps, distinguished from the preachers on the basis of

I Timothy 5.17, where Calvin's commentary runs: 'There were at that time two kinds of elders. . . . There were chosen from among the people men of worth and of good character, who united with the pastors in a common council and authority.' Calvin is said by some to have invented this office, subsequently searching in the Scriptures for warrant for it. But this is hardly so, when we think of his reading of the Bible—especially of the Old Testament with its mention of 'elders'—his reading of the Fathers and his experience of the *curatores animarum* in Strasbourg. Indeed the 1541 *Projet d'Ordonnances* opens with Bucer's famous list of officers in the Christian church—pastors, teachers, elders and deacons (CO X. 15).

The task of the elder was to be an inspector of behaviour. He would be assigned to a particular parish, and would be required to know and to supervise those who lived there. From time to time he would visit the homes, and once a year would be accompanied by the minister. The care of the elders extended to what we would call matters of hygiene, as well as purely religious concerns.

The wording of the 1537 *Ordonnances* makes it clear that Calvin accepted that the appointment would be made by the Council and from the Council. He did not quite realise his ideal of government of the church by the church, though of course all members of the Council in Geneva would (had to be!) be members of the Church. The 1541 *Ordonnances* show that the Little Council was to carry out the appointment in conjunction with the ministers; the eldership to be made up of two members of this Council itself, four more from the Council of Sixty, and six from the Council of Two Hundred.

They could be called in to settle doctrinal disputes among the ministers—no doubt a difficult task; they saw to it that no one lit a fire in a room without a proper chimney; everything came under their notice from playing skittles at Church-time to wearing flowers in one's hat at a wedding (both forbidden)!

Every Thursday morning the twelve elders with the ministers sat as the Consistory (the President always being a layman) to summon offenders before them. They were granted the use of an officer. Angry scenes often took place. Sometimes Calvin walked out in disgust as rebellious citizens reviled him, the 'newcomer' who would fain rule the city! The record of these
222

Consistory meetings makes fascinating and disturbing reading.[5] A man is imprisoned for saying Masses. An independent soul, who refuses to attend the preaching, is threatened with banishment from Geneva. A barber is reprehended for using charms over the sick. An order is given for segregation of the sexes in the public baths, to prevent immorality. A derisive remark to one of the ministers comes in for a rebuke. Mixed marriages are forbidden. A talkative woman pertly replies that she was a Christian while Calvin was still a barrister. A father is not to be allowed to have his child baptised under the name Balthazar. (Eventually it was called John. After Calvin?) Fortune-tellers, swearers, murderers, all appear and are dealt with.

If some of these cases of discipline sound strange to twentieth-century ears, it should be remembered that Calvin made none of the laws concerned. They were all made under Roman Catholic Geneva before Calvin ever went there. All that he did was to seek to enforce the laws instead of allowing men and women to buy their way round them.

On 1 June 1564 the name of Calvin appears with the cryptic note 'Alle à Dieu le Salmedy 27 de May entre huict et neuf heures du soir'.

The state and discipline

THE power of the church, said Calvin, is limited to excommunication. No civil penalty is to be inflicted by the church, 'for the spiritual kingdom of Christ and civil government are things very different and remote from each other' (*Inst.* IV. xx.1). Yet these two powers are not so separate as might appear from that quotation. To begin with, the members of the church cannot refuse obedience to the state, and the citizens cannot refuse obedience to the teachings of the ministers of the Word. The church can be subject to the state and, inversely, the state to the church to a certain extent, without either losing their original independence and authority. Further, the state to Calvin was Christian, and was instituted by God to enforce both tables of the ten commandments. What, he asks, would have been the point of stopping half-way, omitting that part which deals particularly with the true worship of God, who is the creator of the state? 'This civil government is designed, as long as we live in this

223

JOHN CALVIN

world, to cherish and support the external worship of God, to
preserve the pure doctrine of religion, to defend the constitution
of the Church (*Inst*. IV. xv. 2). The church, though its own
powers are limited to excommunication, may call in the civil
power to inflict more severe penalties.

Accordingly, he does not hesitate to say that magistrates
'have their command from God, that they are invested with His
authority, and are altogether His representatives, and act as His
vice-regents' (*ibid*.). In the 1536 *Institutio*, the same sentiment is
already found. Magistrates are the 'dei . . . vices', and are to see
to cases of idolatry, sacrilege, blasphemy against the truth of
God, and public offences against religion (CO I. 230). Even
if the Scriptures did not teach that the jurisdiction of the magistrates extended to both tables of the law, we might learn it
from heathen writers. 'No government can be happily constituted, unless its first object be the promotion of piety', and the
kings in the Old Testament who earn the praise of the inspired
writers are those whose first care was for the maintenance of
religion (*Inst*. IV. xx. 9).

It is significant that Calvin found Deuteronomy a book for
the times and often preached from it. On 13. 1–5 he says: 'Here
our Lord not only desires us to avoid listening to false teachers,
but even to exterminate such a pest. . . . Those who bear the
sword should bring it forth. . . . Now it seems at first sight that
this law was far too severe; but it is strange that punishment is
quite allowable in the case of words spoken against mortal man,
whereas, when the living God is blasphemed, people would
like that to be left unpunished' (CO XXVII. 243 ff.). The glory
of God demands that these murderers of souls should be severely
punished.

He could not avoid the criticism that this savours too much of
the spirit of the Old Testament, but he replied that it would be
strange if we thought less of the honour of God than did his
ancient people. Nor is God's law any less binding in the new
age. Christ did not spread his kingdom by the sword, but Calvin
argues that this refers to a time when not many mighty were
called into this kingdom. But now when, in fulfilment of the
second Psalm, kings come to submit themselves to the Lord,
should not such kings become fathers to the church and queens
give suck to it? 'In other words, those who bear the sword of
224

justice must take the Church of God under their protection, to keep it pure in doctrine and in worship as prescribed by the Word of God.' They are lax if they neglect this duty. 'When the great are called to the service of God, they should exert themselves in the way their station demands' (CO XXVII. 246).

The sentence of death is justifiable for those who trouble the true religion, if again we think of the glory of God. Here too, Calvin sees the need of defending himself against the charge of being as bad as the Roman Church. They also burn heretics and use the secular arm to support 'true religion'. But to Calvin the difference is obvious. In their case, the Romanists are suppressing the truth of God's Holy Word. This medieval view of the Christian state was to be sharply challenged in England at a later date, and the modern conception of freedom of conscience gained.

Penitential discipline

IN this regard Calvin advocates moderation and deprecates what he considers to be the harshness of the early church. 'It is impossible to excuse the excessive austerity of the ancients, which was utterly at variance with the directions of the Lord, and led to the most dangerous consequences' (*Inst.* IV. xii. 8, 10). Bucer, who pleads for the use of penitential discipline, dismisses the thought that men may in this way merit re-admission. It is rather used to test the sincerity of their repentance. But for Calvin the profession of repentance seems to be enough to cause the renewal of fellowship. Of the early church he writes: 'When they sentenced an offender to solemn repentance and exclusion from Holy Communion, sometimes for three, sometimes for four, sometimes for seven years, and sometimes for the remainder of life—what other consequence could result from it, but either great hypocrisy or extreme despair? In like manner, when any one has fallen for a second time, the refusal to admit him to a second repentance, and his exclusion from the church to the end of his life, was neither useful nor reasonable' (*ibid.*). Severity must be tempered with gentleness, otherwise the remedy becomes a poison.

For Calvin discipline was a necessity in the church. It is like the sinews that bind the body together (*Treatises*, p. 245).

225

JOHN CALVIN

The adversary, knowing the worth of discipline, labours to destroy it. 'Having failed to extinguish pure doctrine again—the soul of the body, as it were—he cuts the nerves by breaking and getting rid of discipline' (CO X. 224).

It is true to say that the sixteenth-century church could not have survived without discipline. Outsiders were convinced when they saw a reformation of behaviour. Naturally, the question arises: Can the twentieth-century church survive without discipline? Or, to put the question another way: Can one speak today about the reconstruction of the church without restoring in all its fulness the function of discipline? But a further question has to be added: Must a discipline restored in the Reformed churches have the same aspect as it had in the sixteenth century?

1. *Calvin directeur d'âmes*, pp. 11, 18.
2. *The Theology of Calvin*, p. 199.
3. See especially *Inst.* IV. xv–xvi.
4. W. D. Maxwell, *John Knox's Genevan Service Book*, 1965.
5. CO XXI. See also J-F. Bergier (ed.) *Registres de la Compagnie des Pasteurs de Genève au Temps de Calvin*, (1964), Vol. I, 1546–1553, and Vol. II, 1552–1564 (eds. R. M. Kingdon, J-F. Bergier and Alain Dufour (1962). and the forthcoming ET by P. E. Hughes.

Index

[This index consists mainly of proper names with a few general subjects not obviously covered by the chapter headings. Where the references are covered in the notes and appendices as well as the main text, the latter references only are given below.]

227

INDEX

Hotman, François, 32
Huddleston, Bishop Trevor, 12 f.
Humanism, 2, 13, 16, 25
Hunter, A. Mitchell, 133, 135

Jonviller, Charles de, 184
Justinian, 9

Knox, John, 31ff., 220

Laud, Archbishop William, 11
Luther, Martin, 4 f., 7, 79 f., 104,
123, 134, 141, 152, 155, 158 f.,
161, 167–170, 183

Marolat, A., 195
Martyr, Peter, 35, 126, 170
McNeill, J. T., 32
Melanchthon, Philip, 4 f., 72, 79 f.,
121 ff., 149, 152 f., 167, 171, 173,
179
Moore, A. L., 11 f.
Münster, Sebastian, 179
Musculus, Wolfgang, 35

Niesel, Wilhelm, 136

Oecolampadius, Johann, 123, 125
Olivétan, Pierre, 192–5
Oxford Dictionary of the Christian
Church, 13

Pascal, Blaisé, 104
Perkins, William, 4, 25 f., 28–30,
35 f.
Pfister, Oscar, 6 ff.
Pfisterer, Ernst, 8
Pietism, 3, 29
Pighius, Albert, 122
Prenter, Regin, 169

Pullan, Leighton, 11 f.
Puritanism, 2 f., 28–33

Raguenier, Denis, 184
Ratramnus, 132
Reuss, E., 178
Rihel, Wendelin, 103, 107, 180 f.

Sadoleto, Cardinal Jacopo, 119
Schmidt, A-M., 171
Seneca, 38–66
Servetus, Miguel, 9 f,, 17, 110 f., 118
Simon, Richard, 2
Smits, Luchesius, 106, 176 f.

Tawney, R. H., 22
Tillet, M. du, 83 f.
Toplady, A. M., 4, 28
Tour, Imbart de la, 6
Troeltsch, E., 22

Ursinus, Zachary, 35

Viret, Pierre, 68, 73, 75 f., 78

Wallace, R. S., 132
Warfield, B. B., 163, 167 ff., 173
Weber, O., 22
Westminster Assembly Divines, 3,
151
Westphal, Joachim, 126, 132, 141
Whale, J. S., 143
Whitefield, George, 4
Whitgift, Archbishop John, 11,
35 f.

Zanchius, Jerome, 25, 30, 35
Zweig, Stefan, 6 ff.
Zwingli, Ulrich, 34, 46, 55, 62, 123,
125 f., 134, 141, 153, 170 f., 183